FINANCE IN RURAL CHINA

This book offers insights into the scholarly debates on formal and informal finance in rural China and fills a gap in the existing literature.

The book provides an overview of the overall development of rural finance in China and explains the necessity of embarking on the pathway toward rural financial pluralization through the "Local Knowledge Paradigm". The authors also analyze formal and informal financial development and inclusive finance (including digital inclusive finance) in rural China in various dimensions.

This book aids the understanding of the structure of the rural financial system and the operations of rural financial service providers in China. It will be a useful reference for those researching and interested in rural economy and rural finance.

Xingyuan Feng is Research Fellow of the Rural Development Institute of the Chinese Academy of Social Sciences (CASS), Deputy Secretary-General of the Center of Small and Medium Scale Banking Institutions of CASS, and Professor at the University of CASS. He received his PhD in economics from the University of Witten/Herdecke, Germany. Xingyuan's main research fields include the Australian School of Economics, Freiburg School, Public Choice, constitutional economics, new institutional economics, evolutionary economics, private sector development, government finance, banking and finance, SME finance, rural finance, as well as local and rural governance.

Guangwen He is Professor of the Department of Finance and Director of the Center for Rural Finance & Microfinance Research at China Agricultural University. He focuses on rural finance, cooperative finance, microfinance & inclusive finance, financial demand & supply of farm households & MSEs and institutional & business innovation of small & medium financial institutions. Guangwen has been very active in field surveys. He was Visiting Professor at Duisburg University, Germany and Visiting Researcher at Norinchukin Bank Research Institute, Japan. He has also provided his expertise in microfinance and rural finance projects of the World Bank, ADB, IFAD, KFW etc., in China.

Tongquan Sun is Research Fellow and Director of the Rural Finance Research Office of the Rural Development Institute (RDI) of the Chinese Academy of Social Sciences (CASS), Professor at the University of CASS and Secretary General of the Rural Development Society of China. He received his bachelor's and master's degree from the University of International Business and Economics (UIBE) in economics and law, respectively, and PhD from the Post-graduate School of CASS in Management. He was a visiting scholar at Duke University's Sanford School of Public Policy in the USA. He is a recipient of the Prize for Rural Development Research in China. He has provided consultancies to the government of China, some international development organizations, such as the World Bank, UNDP, IFAD, ILO, United Nations Resident Coordinator's Office in China and international and national NGOs. His main research interests are microfinance, financial inclusion, rural financial cooperatives, credit guarantee and poverty reduction, etc.

Christer Ljungwall is an economist specializing in international trade, knowledge production and innovation. He is Associate Professor in economics at Gothenburg University, Sweden. He has held several positions over the years, including guest Professor at PKU-HSBC Business School in China; Science Counselor at the Embassy of Sweden in China; Associate Professor at Copenhagen Business School, Denmark; Sr. Economist with the Asian Development Bank; and Research-fellow at Peking University, China. He is the author of numerous academic articles in economics, four books, and more than one hundred reports. His current research work focuses on international trade, knowledge production and innovation and geoeconomics. He is an advisor to governments and businesses and a frequently invited speaker on issues pertaining to Asian economic development and innovation. Dr. Ljungwall received his PhD in economics from Gothenburg University in 2003.

FINANCE IN RURAL CHINA

Xingyuan Feng, Guangwen He, Tongquan Sun and Christer Ljungwall

Routledge
Taylor & Francis Group

LONDON AND NEW YORK

Designed cover image: © Getty Images

First published 2023
by Routledge
4 Park Square, Milton Park, Abingdon, Oxon OX14 4RN

and by Routledge
605 Third Avenue, New York, NY 10158

Routledge is an imprint of the Taylor & Francis Group, an informa business

© 2023 Xingyuan Feng, Guangwen He, Tongquan Sun and Christer Ljungwall

The right of Xingyuan Feng, Guangwen He, Tongquan Sun and Christer Ljungwall to be identified as authors of this work has been asserted in accordance with sections 77 and 78 of the Copyright, Designs and Patents Act 1988.

British Library Cataloguing-in-Publication Data
A catalogue record for this book is available from the British Library

Library of Congress Cataloging-in-Publication Data
Names: Feng, Xingyuan, 1965– author. | He, Guangwen, author. | Sun, Tongquan, author. | Ljungwall, Christer, author.
Title: Finance in rural China / Xingyuan Feng, Guangwen He, Tongquan Sun and Christer Ljungwall.
Description: Abingdon, Oxon ; New York, NY : Routledge, 2023. | Includes bibliographical references and index.
Identifiers: LCCN 2022042184 | ISBN 9781138955592 (hbk) | ISBN 9781032439914 (pbk) | ISBN 9781003369776 (ebk)
Subjects: LCSH: Finance—China. | Rural development—China. | Economic development—China.
Classification: LCC HG187.C6 F46 2023 | DDC 332.0951—dc23/eng/20221209
LC record available at https://lccn.loc.gov/2022042184

ISBN: 978-1-138-95559-2 (hbk)
ISBN: 978-1-032-43991-4 (pbk)
ISBN: 978-1-003-36977-6 (ebk)

DOI: 10.4324/9781003369776

Typeset in Bembo
by Apex CoVantage, LLC

CONTENTS

List of Figures   x
List of Tables   xi
Preface   xiii
List of Contributors   xx

1   Towards a Competitive and Inclusive Financial Market in Rural China:
    A Theory-driven Approach   1
    Xingyuan Feng, Christer Ljungwall and Horst Löchel

    1.   *Introduction 1*
    2.   *Existing Rural Finance Paradigms 2*
         2.1   *The Subsidized Credit Paradigm 2*
         2.2   *The Rural Financial Systems Paradigm 3*
         2.3   *Incomplete Market Paradigm 4*
    3.   *The Local Knowledge Paradigm as a New Rural Finance Paradigm 4*
    4.   *The Structure of China's Rural Financial System 5*
    5.   *Demands for Rural Financial Services 7*
         5.1   *Structure and Diversity of Demand 7*
         5.2   *Meeting the Financing Demand of Farm Households 8*
         5.3   *Meeting the Financing Demand of SMEs in Rural Areas 11*
    6.   *Development of Rural Formal, Semi-formal and Informal Finance 12*
         6.1   *Development of Agricultural Bank of China 12*
         6.2   *Development of Rural Credit Cooperatives 13*
         6.3   *Postal Savings Bank and Policy-Oriented Banks 14*
         6.4   *Development of New Financial Institutions 15*
         6.5   *Development of Informal and Semi-formal Finance 16*
    7.   *Improving Financial Market Mechanisms 17*
    8.   *Concluding Remarks 19*
    References 19

2 70 Years' Evolution of the Rural Financial System of the People's
   Republic of China   22
   Tongquan Sun, Xingyuan Feng and Chong Dong

    1. *The Establishment of Rural Financial System and the Formation of State*
       Banking Institutions 23
       1.1 Strategy and Objectives 23
       1.2 Progress 23
       1.3 Achievements and Deficiencies 24
    2. *The Establishment of a Specialized Banking System and the Initial*
       Formation of a Rural Financial Market 25
       2.1 Reform Strategy and Objectives 25
       2.2 Main Reforms and Implementations 25
       2.3 Achievements and Deficiencies 26
    3. *The Formation of Rural Financial System in Which Different-type*
       Institutions Working Together 27
       3.1 Reform Strategy and Objectives 27
       3.2 Main Reform Contents and Implementations 28
       3.3 Achievements and Deficiencies 30
    4. *The Further Open-up of the Rural Financial Market and the Formation of a*
       Modern Rural Financial System 31
       4.1 Reform Strategy and Objectives 31
       4.2 Main Reform Contents and Implementations 32
       4.3 Achievements and Deficiencies 34
    5. *Construction of a Rural Inclusive Financial System 35*
       5.1 Reform Strategy and Objectives 35
       5.2 Main Reform Contents and Implementations 36
       5.3 Achievements and Deficiencies 38
    6. *Outlook of the Reform and Development of the Chinese Rural Financial*
       System 39
       6.1 Continue to Adopt the Principle and Direction of Marketization
           and Market Opening to Promote the Reform of the Rural Financial
           System 39
       6.2 Continue to Construct Rural Financial System Suitable for Serving the
           "Agriculture, Rural Areas and Farmers" 39
       6.3 Further Strengthen the Construction of Rural Inclusive Financial
           System 40
       6.4 Accelerate to Complete Rural Financial Legislation 41
    References 41

3 Farm Households' Demand for and Access to Loans in Rural China   42
   Guangwen He, Jing He and Pei Guo

    1. *The Problem Statements 42*
    2. *The Source of Data and the Basic Situation of the Sample Farmers 44*
       2.1 Data Source and Sample Description 44
       2.2 Farmers' Production and Operation and Income Characteristics 44
    3. *Evolution of Farmers' Credit Demand and Credit Accessibility 46*

    3.1   *Farmers' Credit Demand Remains Strong and Formal Credit Satisfaction Rate is Still Low 46*

    3.2   *Informal Credit is Still the Main Channel for Farmers to Meet their Credit Demands 47*

    3.3   *The Degree of Formal Financial Satisfaction of Farmers' Productive Credit Demands Has Increased 48*

    3.4   *Collateral and Guarantee Are Still the Main Ways for Farmers to Obtain Formal Credit 49*

    3.5   *The Degree of Self-exclusion of Financial Services for Farmers is Still High 49*

  4.   *The Hierarchical and Structural Characteristics of Farmers' Credit Demand 50*

    4.1   *Demands of Farmers with Different Production and Operation Modes Are Still Relatively Strong 50*

    4.2   *All Types of Farmers' Borrowing Still Rely Heavily on Informal Financial Channels 52*

    4.3   *Farmers at All Levels of Income Have Relatively High Credit Demand 52*

    4.4   *The Credit Demand of Small-scale Farmers Remains Relatively Strong 55*

  5.   *Countermeasures for Deepening Credit Services for Farmers 56*

  References 58

4   Ownership, Governance and Interests of Financial Institutions within the Rural Credit Cooperative System   60
   Xingyuan Feng

  1.   *An Overview of the Reform Process 60*

  2.   *Policy Impacts: Advantages and Disadvantages 63*

  3.   *Current Ownership Structures of RCCs and Rural Cooperative Banks are Detrimental to Operations 64*

  4.   *Distribution of Responsibility, Rights and Interests of Financial Institutions within the RCC System 68*

  5.   *Opportunities Remain for New and Genuine Rural Credit Cooperatives to Prosper 70*

  6.   *Downscaling Branches and Services Fit Best the Interests of RCC Institutions 72*

  References 73

5   Improving the Financial Sustainability of the Financial Institutions within the RCC System: Problems and Policy Options   74
   Xingyuan Feng and Xiang Yan

  1.   *Introduction 74*

  2.   *Factors Affecting the Sustainable Development of the RCC Institutions 75*

    2.1   *Ownership Structure and Governance of the RCC Institutions 75*

    2.2   *Risk Factors 76*

    2.3   *Other Factors 78*

3. Countermeasures to Promote the Sustainable Development of RCC
    Institutions 80
    3.1 Improving the Management and Business Operation of RCC
         Institutions 80
    3.2 Further Pushing Forward the Reform of the RCC Institutions 82
    References 84

6 The Development of Digital Inclusive Finance in Chinese Counties:
   Index Construction, Measurement and Analysis   85
   Xingyuan Feng, Tongquan Sun, Chong Dong and Xiang Yan

    1. Introduction 85
    2. Concept Definition and Literature Review 86
    3. Construction and Measurement Method of Digital Inclusive Financial
        Development Index of Chinese Counties 87
        3.1 Compiling Principles of Digital Inclusive Financial Development Index
             of Chinese Counties 87
        3.2 Data Sources 88
        3.3 Construction of the Digital Inclusive Financial Development Index
             System for Chinese Counties 88
        3.4 Determination of Weights 92
        3.5 Measurement Method of Index Score 94
    4. Measurement Results and Analysis of Scores of Indicators at All Levels of the
        Digital Inclusive Financial Development Index System 95
        4.1 The Overall Situation of the Development of County Digital Inclusive
             Finance in China 95
        4.2 Comparison of Digital Inclusive Financial Development in Different
             Regions and Counties 98
        4.3 Development of Digital Inclusive Finance in Different Provinces and
             Counties 99
        4.4 Analysis of the Top 100 Counties in the Development of Digital
             Inclusive Finance of Chinese Counties 101
    5. Conclusions and Policy Considerations 105
        5.1 Conclusion 105
        5.2 Policy Considerations 106
    References 107

7 China's Financing Support for Poverty Alleviation   109
   Tongquan Sun

    1. Introduction 109
        1.1 Lack of Funds for Development in the Rural Poor Areas
             of China 109
        1.2 The Importance of Finance for Poverty Alleviation and
             Development 109
    2. Specialized Financial Policies for Poverty Alleviation 110
        2.1 Credits for Poverty Alleviation 110
        2.2 The Policy of Insurance for Poverty Alleviation 115
        2.3 Participation of Capital Market for Poverty Alleviation 116

3. *The Evolution of Comprehensive and Targeted Financial Policies for Poverty Alleviation 116*
    3.1 *Financial Poverty Alleviation Policy as a Basic Public Financial Service 116*
    3.2 *Policies for Developing Inclusive Finance 117*
    3.3 *Complete, Comprehensive and Targeted Financial Poverty Alleviation Policies 118*
4. *Monetary, Regulatory and Fiscal and Tax Support Policies in Compliance with Financial Poverty Alleviation 120*
    4.1 *Monetary Policy 120*
    4.2 *Financial Regulatory Policies 121*
    4.3 *Fiscal and Tax Policies 122*
5. *Progress and Effectiveness of Finance for Poverty Alleviation 123*
    5.1 *Government-led Subsidized Loans 123*
    5.2 *Microfinance of Non-governmental Organizations 125*
    5.3 *Rural Mutual Funds in Poor Villages 126*
    5.4 *New Mechanism of Policy-Oriented Banks 127*
    5.5 *Innovation in Financial Mechanism and Products of Other Commercial Banks 128*
    5.6 *Innovation of Insurance Products for Poverty Alleviation 129*
    5.7 *Role of Capital Market for Poverty Alleviation 129*
    5.8 *Role of Rural Internet Finance 130*
    5.9 *Stimulation by the Monetary and Regulatory Policies 130*
6. *Summary 131*
    6.1 *Experiences 131*
    6.2 *Outlook for the Future 132*
Reference 133

Index   *134*

FIGURES

3.1 Farmers' Credit Demands and Their Satisfaction Level and Channels 47

4.1 Increased Top-Down Management of RCCs after the Introduction of Alliances 68

4.2 Organizational Structure of Rural Credit Cooperative Associations with Their Primary Rural Credit Cooperatives within Chinese Counties or County-level Cities 69

4.3 The Internal Management Structure of a Standard Genuine Rural Credit Cooperative According to the Principle of Cooperative Finance 71

6.1 Median Scores of the Overall Index and Three Area Indices of All Chinese Counties from 2017 to 2019 96

6.2 Median Scores of the Component Indicators of the Three Area Indices in All Chinese Counties from 2017 to 2019 97

6.3 Median Scores of the Overall Index of Macro Regions of China from 2017 to 2019 98

6.4 Median Scores of the Overall Index of Different Provinces from 2017 to 2019 100

6.5 Comparison of the Median Scores of the Overall Index and Area Indices of Top 100, Non-top 100 and the Last 100 Counties in 2019 104

6.6 Comparison of Median Scores of Component Indicators of Top 100 Counties, Non-top 100 Counties and the Last 100 Counties in 2019 104

TABLES

1.1	Financial institutions in rural China	5
1.2	Categories, types and number of rural banking financial institutions in China (by the end of 2016)	6
1.3	Demand for financial service in rural areas	7
1.4	Farm household loans and their size	9
1.5	Farm households' reason for not applying for a loan	9
1.6	Reason to reject farm households' loan applications	9
1.7	Reason for not demanding loans	10
1.8	Average borrowing and lending interest rates in informal sector in 2006 (%)	10
1.9	Factors constraining the development of rural enterprises (%)	11
1.10	Size and performance of main rural financial institutions	12
3.1	Farmers' production and operation types and income status	45
3.2	Analysis of formal and informal credit use by farmers	48
3.3	Analysis of formal credit lending methods and amounts for farmers	49
3.4	Analysis of the causes of credit rationing and constraints of farm households	50
3.5	Credit demand of farm households and their credit rationing in the perspective of production diversification	51
3.6	Analysis of farmers' borrowing sources under production and business diversification	53
3.7	Status of credit demand, credit rationing and its channel to meet the demand of farm households with different incomes	54
3.8	Analysis of credit demand, credit rationing and their borrowing channels of farmers with different land cultivation scale	56
4.1	Comparison of different pilot restructuring models – Zhangjiagang, Yinzhou and Danyang	65
6.1	Structure of the digital inclusive financial development index system for chinese counties	89
6.2	Weights for the scores of indicators of the digital inclusive financial development index system for chinese counties	93
6.3	Development trend of the median scores of the overall index of different macro regions from 2017 to 2019	99

6.4 Median scores and ranking of the overall index of different provinces
from 2017 to 2019   100
6.5 Median scores of the overall index and area indices of the top 100 counties
in 2019   102
7.1 Amounts of loans for poverty alleviation and specialized fiscal funds for poverty
alleviation (Years 1986–2013)   123

PREFACE

Rural finance is a hot research topic in contemporary China. It is expected that rural finance should fuel the implementation of the eye-catching Rural Revitalization Strategy launched by the CCP in 2017. However, little has been published internationally on rural finance in China.

It has been over 40 years since China launched its reform and opening up in 1978. Tremendous changes took place in China, especially in its rural area. According to Chinese statistics, the per capita annual disposable income of rural residents reached a record high of 18,931 yuan in 2021, while it was only 133.6 yuan in 1978. According to the State Council Information Office of the People's Republic of China (2021), at the end of 2020, through eight years of hard work, China achieved the goal of eliminating extreme poverty. It declares that the 98.99 million people in rural areas who were living below the current poverty threshold all shook off poverty, and all the 128,000 impoverished villages and 832 designated poor counties got rid of poverty".

Rural finance played an important role in attaining the above achievements. In general, economic development supports financial development and vice versa. This cumulative causation effect is obvious in rural China.

In 1978, since China had been implementing a planned economic system before, there was only one bank in China, which was the People's Bank of China (PBC, zhongguo renmin yinhang). Rural Credit Cooperatives (RCCs, nongcun xinyong hezuoshe) were managed as grassroots-level branches of the PBC. Several rounds of rural financial reforms took place then after. It is worth mentioning that the Agricultural Bank of China (ABC, zhongguo nongye yinhang) was rehabilitated only in 1979, while Rural Credit Cooperatives were separated from the ABC in 1996.

The first decade of the 21st century marked a key period for rural financial reforms which brought about a financial diversification we've never seen before in rural China. One key reform was the RCC reform. RCCs were restructured into rural credit cooperatives with a unified legal-person status within their respective county-level jurisdictions (nongcun xinyongshe; with cooperative system), rural commercial banks (nongcun shangye yinhang; with shareholding system) and rural cooperative banks (nongcun hezuo yinhang; with shareholding cooperative system). In 2010, RCCs and rural cooperative banks were required by the government to abandon their cooperative or shareholding cooperative system and adopt the shareholding system. All of those which are qualified have to be transformed into rural commercial banks. With the RCC reforms, the number of financial institutions with legal entity status within the RCC system (in the following "RCC institutions") dropped from 40,141 in 2000 to 2,207 in 2020. According to statistics, their delivery of financial services in terms of total loan balance expanded from RMB 1.05 trillion at the end of

2000 to RMB 38.9 trillion (total loan balance related to rural development, agriculture and farm households) at the end of 2020.

On one side, the RCC institutions dominate in credit market of most Chinese counties or county-level cities. On the other side, the government introduced some new types of financial institutions. With a new entry policy of the then China Banking Regulatory Commission in 2006, three new types of legal-entity financial institutions were introduced: village banks (cunzhen yinhang), loan companies (daikuan gongsi) and rural mutual fund associations (nongcun zijin huizhushe). By the end of 2020, there were 1637 village banks, 13 loan companies and 41 mutual fund associations. Besides them, with another new entry policy of the PBC and the China Banking Regulatory Commission in 2008, microloan companies were introduced as another new type of financial institution.[1] By the end of 2020, there were 6,453 microloan companies. The number of village banks and microloan companies is significant. However, their individual size is very limited. They do improve the institutional landscape of the financial market in rural China since they contributed to financial pluralization in China.

Farmers are encouraged by government policies to establish new types of credit cooperative organizations, such as those within some farmers' specialized cooperatives (nongmin zhuanye hezuoshe) or supply cooperatives (gongxiao she), and rural mutual-fund societies (zijin huzhu hui). These new types of credit cooperatives are mini-sized. They also contributed to financial pluralization in rural China.

In recent years, the Chinese government has enforced quite successfully a pro-active national strategy of developing inclusive finance (puhui jinrong) across China, especially in rural areas. China is now one of the leading countries of the world in upholding and implementing a national strategy for developing inclusive finance. In 2013, the Third Plenary Session of the 18th Central Committee of the Communist Party of China (CPC) took "developing inclusive finance" as the direction of financial reform, which implies that the Central Committee raised the development of an inclusive finance system to the level of a national strategy. In 2015, the Central Committee Document No. stressed "strengthening rural inclusive finance", and in December of the same year, the State Council released the "Development Plan for Promoting Inclusive Finance (2016–2020)". In 2016, the Central Committee Document No. 1 once again articulated "developing rural inclusive finance". In 2018, the Central Committee Document No 1 stressed that "inclusive finance should focus on the countryside". In September of the same year, the State Council issued the "Strategic Plan for Rural Revitalization (2018–2022)", with one focus on "developing rural inclusive finance". The 2019 Central Committee Document No. 1 requested that "the growth rate of inclusive loans should be generally higher than the average growth rate of all the various loans". With the enforcement of these CPC and government policies, all financial institutions are requested to improve their loan services in line with inclusive finance principles. Especially the state-controlled commercial banks (SCCBs) set up a special business department for serving rural areas, agriculture and farm households, or one for inclusive finance to deliver inclusive loan services in rural areas. More competition in the loan market was thus introduced in rural China. All financial institutions are subject to the appraisal by the government of their meeting the requirements for delivering inclusive financial services. At the same time, loans serving the rural area, agriculture and farm households or small and micro enterprises enjoy special tax benefits. RCC institutions enjoy a special deposit reserve ratio which is lower than other banks.

The development of inclusive finance has been fueled by the rapid development of the ICT sector (especially the mobile internet) and the rapid growth in the number of mobile phone users, mobile payments and FinTech, especially since 2014. China is now one of the leading countries of the world in the development of digital economy and digital finance, and thus of digital inclusive finance which can be understood as an integration of inclusive finance and the application of digital technologies. With the popularity of mobile internet, smartphones and mobile payments in urban and rural areas in recent years, various financial institutions (led by the Ant Group) are competing to introduce FinTech and promote digital transformation and the development of digital inclusive finance. The G20 High-Level Principles for Digital Financial Inclusion adopted by G20 leaders in Hangzhou in 2016 are a catalyst for actions in China to drive the adoption of digital approaches to achieve financial inclusion goals. The government has increasingly emphasized the development of rural digital financial inclusion. The 2020 Central Committee Document No. 1 articulated to steadily expand the pilot reform toward the development of inclusive finance in rural areas and accelerate the construction of an inclusive financial service system that combines online and offline services and embeds schemes of risk sharing between banks, insurance companies and agricultural loan guarantee companies. The No. 1 document in 2021 even stressed "developing rural digital inclusive finance".

Both the government's enforcement of the development of a rural inclusive finance system or even rural digital financial inclusion and the banking industry's own active efforts in pushing forward digital transformation and developing digital financial inclusion out of the banking institutions' own consideration of the necessity have led to the formation of a rural inclusive finance system and its digitization. The development of rural digital inclusive financial services has become the common strategic choice and the key grasps of FinTech banks, other FinTech companies and traditional rural financial institutions. At present, China's rural inclusive financial system is in the process of continuous improvement, and digital inclusive finance has been an important part of the rural inclusive financial system, and the main body of the future rural inclusive financial system must be rural digital inclusive finance.

Currently, there are quite a lot of banking financial institutions in most Chinese counties or county-level cities, including branches of state-controlled commercial banks, other large or medium-sized commercial banks, RCC institutions, village banks, etc. In 2020, RCC institutions owned 75,165 business outlets, thus the largest number of business outlets in rural China, followed by the Postal Savings Bank of China (PSBC, zhongguo youzheng chuxu yinhang) with almost 40,000 business outlets across China, 70% out of which are scattered in rural areas. More outlets mean closeness to the demand side and the status of being rooted in a rural grassroots community. However, it also means higher costs for maintaining these outlets, personnel and their services, especially for RCC institutions (PSBC shares partly working places with the Postal Service System).

The competition between rural financial institutions is fierce at the current time. Different digitization strategies are adopted by different financial institutions. While MYBank (under the Ant Group) relies on its advantage in FinTech technologies and big data it generates to deliver online financial services, especially online credit loans to rural areas, RCC institutions and PSBC branches, with their many outlets, emphasize a combination of online and offline services in most counties or county-level cities. In contrast, the branches of the Construction Bank of China (zhongguo jianshe yinhang), with fewer outlets in counties or county-level cities, deliver multiple digital loan products without sending many personals to villages. In the application of FinTech technologies, rural small and medium-sized banking institutions, such as RCC institutions and village banks, are, in general, lagging behind.

However, the pluralization of financial institutions in terms of their number in a rural jurisdiction and their digital transformation themselves don't necessarily mean a diversified and tailored delivery of financial services to meet the diversified demand of the rural population, especially the farm households, the new types of agricultural holdings (big specialized farm households, family farms, farmers' cooperatives, agricultural and agribusiness enterprises) and Small and Medium-sized Enterprises (SMEs) in rural areas. A part of competition between financial institutions takes place in the realm of winning the existing bank customers, while another part of competition is related to winning additional customers. There is no real credit cooperative or credit cooperative union which operates across a wide area. There is a lack of real cooperatives in Chinese counties or county-level cities.

Although formal financial institutions have been developed significantly in rural China, informal finance has been playing a very important role in meeting financial demand in rural China. The recent government policies are characterized by lowering the upper limit of the allowed interest rates, closing down interest-bearing informal financial business, especially informal financial organizations, and cracking down on any illegal forms of debt collection.

This monograph is an attempt to discuss and analyze the development of financial development and reform in rural China. Among the four authors, Prof. Xingyuan Feng, Prof. Guangwen He and Prof. Tongquan Sun has been well-known in the fields of rural development and rural finance in China, while Prof. Christer Ljungwall is well-established as an expert of China, studying in the field of economic and financial development in China, focusing on development finance and development economics. All four authors published widely.

The monograph contains papers completed by the authors in recent years. Some of them got updated, while some others remain in their original form. It consists of seven chapters:

- Chapter I: Towards a Competitive and Inclusive Financial Market in Rural China: A Theory-driven Approach;
- Chapter II: 70 Years' Evolution of the Rural Financial System of the People's Republic of China;
- Chapter III: Farm Households' Demand for and Access to Loans in Rural China;
- Chapter IV: Ownership, Governance and Interests of Financial Institutions within the Rural Credit Cooperative System in China;
- Chapter V: Improving the Financial Sustainability of the Financial Institutions within the RCC System of China: Problems and Policy Option;
- Chapter VI: The Development of Digital Inclusive Finance in Chinese Counties: Index Construction, Measurement and Analysis;
- Chapter VII: China's Financing Support for Poverty Alleviation.

These chapters constitute a rough picture of the situation and problems of the financial development and reform in rural China.

Chapter I, "Towards a Competitive and Inclusive Financial Market in Rural China: A Theory-driven Approach", serves as an introduction to the main ideas the authors would like to convey to the readers. It provides an analytical framework for the whole book and gives an overview of the demand and supply of financial services in rural China. The authors review existing rural finance paradigms, such as the Subsidized Credit Paradigm and the Rural Financial Systems Paradigm, and propose an alternative paradigm, the Local Knowledge Paradigm, based on Hayek's notion of local knowledge. The new paradigm suggests that further diversification of rural financial institutions and the formation of a competitive and inclusive rural financial market are important prerequisites for farmers and small and medium-sized enterprises to be able to fully capture the benefits from their economic activities. By employing this new paradigm, the authors further analyze the structure of China's rural financial system, the demand of China's rural financial services, the development of rural formal, semi-formal and informal finance and some considerations of how to improve the functioning of China's rural financial market.

Chapter II, "70 Years' Evolution of the Rural Financial System of the People's Republic of China", analyzes the evolution of the rural financial system in the 70 years from 1949, the founding year of the People's Republic of China, to 2019. Before the reform and opening up, the evolution of the PRC's rural financial system can be divided into two stages: first, the initial establishment of the rural financial system, with state-owned banks as the main body, supplemented by credit cooperatives and informal lending; second, the formation of a planning system of integrated state banks. After the reform and opening up, The PRC's rural financial system has evolved in the path of the marketization of rural financial institutions and the opening up of the rural financial market. It has gone through four sub-stages of development, namely, the initial formation of the rural financial market, the functional division and coordination of different financial institutions, the initial formation of the modern rural financial market and the development of an inclusive financial system. Overall, the PRC's rural financial system has been developing towards a multi-level and sustainable system with a wide coverage of financial services. It has been becoming more inclusive. Nevertheless, it is still a long way to build a rural financial system that meets the requirements for serving "agriculture, rural areas and farmers" well and meets, to a high degree, the diversified financial demands in rural China.

Chapter III "Farm Households' Demand for and Access to Loans in Rural China" analyzes a survey on farm households' demand for and access to loans in rural China. Based on the survey data of 1,730 farm households in 9 counties of three provinces, this research shows that the demand for farmers' credit is still strong, informal credit is still the main channel for farmers to meet their credit demand, farmers' credit rationing is still serious, mortgage and guarantee are still the main way for farm households to obtain formal credit, the availability of farm households' formal credit is still low, and the degree of self-exclusion of farmers' financial services is still high. The credit demand of farmers with different production and operation modes and income levels and small-scale farmers is still relatively strong. In order to improve the availability of farmers' credit, it is necessary to further relax market access control from the perspective of financial supply, integrate county-level financial supervisions, implement special financial institutional arrangements conducive to improving farmers' and small and micro enterprises' access to credit, and conduct the structural adjustments on the demand side.

Chapter IV, "Ownership, Governance and Interests of Financial Institutions within the Rural Credit Cooperative System", analyzes the situation and problems of the ownership structure, governance and interests of the RCC institutions in rural China. The overall reform of rural credit cooperatives (RCCs) has been a success to a certain extent since 2003. RCCs were restructured into rural commercial banks, rural cooperative banks and rural credit cooperatives with a single judicial person status within respective county-level jurisdictions. The reform approach is seriously government-centered, not well respecting RCCs' own autonomy. After the restructuring, the problems with "insider control" and "outsider control" persist within RCCs, rural cooperative banks and rural commercial banks, and the relationship between the responsibilities, rights, and interests accrued to different stakeholders are unbalanced and distorted. The 2010 reform policy requires that all rural credit cooperatives and rural cooperative banks are to be transformed into rural commercial banks, while the provincial associations of credit cooperatives which have the task of managing RCCs, rural cooperative banks and rural commercial banks within their respective provinces should focus on executing their service functions. The direction of such policy is not wrong since the RCCs and rural cooperative banks are not able to comply with the principles of cooperatives, and the provincial associations have no right to intervene in the micro-management of these rural financial institutions. The government needs to respect the autonomy of rural credit cooperatives and rural cooperative banks themselves. Only takings this step would straighten out the distorted relationship between the responsibilities, rights and interests accrued to different stakeholders of RCCs and rural cooperative banks. In addition, there is a huge space for the development of new authentic rural credit cooperatives. One should not refuse to take this step because of the existence of a large number of RCCs and rural cooperative banks which are not able to operate in accordance with the principles of cooperatives.

Chapter V, "Improving the Financial Sustainability of the Financial Institutions Within the RCC System: Problems and Policy Options", analyzes the status quo of and problems with the financial sustainability of the financial institutions within the RCC System. RCC institutions are the ones with the largest number and the widest coverage in China. With a reform introduced by the China

Banking and Insurance Regulatory Commission in 2010, all rural cooperative banks and rural credit cooperatives were transformed into shareholding entities without any element of a cooperative system, which implies that all of the RCC institutions are now shareholding entities without any element of a cooperative system, no matter whether their names are coined with the term "cooperative". The RCC institutions are the main force of the current rural financial market and play an important role in supporting rural revitalization and agricultural and rural modernization. In comparison with 2003, the beginning year of the RCC reform, the business operations and asset conditions of the RCC institutions improved significantly in general. However, these financial institutions still face big challenges in their business operations and development. There are still a series of problems relating to their ownership and governance, and some are vulnerable and also face severe financial risks. This paper expounds the above problems and analyzes their background and origins.

The direction of the development of the financial system is an inclusive financial system. Digital infrastructure is the core of financial inclusion. The research and improvement of the digital infrastructure of inclusive finance are not only conducive to the construction and operation of the current inclusive financial system but also a priority for the future.

Chapter VI, "The Development of Digital Inclusive Finance in Chinese Counties: Index Construction, Measurement and Analysis", introduces the construction and measurement of the first digital inclusive financial development index for Chinese counties. In China, there has still been a lack of an index evaluation system which systematically measures the development of digital inclusive finance in Chinese counties. Based on the MYBank (Ant Group) business data of digital inclusive finance of 1884 counties (county-level cities and autonomous counties) and their socioeconomic statistics, this paper constructs an index system of the development of digital inclusive finance in Chinese counties from the dimensions of the breadth and depth of the outreach of, and the quality of digital inclusive finance, and puts forward the method of measuring the scores of the indicators at all levels in this index system. This paper obtains thus the scores of these counties for the period of 2017~2019, which systematically reflects the development of digital inclusive finance in these counties. The research shows that the overall development of digital inclusive finance of counties has been greatly improved in all the macro regions and provinces of China, but there are obvious differences among the macro regions and provinces; the breadth and depth of the outreach of digital inclusive finance are greatly improved, and the improvement of service quality is relatively insufficient; the development of digital loans and the approval of line of digital credit is the fastest, followed by the development of mobile payment, while the development of digital wealth management and digital insurance is relatively slow. Generally speaking, there is a huge space left for the development of digital inclusive financial services in China. It is necessary to further strengthen the construction of digital inclusive financial infrastructure in Chinese counties and improve a relevant framework of rules and national and local laws and policies, the system of digital inclusive financial services and the literacy of the residents relating their knowledge of digital inclusive finance in these counties.

Chapter VII, "China's Financing Support for Poverty Alleviation", reviews the development and evolution of China's financial policies for poverty alleviation since the reform and opening up 40 years ago, introduces and analyzes the main methods, and holds that finance plays an increasingly important role in China's poverty alleviation. This trend is consistent with China's transformation from a planned to market economic system, and it is also part of China's financial system reform. It provides important support for the implementation of China's development-oriented poverty alleviation strategy. The policies and methods continue to develop with China's economic development and poverty alleviation practice. The authors not only paid attention to solving the financing problems of poor families but also to the role of industrial and regional economic development. This chapter discusses both the improvement of material conditions and institutional development policies conducive to the poor. These policies not only focus on the causes that directly lead to poverty but also on the environmental factors and basic conditions. These policies not only refer to specific and direct poverty alleviation intervention but also to the construction of a comprehensive, systematic and comprehensive inclusive financial system.

The whole book contains many valuable, authoritative data collected from field surveys. It will contribute to the reader's understanding of the structure of the rural financial system and the operation of rural financial service providers in China. Most importantly, it provides the global academic community with an insight into scholarly debates and perspectives on finance in rural China, which have been underrepresented in English literature. It should thus constitute a valuable contribution to the small but growing body of English literature on financial development and reform, especially financial inclusion in rural China.

The book will be interesting to academic departments or development practitioners focusing on rural financial services (including microcredit) globally and in China specifically. The book would be of particular interest to the Asia-Pacific region and also to academics and practitioners in the global South. Because the subject of financial services as a means of, or impediment to, development is a popular and timely subject, and because of the increasing interest in the "Chinese Model" of development, it is expected that the book will be relatively well received.

The book would mainly appeal to graduate students (in particular Ph.D. students), academics and development finance practitioners doing independent research on rural development in China or elsewhere. Some of the chapters could be useful if getting assigned to reading lists for undergraduate and/or master's courses on Chinese rural development, Chinese business or development studies more generally.

We are grateful to Ms Yongling Lam, the editor of this book, and Mr Payal Bharti, her colleague at Routledge, for their patience and great help in bringing our manuscript to this final product.

Xingyuan Feng, Guangwen He, Tongquan Sun and Christer Ljungwall

Beijing/Stockholm, May 2022

Note

1 Between 2005 and 2008, several microloan companies were established in pilot reform guided by the PBC.

CONTRIBUTORS

Xingyuan Feng is Professor at the Rural Development Institute, Professor of Graduate School, Deputy Secretary-General of the Center of Small and Medium Scale Banking Institutions of the Chinese Academy of Social Sciences (CASS), and Director of the Committee of Rural Finance of the Rural Development Society of China (RDSC). He received his PhD in economics from the University of Witten/Herdecke, Germany. Xingyuan's main research fields include the Australian School of Economics, Freiburg School, Public Choice, constitutional economics, new institutional economics, evolutionary economics, private sector development, government finance, banking and finance, SME finance, rural finance, as well as local and rural governance.

Guangwen He is Professor of the Department of Finance and Director of the Center for Rural Finance & Microfinance Research at China Agricultural University. He focuses on rural finance, cooperative finance, microfinance & inclusive finance, financial demand & supply of farm households & MSEs and institutional & business innovation of small & medium financial institutions. Guangwen has been very active in field surveys. He was Visiting Professor at Duisburg University, Germany and Visiting Researcher at Norinchukin Bank Research Institute, Japan. He has also provided his expertise in microfinance and rural finance projects of the World Bank, ADB, IFAD, KFW and etc., in China.

Tongquan Sun is Research Fellow and Director of the Rural Finance Research Office of the Rural Development Institute (RDI) of the Chinese Academy of Social Sciences (CASS), Professor at the University of CASS and Secretary General of the Rural Development Society of China. He received his bachelor's and master's degree from the University of International Business and Economics (UIBE) in economics and law, respectively, and PhD from the Post-graduate School of CASS in Management. He was a visiting scholar at Duke University's Sanford School of Public Policy in the USA. He is a recipient of the Prize for Rural Development Research in China. He has provided consultancies to the government of China, some international development organizations, such as the World Bank, UNDP, IFAD, ILO, United Nations Resident Coordinator's Office in China and international and national NGOs. His main research interests are microfinance, financial inclusion, rural financial cooperatives, credit guarantee and poverty reduction, etc.

Christer Ljungwall is an economist specializing in international trade, knowledge production and innovation. He is Associate Professor in economics at Gothenburg University, Sweden.

He has held several positions over the years, including guest Professor at PKU-HSBC Business School in P.R. China; Science Counselor at the Embassy of Sweden in P.R. China; Associate Professor at Copenhagen Business School, Denmark; Sr. Economist with the Asian Development Bank; and Research-fellow at Peking University P.R. China. He is the author of numerous academic articles in economics, four books, and more than one hundred reports. His current research work focuses on international trade, knowledge production and innovation and geoeconomics. He is an advisor to governments and businesses and a frequently invited speaker on issues pertaining to Asian economic development and innovation. Dr. Ljungwall received his PhD in economics from Gothenburg University in 2003.

Dr. Horst Löchel is a Professor of Economics at Frankfurt School of Finance & Management in Germany and Co-Chairman of the Sino-German Center. He is also a member of the Board of Directors of the Shanghai International Banking and Finance Institute (SIBFI), where he acts as the Chairman from 2004 to 2012. From 2009 to 2011 he was appointed as the Director of the German Centre of Banking and Finance at China Europe International Business School (CEIBS) in Shanghai, where he was a Visiting Professor until 2019 as well. Before Frankfurt School, he was Professor of Economics and Acting Head of the Banking and Finance Department at the University of Cooperative Education in Berlin. He received his Ph.D (Dr. rer. pol.) from Goethe-University in Frankfurt. His research focusses on the development of China's economy and German-China economic relations.

Pei Guo, PhD, Professor for Department of Finance, College of Economics & Management at China Agricultural University. He focuses on rural finance, microfinance, development finance, value chain finance and land reform in China. He had also provided his expertise in microfinance and value chain finance projects of ADB, IFAD, World Bank, UNDP and etc., in China. He has cooperated with Taobao for many years, studying e-commerce and financial services.

Jing He, PhD, Professor and Chair for Department of Finance, College of Economics & Management at China Agricultural University. She focuses on rural finance, cooperative finance, microfinance & inclusive finance, digital finance. Jing yearly she organizes a field survey about the supply and demand of rural farm household in nine counties of three provinces in China and she had also provided her expertise in inclusive finance and digital finance projects of ADB, UNDP and etc., in China. She has long-term cooperation with Ant Financial Services to study rural digital finance.

Chong Dong is an Assistant Research Fellow of the Rural Development Institute at the Chinese Academy of Social Sciences (CASS) and Secretary-General of the Committee of Rural Finance of the Rural Development Society of China (RDSC). She focuses on rural finance, cooperative finance, microfinance & inclusive finance, value chain finance and agricultural insurance. Dong Chong has been very active in field surveys. She had also provided her expertise in value chain finance and rural finance projects of ADB, UNDP and etc., in China.

Xiang Yan is a Postdoctoral Fellow in the Institute of Finance & Banking, Chinese Academy of Social Sciences. He got his PhD in economics from the University of the Chinese Academy of Social Sciences. His main research fields are rural finance, inclusive finance, rural small & medium financial institutions.

1

TOWARDS A COMPETITIVE AND INCLUSIVE FINANCIAL MARKET IN RURAL CHINA

A Theory-driven Approach[1]

Xingyuan Feng, Christer Ljungwall and Horst Löchel

1. Introduction

China's rural financial system has changed dramatically over the last 40 years. Great progress has been made with financial pluralization in terms of an increasing number of financial institutions operating in respective counties or other county-level jurisdictions. This was made possible partly because new market entry policies have been launched since the mid-2000s for a limited number of new types of formal and semi-formal financial institutions, making it possible for them to absorb capital from the informal finance sector. The formal financial sector has become more robust than before, with the ownership system of rural credit cooperatives (RCCs, nongcun xinyong hezuoshe) got gradually restructured, and the new entities that came out of the restructuring became more market-oriented since 2001. Financial institutions within the RCC system are changing entirely to shareholding entities, given the fact that they lost the characteristics of real credit cooperatives anyhow. Furthermore, despite legal uncertainty, unregistered rural mutual fund societies (nongcun zijin huzhuhui) became flourishing in many rural communities, encouraged by the favorable rural finance policy proclaimed by the CCP. They are real credit cooperatives. Yet, their respective size is very small. At the same time, the rate ceiling for informal lending was changed by the Supreme Court in 2015 to a more tolerant level. And the death penalty for the crime of "fund-raising fraud" was abolished in the 2015 amendments of the Criminal Law.

In comparison with the rural financial system of a dozen years ago, a much better financial ecosystem is developed, which is quite conducive to the financial sector's excising better functions (Bodie et al., 2009). Despite the above progress China's rural finance reform has made, China's rural financial sector still lags behind the rural socio-economic development and is unable to meet the changing, multi-layered and diversified demands for financial services in rural areas. Farmers and small and medium-sized enterprises (SMEs) have an important position in the Chinese economy, but their role is impeded by limited access to formal finance and the general underdevelopment of rural financial markets (Feng et al., 2013).[2] That's one reason why informal finance still plays an important role for rural economic agents in China.

A well-developed financial system is key to an efficient allocation of social resources (Shaw, 1973; Goldsmith, 1969; Levine, 2005). If financial transaction mechanisms are underdeveloped, this will inevitably harm the development of an economy. And formal, semi-formal and informal finance are integrated parts of such a system. Their healthy and robust development is the key to the overall development of a better rural financial ecosystem.

DOI: 10.4324/9781003369776-1

In this introduction, we review existing rural finance paradigms and propose an alternative paradigm based on Hayek's notion of local knowledge (Hayek, 1945, 1948) which we denote the "Local Knowledge Paradigm". With respect to the resulting policy implications, this alternative paradigm suggests that further diversification of rural financial institutions and the formation of a competitive commercial and cooperative rural financial sector are important prerequisites in order to fully exploit the potential of markets. Such competitive rural financial structures do not exclude special government policy-oriented finance as a complement to better meet the demand for rural financial services.

This introduction proceeds as follows: Section 2 reviews the theoretical foundation of rural finance, i.e., existing paradigms. In Section 3, we subsequently introduce the new rural finance paradigm. Section 4 discusses the current structure of the rural financial system, followed by an analysis of the demand for financial services in rural areas in Section 5. Section 6 describes the development of rural finance institutions and the informal financial sector and their role in the supply of financial services in rural China and, in accordance with the Local Knowledge Paradigm, highlights the importance of a high degree of diversification of rural financial institutions. Hereinafter, Section 7 presents the policy implications resulting from our analysis in order to improve the rural financial system in China. Section 8 finally concludes.

2. Existing Rural Finance Paradigms

Rural finance theory is derived more from practices and experiences, and, therefore, rural finance paradigms always involve a dual dimension, i.e., they combine theoretical and practical components. Their rejection, modification or acceptance is often subject to an evolutionary process of trial and error (Popper, 2004). Nevertheless, rural finance paradigms play an important role in providing policy guidance for decisions fostering access to finance in rural areas.

There are two representative rural finance paradigms to date, the *Subsidized Credit Paradigm* and the *Rural Financial Systems Paradigm*. These two paradigms follow the path of traditional development finance theories, for example, Shaw's theory of financial deepening (Shaw, 1973) and McKinnon's theory of financial liberalization (McKinnon, 1973). Both theories point out the need to eliminate financial repression and enhance financial market deepening and liberalization in developing countries. In addition, though not an explicit rural market paradigm, Stiglitz's Incomplete Market Paradigm (Stiglitz and Weiss, 1981; Stiglitz, 1989; Greenwald and Stiglitz, 1986; Zhang and Heufers, 2002) has important implications for rural financial development. In particular, it lends support to government intervention in incomplete financial markets to do away with inefficiencies in the allocation mechanism.

2.1 The Subsidized Credit Paradigm

The Subsidized Credit Paradigm as a traditional theory dominated discussion on rural finance before the 1980s. It is based on the implicit assumption that farm households, especially the poor, lack adequate saving opportunities. The chronic lack of capital poses a permanent problem to rural areas. This paradigm correctly emphasizes that income uncertainty is high in the agricultural sector but incorrectly concludes that the sector cannot be an interesting target for commercial banks as agricultural profits generally are far too low (Yaron and Benjamin, 1997; Yaron et al., 1997; Zhang and Heufers, 2002). As a matter of fact, however, many agricultural activities are able to generate enough returns to cover the cost of capital.

Based on its underlying assumptions mentioned above, the Subsidized Credit Paradigm concludes that it is necessary to inject capital from outside rural areas and to establish special non-profit financial institutions that assume the task of funds allocation in order to increase agricultural production and alleviate rural poverty. According to this theory, interest rates of loans for agricultural production must be lower than in other industries in order to reduce the structural income gap between the different sectors. This paradigm implies that informal finance with high interest rates makes poor farmers even poorer and hampers agricultural development still further. Under such a framework, the government provides through rural bank branches and credit cooperatives a large number of low-interest policy funds for rural areas, with special subsidized loans targeting the poor.

Nevertheless, the assumptions underlying the Subsidized Credit Paradigm are inaccurate. In fact, there is a demand for savings opportunities by rural farm households, including the poor. Experiences from several Asian countries show that most poor people will save if they are offered adequate opportunities and incentives (Adams and Fitchett, 1992). Furthermore, low-interest loan policies do rather poor in promoting agricultural production and in effectuating a pro-poor income redistribution (Yaron and Benjamin, 1997). As the uses of funds for loans are fungible, low-interest loans are unlikely to promote particular agricultural activities. Indeed, often it is not the poor agricultural population in rural areas that emerges as the main beneficiaries of low-interest loans but rather wealthier farmers in need of large amounts of credit that may divert away and exploit the interest subsidy of low-interest loans (Vogel, 1984). Many subsidized credits are even channeled to initially commercially profitable projects and thus crowd out conventional commercial finance. The subsidized credits result in adverse selection problems and cause distortion in rural financial markets. The concept of subsidized credits also intensifies the misconception of financial institutions that agriculture inevitably is a low-return industry, further hampering farmers' access to finance and thus further increasing their dependence on government subsidies.

2.2 The Rural Financial Systems Paradigm

During the 1980s, the Rural Financial Systems Paradigm gradually replaced the Subsidized Credit Paradigm. Being built from exactly opposite theoretical assumptions than its predecessor paradigm, the rural Financial System Paradigm emphasizes the role of financial markets (Yaron et al., 1997; Zhang and Heufers, 2002). According to its logic, there is no need to channel subsidized credits to rural areas as rural farm households have saving ability.[3] Even more, a low-interest policy rather will prevent people from depositing in financial institutions and consequently will curb financial development. In addition, it is natural that the interest rate of informal lending is high, as considerably higher opportunity costs come along with informal lending in rural areas.

The Rural Financial Systems Paradigm focuses on the importance of rural financial reform. First, financial institutions in rural areas play an important role in rural finance, especially for the mobilization of savings, which is of utmost importance. Second, interest rates must be determined by the market, and the real deposit rates need to be positive in order to attract savings and balance the demand for and supply of funds. Third, whether or not a rural financial system is successful should be assessed by its financial institutions' performance as well as the degree of autonomy and sustainability of their business operations. Fourth, there is no need to implement a directed loan system for specific target groups. Finally; fifth, informal finance has its legitimacy and thus should not be completely eliminated, but rather, informal structures should be embedded into the overall rural financial system.

The two paradigms presented above have aroused much interest since the 1980s. Although the Subsidized Credit Paradigm is still supported by governments in a large number of developing countries, the Rural Financial Systems Paradigm has become the mainstream view within the international rural finance circle.

2.3 Incomplete Market Paradigm

Stiglitz's *Incomplete Market Paradigm* stresses that some social and non-market factors are needed to foster an efficient financial market. In its basic framework, it understands financial markets as markets characterized by imperfect information. In particular, lenders (financial institutions) do not dispose of full knowledge about borrowers, i.e., there is imperfect information potentially hampering the efficiency of the market mechanism and leading to socially undesirable financial market outcomes. According to this paradigm, in order to remedy this type of so-called "market failure", there is a need to implement appropriate government intervention schemes in the financial market. Non-market measures such as getting borrowers organized can be adopted as well (Stiglitz and Weiss, 1981; Stiglitz, 1989; Zhang and Heufers, 2002).

Stiglitz's extensive work on incomplete markets and information asymmetry between lenders and borrowers has had a significant influence on finance research. Besides, a related field of study, information economics, has also become an important tool in financial market analysis. Stiglitz concludes that government intervention in a market under imperfect information is imperative as it is able to mitigate information asymmetries.

3. The Local Knowledge Paradigm as a New Rural Finance Paradigm

However, the government also faces information asymmetry problems, and it has no advantage over market players in using local knowledge. Local knowledge refers to dispersed knowledge "which is and remains widely dispersed among individuals" (Hayek, 1973: 15) and "the knowledge of the particular circumstances of time and place" (Hayek, 1948). Furthermore, Stiglitz regards information asymmetry as an obstacle to the attainment of certain market outcomes. However, behind information asymmetry is often the local knowledge that can be utilized by market players, especially if new market mechanisms are discovered. Here competition can be utilized as a discovering procedure in Hayekian sense (Hayek, 1968).

In rural financial markets, the prevalence of local knowledge means that there exist situations that are characterized by information asymmetry between a borrower and a formal lender. However, this does not automatically provide a justification for government intervention, as a more developed market could potentially do away with these inefficiencies. For Hayek (1973: 15), local knowledge or dispersed knowledge is a resource which can be utilized by market actors. One can rightfully utilize and explore market processes and market mechanisms to discover and utilize local knowledge (Kirzner, 1973, 1992) and thus reduce the information asymmetry in rural financial markets. In contrast to the Imperfect Market Paradigm, the Local Knowledge Paradigm emphasizes the concept of local knowledge rooted in Hayek's epistemology. It echoes the aforementioned rural financial market paradigm but focuses explicitly on how to solve inefficiencies in the market process brought about by imperfect competition and imperfect information by discovering and exploiting local knowledge.

Hayek stressed that competition is a discovery procedure (Hayek, 1968). In particular, competition is a procedure of discovering information and thus reducing imperfect information and information asymmetry. Competition in rural financial markets can also manifest itself as a discovery procedure. According to Hayek's local knowledge notion, also known as the Market Process Paradigm, competition can help discover knowledge, promote its dissemination, and enhance cooperation (Hayek, 1937, 1945, 1948). Accordingly, agents engaging in peer relational transactions (including spot financial transactions) at a specific time and location can best explore and use local knowledge to reduce information asymmetry.

Effective implementation of the Local Knowledge Paradigm in China implies a fundamental change in both the organizational and operational structure of financial institutions and will ultimately result in a more competent rural financial system. In detail, the changes will spur competition within the rural financial sector by increasing financial institutions' degree of diversification and thus establishing a competitive rural financial order. Policy-steered credit schemes can still play a subsidiary role in specific sectors where an efficient competitive financial market cannot be established. Local knowledge, on the other hand, will be exploited more comprehensively, making it possible to prevent problems of information asymmetry and imperfection more effectively.

4. The Structure of China's Rural Financial System

Rural financial institutions in China are classified as formal, semi-formal, and informal financial institutions. Abiding by the definition by Adams and Fitchett (1992), financial institutions which are regulated by the authorities fall into the category of formal institutions, those fully beyond their supervision are called informal and semi-formal institutions are situated between these two categories. Formal financial institutions are generally supervised by financial authorities, such as currently the China Banking and Insurance Regulatory and Administrative Commission (CBIRC), while semi-formal institutions are established upon central or local government approval or licensing and are supervised by the government. Informal finance, on the other hand, is not subject to a regulatory mechanism and is mainly self-governed and controlled by prohibition (or access control) and subsequent cleanup.

With the possible exception of Fintech, many forms of which are informal financial activities, the informal sector has a much greater extent of local features (Feng et al., 2013).[4] This is also compatible with respect to the endogeneity of these informal financial institutions or activities. Moreover, formal financial institutions are generally of a much larger scale, operate over a greater geographical area and are more systemized than their counterparts in the informal sector.

It should be noted, however, that technical advances in information technology increase the action radius of informal finance. This is especially the case with regard to FinTech. Table 1.1 provides an overview of the different types of financial institutions and activities in China.

TABLE 1.1 Financial institutions in rural China

Formal finance	Semi-formal finance	Informal finance
Rural branches of the "Big Four State-owned Commercial Banks"[1]	Credit companies wholly owned by domestic banks	Informal direct borrowing
State Development Bank	Microcredit companies	Informal lending intermediaries
Agricultural Development Bank of China (ADBC)	Registered pawn houses	Informal lenders[4]
Rural credit cooperatives[2]	Registered community development funds	Rotating savings and credit associations
Rural cooperative banks[2]	Registered credit guarantee companies	Mutual funds
Rural commercial banks[2]	Registered investment companies	Unregistered rural mutual fund societies
City commercial banks[3]	Pawn shops	Microcredit programs
Postal Savings Bank of China	Registered microfinance institutions	Unregistered microcredit institutions
Joint-stock commercial banks	Registered rural mutual fund societies (nongcun zijin huzhuhui)	"Underground banks"[5]
Village banks	Registered Fintech platform companies	Informal discounting services
Rural mutual fund associations (nongcun zijin huzhushe)		Informal Fintech activities and organizations
Branches of securities companies		Trade credits, etc.
Branches of insurance companies		

Source: The authors.

Note: 1. "Big Four State-owned Commercial Banks" include Bank of China, China Industrial and Commercial Bank, China Construction Bank and Agricultural Bank of China. 2. Rural credit cooperatives, rural cooperative banks and rural commercial banks are regarded as "financial institutions within the RCC system". The rural cooperative banks and rural commercial banks are an outcome of the restructuring of rural credit cooperatives in many counties or cities since 2001. 3. Most city commercial banks are the outcome of the restructuring of city credit cooperatives in some cities. 4. "Informal lenders" are individuals specialized in informal lending businesses. 5. "Underground banks" involve various types of entities doing private saving and lending businesses or running foreign exchange conversion businesses without government approval. Their businesses are illegal according to Chinese law and regulations.

From the viewpoint of the enforcement mechanism of financial contracts, formal financial institutions rely mainly on formal sanctions such as those provided by laws and regulations, while semi-formal institutions, though subject to the use of laws and regulations, first and foremost, implement informal sanctions in order to enforce financial contracts. In contrast to formal and informal institutions, informal financial organizations and activities are, first, subject to informal sanctions such as peer pressures and then formal sanctions.

From the viewpoint of epistemology, formal finance relies on both global and local knowledge, although the sector has problems in fully exploiting the potential of local knowledge. Semi-formal and informal finance, on the other hand, greatly benefit from the extensive use of local knowledge. As mentioned above, large formal financial institutions can enhance their ability to use local knowledge by downscaling financial operations and services. In this aspect, Rural Credit Cooperatives (RCCs) are doing better than the Agricultural Bank of China (ABC) in serving small farm households since RCCs' operations are locally rooted to a greater extent.

Table 1.2 shows various categories, types and numbers of rural banking financial institutions. The major players are in the first place rural credit cooperatives, rural cooperative banks and rural commercial banks, which are regarded as "financial institutions within RCC system" in the lending business for farm households and rural micro and small enterprises. In general, there is only one RCC, rural cooperative bank or rural commercial bank operating in each county.

TABLE 1.2 Categories, types and number of rural banking financial institutions in China (by the end of 2016)

Category	Name	Types by size	Number
Policy-oriented banks	State Development Bank	Big Bank	1
	Agricultural Development Bank of China	Big bank	1
Commercial banks	"Big Four" State-owned Commercial Banks (Rural branches, including those of the Agricultural Bank of China)	Big banks	4
	China Postal Savings Bank of	Big bank	1
	Rural commercial banks	Mostly small and medium banks	1114
	Village banks	Small banks	1443
Cooperative financial institutions	Rural cooperative banks	Small and medium financial institutions	40
	Rural credit cooperatives	Small and medium financial institutions	1125
	Rural or town mutual fund associations	Small and medium financial institutions	48
Semi-formal financial institutions	Credit companies	Small semi-formal financial institutions	13
	Microcredit companies	Small semi-formal financial institutions	8,673
	Registered P2P lending platform companies	Small semi-formal financial institutions	2,448★

★ Registered P2P lending platform companies are a kind of registered Fintech platform companies which had been regulated strictly by the government since 2016. There were 2,448 registered P2P lending platform companies which were still running normal businesses by the end of 2016.

Source: China Banking Regulatory Commission. Annual Report of the China Banking Regulatory Commission 2016, July 25, 2017; People's Bank of China. Report of the Statistical Data of Microcredit Companies 2016, January 25, 2017; Yingcan Consulting. Annual Report of the P2P Lending Industry 2016, January 6, 2017.

5. Demands for Rural Financial Services

5.1 Structure and Diversity of Demand

Demands for financial services in rural areas depend on multiple factors and arise from the different needs of farm households, rural enterprises, villages, as well as township and county governments. Living expenses and small agricultural loans constitute the main demand for credit amongst farm households. Studies such as Han (2009) have shown that the average credit needs of farm households are small in volume and geographically widely distributed, have short maturity and exhibit seasonal characteristics. Moreover, credit is used for a wide range of living and production purposes. Farm households which run an agribusiness demand mainly larger loans for specialization and expanding their scale of production.

The situation is different with rural micro and small enterprises. Micro and small enterprises demand credit for starting their businesses, keeping operating, expanding their production, and entering markets. The credit volumes demanded are relatively small in comparison to that required by medium and large enterprises focusing on tapping new markets or maintaining or expanding their current business. From an epistemological point of view, any form of financial institution which is relatively good at utilizing local knowledge is more capable of meeting the demand of these micro and small enterprises for loans: Such financial institutions tend to better utilize the financial tools currently at their disposal and identify and manage clients. With respect to larger enterprises, financial institutions, in the context of their lending decisions, rather rely on global knowledge.

Financial service providers which emphasize the use of local knowledge, on the other hand, are better able to adapt to the specific needs of farm households and rural micro and small enterprises in their geographical proximity. They limit their business scope to a small range of financial products, especially loan business. Yet, to facilitate access to rural finance and in order to broaden finance opportunities for rural economic agents, more diversified financial institutions are needed. However, a mere expansion of the number of local financial institutions alone will not do away with the problem of limited access to financial services for farm households and SMEs in rural areas. For these institutions to effectively contribute to an efficient rural financial system, they must amend their financial services offered by complementing financial instruments such as agricultural credit insurance mechanisms. Table 1.3 summarizes the diversified financial services demanded by farm households, rural enterprises, local governments, and village organizations.

TABLE 1.3 Demand for financial service in rural areas

Users of Rural Financial Services			Main Type of Loan Demands
Farm households	Poor farm households		Living expenses and small loans
	Ordinary farm Households	Traditional farming	Living expenses and small loans
		Farm households running agribusinesses	Specialization and expanding scale of production
Rural enterprises	Micro and small enterprises		Starting, maintaining and expanding business
	Medium to large enterprises		New market entry; maintaining and expanding current production/business
	Leading enterprises	In early stage of development	Expanding specialized technology-intensive production and expanding overall production/business
		In developed stage	Expanding specialized technology-intensive production and expanding overall production/business, maintaining or expanding market share/entry to new markets

(Continued)

TABLE 1.3 (Continued)

Users of Rural Financial Services		Main Type of Loan Demands
Local government	Provincial, county and township governments	Infrastructure, new loans to pay off old loans
Village organization	Villagers' committee and village economic cooperatives	Infrastructure (roads, schools and village office buildings, etc.)

Source: The authors.

5.2 Meeting the Financing Demand of Farm Households

Although the situation is improving, the coverage of formal financial institutions in China's rural areas remains limited. In 2017, the China Agricultural University investigated 2,093 farm households in 54 villages of 3 provinces, i.e., Shandong, Henan and Guangxi, and obtained 1,730 effective sample households. 705 households of them (40.75%) had credit demand. Of the 705 households with credit demand, 485 (68.8%) can be satisfied through formal and informal channels. Of the 485 households with credit support, only 165 (34.02%) obtained sufficient credit support from formal financial institutions. Although 60 households can obtain formal credit support, the amount of their loans cannot meet their financial needs, and they need to be supplemented through informal credit. In addition, 260 farmers are unable to obtain formal credit support and are totally dependent on informal credit (He et al., 2008).

According to a 2006 survey organized by the People's Bank of China (in the following PBC survey), only some 10% of farm households receive credit from formal financial institutions, whereas the figure for farm households having received informal loans is close to 25%.[5] According to data from the China Banking Regulatory Commission, of the more than 230 million Chinese households, more than 120 million claimed to be in direct need of credit in 2007. About 32% of total households thereby satisfy their need for credit by accessing rural cooperatives and farmers' mutually guaranteed loans (Hu, 2009). The PBC survey also shows that, in general, the average loan volume that farm households borrow from the formal financial sector is close to 50% higher than from the informal financial sector. Table 1.4 summarizes the origin and size of farm household loans.

According to the PBC survey (People's Bank of China, 2009), regarding the purpose of lending, farm households' credit needs for meeting living expenses account for 45% of their total loan demand, thus exceeding their credit need for productive (41%) and other purposes (11%). Loans supplied to farm households by formal financial institutions are far from being sufficient, and the extent of credit rationing remains severe.[6] The average loan for a household amounts to 10,906 RMB, with more than 52% of all households drawing on loans in excess of 5,000 RMB, 20% on loans between 10,000–20,000 RMB and less than 3.5% having loans higher than 30,000 RMB. When asked how much money they were willing to borrow under the existing mortgage and guaranty conditions, farm households' answers ranged around 22,000 RMB on average. Thus, as becomes apparent, the credit needs voiced by farm households are far from being satisfied. At the same time, several farm households with effective credit demand find themselves unable to find appropriate credit instruments that suit their needs. Table 1.5 summarizes the main reasons farm households were willing to take loans that prevented them from applying for credit with formal financial institutions.

The main reason why farm households don't succeed in receiving loans from formal financial institutions essentially is the lack of "guanxi"[7] and having no mortgage or guarantee for getting loans (see Table 1.6). Another reason is credit rationing in the formal sector. Yet, in using detailed information on farmers' investment projects and exploiting local knowledge of farmers' credit records,

TABLE 1.4 Farm household loans and their size

	Formal and informal sector	Formal sector	Informal sector
Percentage of farm households having taken loans in all households	30.8%		
Percentage of farm households having taken loans in all households		10.4%	23.8%
Average amount of a loan in RMB	6,606	8,589	4,624

Source: People's Bank's Survey on the Borrowing Situation of Farm Households, 2009.

Note: Interest-free borrowings are included in informal loans. "Informal" refers to "informal and semi-formal" if one contrasts "informal" to "formal" only. This applies to the whole book unless "semi-formal" is mentioned explicitly.

TABLE 1.5 Farm households' reason for not applying for a loan

Reasons	Percentage (%)
Afraid of failing to repay the loans	10.72
Interest rate and other costs too high	37.1
Afraid of not getting loan application approved	18.54
Other reasons	32.92
Total	100.00

Source: People's Bank's Survey on the Borrowing Situation of Farm Households, 2009.

TABLE 1.6 Reason to reject farm households' loan applications

Reasons	Percentage (%)
Having no mortgage or guarantee	23.83
Lack of guanxi	33.36
Too poor	7.73
There were old loans which hadn't been paid off	7.57
Other reasons	27.51

Source: People's Bank's Survey on the Borrowing Situation of Farm Households, 2009.

formal financial institutions could do much better in meeting farmers' credit needs. For example, by downscaling their financial products and services, formal financial institutions can refine their credit rating system and enlarge loan coverage. The government furthermore could encourage farm households to establish formal grassroots financial institutions of their own. By fully exploiting internal local knowledge and the information symmetry among farmers, the formal grassroots financial institutions could establish an efficient intermediary providing financial services to farmers.

As Table 1.7 illustrates, there also is a high but still unexploited loan demand from farm households. The main reasons why many farm households can but do not want to borrow money are that they, in descending order: (i) have enough financial resources to meet current production and living demands; (ii) are unfamiliar with borrowing; (iii) have no profitable projects to develop; or (iv) can accumulate enough money by labor.

Most loans (93%) farm households receive from peers are interest-free. Among loans bearing interest, high rates are charged in very rare cases. The average interest rate of farmers' borrowing from peers for maturities between six and twelve months was 9.3% in 2006, and the average interest

TABLE 1.7 Reason for not demanding loans

Reasons	Percentage (%)
Have abundant money to meet current production and living demands	60.5
Don't have any profitable investment project	12.5
Don't want to become used to borrowing money	14.0
Can earn enough money by working as migrant labor	10.1
Others	2.9
Total	100.0

Source: People's Bank's Survey on the Borrowing Situation of Farm Households, 2009.

TABLE 1.8 Average borrowing and lending interest rates in informal sector in 2006 (%)

Loan term / Interest rate	½ year	½ – 1 year	1–3 years	3–5 years	5 years and above
Borrowing	9.2	9.3	8.4	9.4	6.6
Lending	10.1	10.4	10.6	–	–

Source: People's Bank's Survey on the Borrowing Situation of Farm Households, 2009.

rate for the one-year maturity was 10.4%. In fact, interest rates of loans between farm households, on average, have been higher than that of loans from formal financial institutions. Table 1.8 provides information on the average annual interest rates charged.

Notably, 49% of farmers taking loans (including from formal financial institutions) had overdue debts in 2006. The two main reasons for farm households not repaying their debt in time are the lack of enforcement mechanisms and unpredicted family expenses. Moreover, relatives and friends account for more than 83% of the creditors for farm households' first loans. These creditors, in turn, collect their receivables mainly when the debtors have the money available (62%) or in terms of a one-time payment (32%). As a result, the overdue rate appears to be quite high. This figure, although related, is not to be confused with the loan default rate. While the former is the percentage of borrowers who fail to pay their debts in time, the latter captures the ratio of outstanding loans debtors have failed to pay in time to total outstanding loans of a respective financial institution (formal or informal). Moreover, overdue behavior is not synonymous with breaking a contract, taking into consideration that both borrowing and repayment behavior should be monitored against the background of local culture and customs.

In the social network of a close community of a rural area, lending is often a reciprocal social exchange: It is a favor of the lending person granted to the borrowing person who promises to repay; however, the borrower, in her/his requesting a borrowing, she/he often only requests the return of a favor she/he granted beforehand to the lender. Such lending customs are reflected by the fact that most loans are interest-free, most creditors do not have a written receipt, and debtors are able to delay the repayment when they don't dispose of enough money at the time payment is due. Besides, in accordance with Chinese customs, most farm debtors who delay their debt repayment do not deny their obligation but recognize their unlimited liability. While this is different from Chinese formal civil and contract law, this does not mean that the lending parties cannot resort to formal laws.

Hence, though the loan default rate of formal financial institutions (RCCs, for example) appears to be high, especially in regard to small credits, this figure can only be interpreted appropriately considering Chinese farmers' credit culture and customs. Many farmers are able to pay the interest but have limited ability to pay the principal. Loan officers generally just extend these loans' periods considering their personal income and the interests of the RCC. In this way, bad loans are disguised as standard loans. As a result, although the loan default rates of farm debtors appear to be high, they rarely constitute a high volume of bad loans. On the other hand, formal financial institutions are forced to pay attention to the matter. Education on modern credit culture is needed among farmers, and a strict credit discipline is required to eliminate high default rates.

5.3 Meeting the Financing Demand of SMEs in Rural Areas

A number of studies, such as Feng et al. (2006), Han (2009) and Li (2014), have shown that lack of credit is a major constraint for SMEs in rural areas. Further factors restricting the development of enterprises are weak external demand, frequent changes in macroeconomic policies, unfair competition, exchange rate fluctuation, weak technologies, a high tax burden, lack of information and adverse government intervention, among others (Feng and Zhang, 2018). Both formal and informal loans are important for SMEs.

According to the data of the Report on the "Small and Micro Enterprise Index" released by ChinaPnR Ltd. and Southwest University of Business and Economics in 2014, 45.2% of the surveyed small and micro enterprises in rural areas have borrowed bank loans (including loans from rural credit cooperatives), the average amount of a loan is 57,900 RMB, and 54.8% of the surveyed enterprises borrowed funds from the informal financial sector, the average amount of the funds is 70,200 RMB. Data show that the average annual interest rate of their interest-bearing borrowings from the informal financial sector is 18.8%, which is double the annual bank lending rate (9.4%) (Li, 2014).

Han's survey data reveals that 37% of rural enterprises borrow from rural credit cooperatives while 10% access credit from the Agricultural Bank of China. The proportion of loans to rural SMEs from formal financial institutions accounted for 52%. Accordingly, informal lending accounted for 48% of total credit.

Regardless of whether we consider formal or informal finance, credit rationing of rural enterprises is widespread, and the new lending supply is far from sufficient to meet the demand of SMEs. According to Han (2009), there are three major problems rural enterprises face in applying for loans: First, the proportion of companies that have access to credit supplied by banks or RCCs is small, and their credit lines are too small. Second, the collateral requirements stipulated by formal institutions make it difficult for small enterprises to borrow. Third, because informal channels in rural areas mainly consist of friends and families, specialized informal lenders and other individual loan providers, the scale of informal finance is limited. Key factors in formal financial institutions' lending decisions are the availability of sufficient collateral, a satisfactory scale and performance, as well as good past credit records Feng (2006). Table 1.9 provides additional information on factors rural enterprises consider as constraints to their development.

TABLE 1.9 Factors constraining the development of rural enterprises (%)

Lack of funds	Backward technology	Insufficient market space	Insufficient access to information	Government intervention	Heavy tax burden	Unskilled labor	Other
64.2	30.7	39.6	14.5	10.1	23.5	15.2	4.4

Source: Han (2009).

Note: The sum can be greater than 100 as a result of the questionnaire design. 8.3% are enterprises whose annual sales exceed 30 million RMB.

6. Development of Rural Formal, Semi-formal and Informal Finance

6.1 Development of Agricultural Bank of China

The development of rural financial institutions started from scratch with the founding of the People's Republic of China and has gone along a zigzag path since then. Both the Agricultural Bank of China and the rural credit cooperatives have been major rural financial institutions. The predecessor of the Agricultural Bank was called the Agricultural Cooperative Bank of China, which was founded in August 1951. The Agricultural Bank received its current name in 1955. From 1951 to 1965, the bank was established and then merged into the People's Bank of China three times.

During the "Cultural Revolution" from 1966 to 1976, the People's Bank served as the only bank in China. It contained various specialized branches to take care of fund supply according to a central plan for corresponding sectors such as agriculture, industry and commerce, construction, and international transactions.

On February 23, 1979, it was established for the fourth time as a state-owned national bank specializing in agricultural lending. In 1993, the bank was changed into a state-owned commercial bank, known as one of the "Big Four" banks in China. From 1997 to 2006, the bank withdrew from many county-level jurisdictions or sub-county-level jurisdictions according to the decision of the 1997 Annual Finance Work Meeting of the Central Committee of the CCP. In September 1997, the bank started to experiment with its rural financial service delivery in Jilin, Anhui and six other provinces to follow the decision of the Third All-China Finance Work Meeting held in January 2007. According to this decision, the Agricultural Bank of China is to orient itself to servicing the agricultural, farm households' and rural development. In July 2010, the bank got listed in Shanghai and Hong Kong. Table 1.10 shows the size and performance of ABC in the rural financial sector of China.

TABLE 1.10 Size and performance of main rural financial institutions

	Number of banking financial institutions as legal person entities	Number of branches/ offices	Balance of loans related to agricultural, farm households' and rural development (100 million RMB)	Rate of non-performing loan (%)	Total assets (100 million RMB)	Equity (100 million RMB)	Post-tax profits (100 million RMB)	Number of employees
Agricultural Bank of China	1[1]	23,682[1]	27,600	3.02	1957,01[1]	13,216[1]	1841[1]	496,698[1]
Postal Savings Bank of China	1[1]	40,000[1]	9,174	0.87[2]	82,700[1]	44,219	398	171,551[3]
Rural commercial banks	1,114	49,307	53,096	2.9	202,680	15,167	1785	558,172
Rural cooperative banks	40	1,381	1,767	3.3	4359	363	38	13,561
Rural credit cooperatives	1125	28,285	27039	8	79,496	4698	519	297,083

	Number of banking financial institutions as legal person entities	Number of branches/offices	Balance of loans related to agricultural, farm households' and rural development (100 million RMB)	Rate of non-performing loan (%)	Total assets (100 million RMB)	Equity (100 million RMB)	Post-tax profits (100 million RMB)	Number of employees
Village banks	1,443	4,716	5,550	2	12,000			81,521
Total	3,724	147,371	124,226		1,300,125			1,618,586

Source: China Banking Regulatory Commission: Annual Report 2016, 2017; Agricultural Bank of China: Annual Report 2016, 2017; Postal Savings Bank of China: Annual Report 2016, 2017.

Note: 1. These indicators of the bank's size and business performance refer to the whole of China, including the urban and rural areas. 2. This figure is the rate of a non-performing loan in the balance of all loans, not only including the loan for agricultural, farm households and rural development. 3. Basic Information of Listed Company, September 30, 2016, http://stockpage.10jqka.com.cn/HK1658/.

6.2 Development of Rural Credit Cooperatives

The first rural credit cooperatives since the founding of the New China were also established in 1951, running basically in accordance with cooperative principles, with members being mainly farmers who paid membership shares. However, their activities were seriously affected by their external governance structure: They were centrally administered by the People's Bank of China till 1958, then were merged into credit departments (xinyong bu) of the People's Communes with grassroots branches of state-owned banks and these credit departments in 1958. In 1959 the rural credit cooperatives were separated from the credit departments and managed by production brigades. In 1962, they began to be administered by the People's Bank of China again. From 1966 to 1974, the operation of rural credit cooperatives was chaotic and heavily affected by the "Cultural Revolution". They were even managed by "poor and lower-middle peasants". From June 1974 to 1977, they were encouraged to operate more autonomously. However, they were managed by the People's Bank as grassroots branches of that bank in rural areas in 1978, according to the 1977 State Council decision "Several Provisions on Rectifying and Strengthening Banking Work". They were, at that time, fully run by the government. They were managed by the Agricultural Bank of China since that bank was separated from the People's Bank in 1979 and increased their self-operation since then.

Only in August 1984 did rural credit cooperatives start to rehabilitate their three characteristics of being organized by the mass, democratically managed and flexibly operated in accordance with the State Council's approval of the Agricultural Bank's path-breaking "Report on the Reform of Management System for Rural Credit Cooperatives". One of the most important breakthroughs was that rural credit cooperative associations were established at the county level. With the introduction of the associations, the degree of autonomy of rural credit cooperatives increased. In 1989, rural credit cooperatives were further standardized and consolidated in the direction of autonomous business decisions and operations. In August 1996, the Inter-ministerial Coordination Group for Rural Financial System Reform of the State Council issued the "Notice of the Implementation Plan of the Separation of Rural Credit Cooperatives from the Agricultural Bank of China" and officially declared the rural credit cooperatives to be decoupled from the Agricultural Bank of China. All rural credit cooperatives and their county-level associations have been gradually decoupled from the Agricultural Bank of China then after. In June 1997, the People's Bank established the Administrative Bureau for Supervising Rural Cooperative Finance. It was responsible for leading the new round of RCC reform in the direction of enhancing its cooperative system, self-management and self-discipline. At the same time, the bureau took on the function of supervising the RCCs.

In 1999, the first provincial-level business associations of rural credit cooperatives (xinyong hezuo xiehui) were established in Heilongjiang, Shaanxi, Sichuan, Zhejiang and Fujian, which took over the function of the sectoral management of RCCs. Also, the Rural Credit Cooperative Association of the Ningxia Hui-Nationality Autonomous Region, the first provincial-level rural credit cooperative association, was established in the same year. On August 10, 2007, the Hainan Rural Credit Cooperative Association was established as the last provincial-level association, which symbolized the completion of the reform of establishing provincial-level associations across China.

The experiments with the ownership structure reform of RCCs started in 2000. In the same year, all the 1746 rural credit cooperatives were merged with their county-level associations as unified entities in a single legal person status in their respective county-level jurisdictions. In 2001, the first rural commercial banks were transformed from RCCAs and founded in Zhangjiagang, Changshu and Jiangying city. In the same year, Yinzhou Rural Credit Association started its experiment of transforming itself into a rural cooperative bank. This first rural cooperative bank opened its business on April 8, 2003. On June 27, 2003, the State Council launched a full-fledged reform of RCCs; while poor-performing RCCs were to be consolidated or even liquidated, others were to be transformed into rural credit cooperative associations as unified entities in single legal person status within respective counties, rural cooperative banks and rural commercial banks. During the reform, part of the losses made by RCCs was covered by the central government and local governments.

On November 9, 2010, the China Banking Regulatory Commission released "Guiding Opinions of the China Banking Regulatory Commission on Accelerating Equity Reform of Rural Cooperative Financial Institutions". According to this document, the rural cooperative financial institutions should formulate a plan for equity reform, speed up the transformation of qualification shares, and abolish them before the end of 2015. In the future, no new rural cooperative banks will be established. Rural credit cooperative associations and rural cooperative banks which meet the qualification of becoming rural commercial banks should be converted into such banks directly. If the conditions are not met, their qualification shares should be converted into investment shares as soon as possible, and they should be transformed into rural credit associations (nongcun xinyong she) under the shareholding system. This document shows no cooperative elements will be retained after the equity reform of rural credit cooperate associations and rural cooperative banks.

After this new round of RCC reform in 2003, the financial situation of RCCs or their successors improved significantly. But all of them became profit-oriented, far away from complying with the cooperative principles. Also, with the withdrawal of the ABC from many county-level jurisdictions since 1997, RCCs, rural commercial banks, and rural cooperative banks became monopolies or quasi-monopolies in the agricultural lending business in the formal financial sector of rural areas.

6.3 Postal Savings Bank and Policy-Oriented Banks

While RCCs, rural commercial banks, and rural cooperative banks became monopolies or quasi-monopolies in agricultural lending in their respective counties or other county-level jurisdictions, their only major challenger in absorbing deposits is the Postal Savings Bank of China. This is because the bank enjoys a high density of service outlets. According to this bank's "Social Responsibility Report 2018", by the end of 2017, the Postal Savings Bank has nearly 4 million service outlets, 143,000 rural deposit withdrawal services and nearly 120 self-help automats across China. According to the "Annual Report of the Postal Savings Bank 2017", it absorbed a balance of personal deposits amounting to 6,200 billion RMB and disbursed personal loans amounting to 1,580 billion

RMB by the end of 2016 across China. The balance of loans for agricultural, farm households and rural development was 917.4 billion RMB at the same point in time. A large part of deposits was taken from the rural area, so the bank was criticized as the "water pump" which has pumped financial funds out of the rural area (Li, 2018). The Postal Savings Bank was established in 2007. It originated from the former postal savings services, which was a part of the General Post Office of China. Around three fourth of the outlets of the postal savings bank are not separated from the China Post Group Co. (Li, ibid), the successor of the General Post Office of China, in managing postal and postal savings business operations, which implies heavy subsidy to the postal savings units from the China Post Group Co.

The Agricultural Development Bank of China is the only policy-oriented bank promoting agricultural development in China. It was founded in November 1994. It is responsible for providing credit support for the national purchase, sale and storage of grain and cotton. By 2013, its new business development model was formed: it is mainly to provide credit support for the national purchase, sale and storage of grain and cotton; at the same time, its main business is to be accompanied by two other business fields: its support for the agricultural modernization and agribusiness development and for the construction of agricultural and rural infrastructure. Currently, it has branches at provincial, prefecture and county levels across China.

Another policy-oriented national bank is the State Development Bank which focuses on financial support for the implementation of long- and mid-term development strategies in China. It provides some local financial institutions or local government investment and financing vehicle companies with a total credit line under the condition that local financial institutions or local government-designated representative institutions provide guarantees for the repayment.[8]

6.4 Development of New Financial Institutions

The number of financial institutions in China is now quite large. However, very few financial institutions really take care of disbursing loans for agricultural, farm households' and rural development in each county or other county-level jurisdictions. State-owned commercial banks (including ABC), national-level shareholding commercial banks and city banks are present within Chinese counties but focus on lending to larger industrial and commercial companies and government projects. At the same time, informal lending was pervasive since the financial supply of the formal banking sector to farm households was limited. This shortage of fund supply from the formal financial sector is reflected by high interest rates in the informal sector, which can reach for instances easily 18% or more on an annual basis in counties of Zhejiang province if one household is in urgent need of funds. The larger the shortage is, the higher the interest rate of informal lending.

It is a consensus among policy-makers and researchers in rural finance that financial pluralization is needed in rural China. The People's Bank of China started in 2005 with the introduction of small financial institutions serving agricultural, farm households' and rural development, formal and semi-formal, which was also regarded as a new channel to absorb funds from the informal financial sector and divert them into the formal and semi-formal financial sector. Seven microcredit companies (xiaoe daikuan gongsi) were established as a new type of semi-formal financial institution in five provinces in 2005. In 2006, the CBRC started with the experiments of introducing three new types of financial institutions, i.e., village banks (cunzhen yinhang), credit companies (daikuan) and rural mutual fund associations (nongcun zijin huzhushe). In May 2008, the PBC and CRRC jointly launched "Guiding Opinions on the Experiments with Microcredit Companies", which accelerated the development of this type of new financial institution.

By the end of 2016, there were 8,673 microcredit companies, 1,443 village banks, rural (or town) mutual fund associations, and 13 credit companies (Table 1.2). In general, with the introduction of these financial institutions, the structure of the banking sector got diversified and thus improved. Because of the high threshold for the entry of credit companies and rural mutual fund associations (RMFAs),[9] their number was limited. Microcredit companies are lending-only financial institutions, and they are not allowed to take a deposit, which led to a high cost of capital and high lending rate. Accordingly, their business focus is not on the goal of serving primarily agricultural, farm households' and rural development which was set by the government, but on lending to companies which have difficulties with access to formal finance. Village banks focus on small loans for farm households and agricultural development. However, the main initiators should be commercial banks. And their establishment is subject to the approval of the CBRC. This approval system hinders the growth of their number.

6.5 Development of Informal and Semi-formal Finance

As shown in Table 1.5, informal finance has played an important role in financing agricultural, farm households and rural development. Informal financial activities were not active in rural China in the period of the planned economy before China began with the reform and opening-up in 1978. Usury almost vanished. With the reform and opening up, people's commodity production and business activities increased, and so did the demand for capital. All kinds of high-interest loans and fundraising began to rise in the middle and late 1980s. Since the start of China's reform and opening up, the government has paid special attention to the prevention and control of "illegal fund-raising", usury and other "serious speculation" behavior.

In the 1980s, "illegal fund-raising" or usury were regarded as a "crime of speculation". If they were severe, the "criminals" were subject to death sentences. For example, in 1986, Zheng Lefen, a female organizer of rotating savings and credit associations (RoSCAs) in Yueqing county of Wenzhou city, was sentenced to death because of such a "crime of speculation". This name of crime was no more suitable at the time of the development of the commodity economy. Only in 1997 was the name "crime of speculation" abolished.

At the end of 1990s, the central government issued a set of regulations to ban "illegal fund-raising". Also, the 1997 amendments to the Criminal Law include the crimes of "fund-raising fraud" and "illegal taking of deposit from the public", which are the two main crimes in the category of "illegal fund-raising" in rural China. And the 2015 amendments of the Criminal Law made a "Great Step Forward" in that they abolished the death penalty relating to the crime of "fund-raising fraud", which means that there is now no death punishment for "illegal fund-raising".

The Supreme Court made, on August 13, 1991, a judicial explanation that interest of informal lending at an interest rate of a maximum of four times of similar lending rate of the bank is protected while the excessive part is not protected. On August 6, 2015, the ceiling of an interest rate for the protected interests of informal lending was fixed at 24% on an annual basis, while the rate over 36% is not protected. The space between the two rates is so-called that of "natural debt": if the borrower pays voluntarily, the court will not ban it; if she/he requests the return of the paid interest, the court will not support it.

On April 16, 2018, the new China Bank and Insurance Regulatory and Administrative Committee (CBIRC) even jointly issued a "Notice on Regulating Informal Lending Activities and Maintaining Economic and Financial Order" with the Ministry of Public Security, the State Administration of Market Supervision and the People's Bank of China, stating that without the approval of the competent authority, no unit or individual may establish an agency engaged in the loan business or issue loans as a regular business activity. This new regulation marks a new step forbidding any regular lending organizations or lending businesses in informal sector.[10] For instances, according to this Notice, an informal lender is allowed to do lending accidently but not regularly. He is not allowed to establish and maintain a company to do regular lending.

Although government policies are quite suppressive toward some special types of informal financial activities which involve or lead to "illegal fund-raising" or usury or threaten the stability of the so-called "financial order", a large part of informal finance will be further accepted or tolerated and go on playing an important role in financing rural and agricultural development.

Besides the aforementioned informal financial activities and microfinance companies as semi-formal financial institutions, there are many microfinance institutions or programs which can be regarded as informal and semi-formal financial activities. They are important in providing small farm households, especially poor households, with microcredit. These microcredit institutions or programs are often initiated by international organizations, non-governmental organizations, and some governments, and sometimes by some individuals or companies. Its no doubt that they made contributions to the target groups' income generation. However, the total size of the fund has been limited. And only a small part of them was financially sustainable, and very few of them were institutionally sustainable.

To mention are various types of rural mutual fund societies (noncun zijin huzhuhui). They were often established by farm households or cooperatives. They were not approved by the CBRC and were thus different from the rural mutual fund associations approved by the CBRC. However, the development of such societies was encouraged by almost every year's Document No. 1 of the Central Committee of the CCP. They were often not registered anywhere at all or internally registered with some government department such as local bureaus of civil affairs or with local federations of industry of commerce. Some of them operate as mutual lending cooperatives, while some others run as guarantee funds. These rural mutual fund societies and the rural mutual fund associations are real credit cooperatives. In some poor regions, rural mutual fund societies also receive funds from the government. They are required by the government to ensure the access of poor members to loans. According to incomplete statistics, there were 19,397 rural mutual fund societies within poverty villages in 2013 (Zhao, 2015) and 2,159 rural mutual fund societies run by farmers' cooperatives by the end of March 2014 (Zong, 2018). In sum, these various types of rural mutual fund societies are worth paying attention to. Again, the total amount of their funds is still limited.

7. Improving Financial Market Mechanisms

The multilayered demand for financial services on the part of farm households and SMEs requires further development of all types of rural financial institutions. The government's rural finance policies are favorable in this respect but have not yet been implemented to a satisfactory degree. In this respect, the Local Knowledge Paradigm can provide a theoretical basis that helps the government provide an environment apt for the development of sound and diversified rural financial markets. Specific suggestions for improving rural financial market mechanisms include further diversification of rural finance, the shaping of a competitive rural financial order and the building of an inclusive financial system:

Diversification of rural finance: First, rural financial diversification will enable more financial institutions to use their own capability and skills to identify and use local knowledge available to them and meet the demand for rural financial services in their way. Second, the diversification of rural financial institutions will introduce financial, supply-side competition in the rural financial market and, thus, break the monopoly or quasi-monopoly position of RCCs, rural cooperative banks and rural commercial banks in lending to farm households. Competition will foster efficiency and spur financial innovation, as well as lead to an expansion of the supply of financial services and the introduction of risk-based pricing, etc. Third, further diversification is necessary in order to exploit further local knowledge and tailor the supply of financial services to actual demand. Currently, rural financial institutions are more diversified than before. But the financial services they delivered were similar, and credit rationing was pervasive. More self-organized financial institutions are needed, which are close to the demand side and can simply come out of the demand side. More innovative financial institutions are needed, which are innovative in designing new products to activate financial demand that is potential and frozen because of lack of some sideline conditions. For instance, only after the transfer of some knowledge on some market opportunity, and even some skills of production, a poor farm household can discover its demand for some microcredit. Innovative financial institutions can even create new demands on financial services.

Shaping a competitive rural financial order: A competitive rural financial order implies a rural financial pluralization under a fair and open competition order. Under such an order, commercial finance and cooperative finance should play a major role while the government, with its policy-oriented finance, plays a supportive role in accordance with the principle of subsidiarity. Also, a competitive rural financial order implies a high degree of financial autonomy for the market players and an open or low-threshold market entry in rural areas. A competitive financial market is a corresponding market form under a competitive rural financial order. It can best explore and use the scattered local knowledge, utilize a variety of market mechanisms, and improve the financial services for farmers and rural SMEs.

Building up an inclusive financial system: An inclusive financial system implies two dimensions: first, individuals and organizations have access to financial products and services that meet their demands and are delivered in a responsible and sustainable way; second, poor or low-income groups can enjoy this at affordable cost. Many things should be done at three levels:

Macro level: A proper framework of legislation, regulation and supervision for an inclusive financial system should be established and maintained (Helms, 2006). A very positive development is that the State Council released at the end of 2015 "Plan for Promoting the Inclusive Financial Development (2016–2020)". However, currently, a very rigorous and centralized approval system for introducing new financial institutions is present, which is not conducive to the building of a real inclusive financial system. Part of financial institutions should and can be introduced in a decentralized way. Provincial offices of the new CBISAC can take more responsibility for approving the establishment of new financial institutions as far as they will operate mainly within the province where they will get registered. Also, the term "approval" should be understood as the acceptance of the application for the establishment of a new financial institution as soon as a pre-announced set of prerequisites are met by the applicants.

Meso level: The delivery of support services for inclusive finance should be ensured, and a basic financial infrastructure should be built up (Helms, 2006). For instance, the credit rating system should be upgraded. Currently, defaults in repayment of loans from formal financial institutions and a small part of related information are included in the PBC's credit rating system. A large part of related information is scattered among government departments, and even a part is concentrated in some internet platform companies such as Taobao and Jingdong. Information on guarantees and informal lending are not included in the rating system. A full-fledged credit rating system is to be established.

Micro level: There should be a multitude of financial service providers, especially retail financial service providers in rural areas. The latter of which offer services directly to poor and low-income clients (Helms, 2006). First, commercial banks need to substantially improve the supply of financial services to poor and low-income groups by downscaling their branches and services. Second, the current rule of "One RCC, rural cooperative bank, or rural commercial bank operates within one county" should be abolished. RCCs, rural cooperative banks and rural commercial banks can be allowed to operate mainly within their own prefecture-level cities within which they are registered. They can be allowed to operate within the whole province as far as they operate mainly within their own prefecture-level cities within which they are registered. Third, since the rural credit cooperatives, rural commercial banks and rural cooperative banks became all commercialized, there is also a need for the development of new real credit cooperatives. Fourth, all different kinds of new commercial, cooperative credit and guarantee institutions should be introduced that can provide microcredit, guarantees, micro-insurance, and other supplementary financial products and services. They should be helpful for boosting competition in the rural financial market. Fifth, policy-oriented banks should do more in wholesaling funds to other financial institutions. Sixth, well-performing microcredit institutions, microcredit companies and internet platform–based financial service providers can be licensed as banking financial institutions.

8. Concluding Remarks

This introduction shows existing rural finance paradigms, our proposed Local Knowledge Paradigm, the structure of China's rural financial system, the demand of China's rural financial services, the development of rural formal, semi-formal and informal finance and some consideration of how to improve China's rural financial market. We hope this introduction can act as a guide for the following chapters of this book.

Notes

1 Revised based on Xingyuan Feng, Christer Ljungwall, and Horst Löchel. Towards a Diversified and Inclusive Financial Market in Rural China: A Theory-Driven Approach, SGC Working Paper, December 2019, and Xingyuan Feng, Carsten Herrmann-Pillath, and Guangwen He. Toward Financial Pluralization in Rural China – An Analysis Based on "Local Knowledge Paradigm". *China Rural Review*, 2004(5), pp. 17–30.
2 See, for example, Levine (2005) for a discussion on the relationship between financial development and economic growth.
3 For instances, livestocks can be a kind of saving for the poor. There are also rotating savings and credit associations (RoSCAs) in Guizhou which use rice as savings and credit instruments (Feng et al., 2012).
4 In the following, we will not discuss informal Fintech activities which is a fully different type of informal finance in contrast to other informal financial institutions and activities.
5 A total of 20,040 households was surveyed by The People's Bank in 10 provinces nationwide. Here informal loans include loans from informall and potentially semi-formal ones. However, semi-formal channels were very rare and the corresponding amout would be very limited in 2006.
6 Credit rationing describes the situation when a bank limits the supply of loans, although it has enough funds to loan out, and the supply of loans is less than the effective demand of borrowers.
7 According to Luo (2000: 1f), guanxi means broadly "interpersonal linkages with the implication of continued exchange of favors. It includes reciprocal obligations to respond to requests for assistance".
8 According to the Budget Law, local government guarantees are illegal. However, local governments provide implicit guarantees through their companies or institutions.
9 The establishment of RMFAs should be approved directly by the CBRC. However, it seems to distrust this form of banking financial institution.
10 People's Bank of China, Notice of the People's Bank of China on the Failure of Enterprises or Individuals to Handle Financial Transactions, No. Yinfa (1992) 285, November 14, 1992.

References

Adams, D. and Fitchett, D. 1992. *Informal Finance in Low-Income Countries*. Boulder: Westview Press.
Bodie, Z., Merton, R. C., and Cleeton, D. L. 2009. *Financial Economics*, 2nd edition. Upper Saddle River, NJ: Pearson Prentice Hall.
Feng, X., He, G., and Du, Z. 2006. *The Financing of Township and Village Enterprises and Endogenous Informal Financial Organizational and Institutional Innovations*, Chinese edition. Taiyuan: Shanxi Economic Press.
Feng, X., He, G., and Zhao, B. 2013. *A Study on Informal Financial Risks in China*. Beijing: China Social Sciences Press.

Feng, X., Li, L., and He, G. 2012. *Rotating Savings and Credit Associations in China*. Beijing: Economic Science Press.

Feng, X. and Zhang, L. 2018. Quantitative Measurement and Empirical Investigation of the Environment for the Survival and Development of Private Enterprises. *Academic Circle*, Vol. 243, No. 8, pp. 143–154.

Goldsmith, R. W. 1969. *Financial Structure and Development*. New Haven and London: Yale University Press.

Greenwald, B. C. and Stiglitz, J. E. 1986. Externalities in Economies with Imperfect Information and Incomplete Markets. *The Quarterly Journal of Economics*, Vol. 101, No. 2 (May), pp. 229–264.

Han, J. 2009. *China's Rural Finance: A Survey*, Chinese edition. Shanghai: Shanghai Far East Publishing House.

Hayek, F. A. von. 1937. Economics and Knowledge. *Economica*, [New Series], Vol. 4, No. 13 (February, 1937), pp. 33–54.

Hayek, F. A. von. 1945. The Use of Knowledge in Society. *American Economic Review*, Vol. XXXV, No. 4, pp. 519–530.

Hayek, F. A. von. 1948. The Socialist Calculation II: The State of the Debate. In: Friedrich August von Hayek (Ed.): *Individualism and Economic Order*, pp. 148–180. Chicago: Chicago University Press.

Hayek, F. A. von. 1968. Wettbewerb als Entdeckungsverfahren. In: *Kieler Vorträge*, Neue Folge 56, Hrsg. E. Kiel: Schneider.

Hayek, F. A. von. 1973. *Law, Legislation and Liberty: A New Statement of the Liberal Principles of Justice and Political Economy*. London: Routledge & Kegan Paul.

He, G., He, J., and Guo, P. 2008. Reconsider the Farmers' Credit Demand and Their Credit Availability. *Agricultural Economic Problems*, No. 2, pp. 38–49.

Helms, B. 2006. *Access for All: Building Inclusive Financial Systems*. Consultative Group to Assist the Poor, Washington, DC: The World Bank.

Hu, R. 2009. Loans Below RMB 50 000 Will Enjoy Tax-Free Treatment – New Deal of the Ministry of Finance Relating to Rural Finance of China. *The Economic Observer News*, Chinese edition, November 16.

Kirzner, I. M. 1973. *Competition and Entrepreneurship*. Chicago: University of Chicago Press.

Kirzner, I. M. 1992. *The Meaning of Market Process*. London: Routledge.

Levine, R. 2005. Finance and Growth: Theory and Evidence. In: Aghion, P. and Durlauf, S. (Eds.): *Handbook of Economic Growth*. The Netherlands: Elsevier Science.

Li, F. 2014. Small and Micro Enterprises in Rural Areas Are More Difficult to Get Loans. *Sina Column*, August 21. Available at http://finance.sina.com.cn/zl/bank/20140821/153020081121.shtml, Retrieved November 18, 2017.

Li, L. 2018. The Phenomenon of the Postal Savings Bank's Acting as a "Water Pump, and It is Questioned How to Return Benefits to Rural Area". *Jinrong Jie*, Available at http://bank.jrj.com.cn/2014/05/12153817192967.shtml, retrieved on May 18.

Luo, Y. 2000. *Guanxi and Business*. Singapore: World Scientific Publishing Co. Ptc. Ltd.

McKinnon, R. I. 1973. *Money and Capital in Economic Development*. Washington, DC: Brooking Institute.

People's Bank of China. 2009. *The Situation of Farm Households' Borrowing and Lending: A Questionnaire-based Survey Report*, Chinese edition. Beijing: Economic Science Press.

Popper, Karl R. 2004. What is Dialectic? *Mind*, Vol. 49, No. 196, pp. 403–426.

Shaw, E. S. 1973. *Financial Deepening in Economic Development*. New York: Oxford University Press.

Stiglitz, J. 1989. Markets, Market Failures, and Development. *American Economic Review*, Vol. 79, pp. 197–203.

Stiglitz, J. and Weiss, A. 1981. Credit Rationing in Markets with Imperfect Information. *American Economic Review*, Vol. 71, pp. 393–410.

Vogel, R. C. 1984. The Forgotten Half of Rural Finance. In: Adams, Dale W., Graham, Douglas H., and Pischke, J. D. von (Eds.): *Undermining Rural Development with Cheap Credit*. Boulder, CO: Westview Press.

Yaron, J. and Benjamin M. 1997. Developing Rural Financial Markets. *Finance and Development*, IMF, December, pp. 40–43.

Yaron, J., Benjamin, M. P., and Piprek, Jr., G. L. 1997. *Rural Finance: Issues, Design, and Best Practices*. Washington, DC: World Bank.

Yingcan Consulting. 2017. Annual Report of the P2P Lending Industry 2016, January 6.

Zeller, M. 1994. Determinants of Credit Rationing: A Study of Informal Lenders and Formal Credit Groups in Madagascar. *World Development*, Vol. 22, No. 12 (December), pp. 1895–1907.

Zhang, X. and Heufers, R. (eds.). 2002. *Rural Financial Transformation and Innovation – Thoughts on the Rural Cooperative Funds*, Chinese edition. Taiyuan: Shanxi Economic Publishing House.

Zhao, T. 2015. Theory and Practice on Credit Cooperation between Farmer Cooperatives. *China Peasant Cooperative*, No. 5, pp. 22–25.

Zong, G. C. 2018. How to Realize Risk Prevention and Control for Mutual Fund Organizations? Available at http://www.360doc.com/content/18/0902/03/15372357_783170088.shtml, retrieved on November 15, 2022.

2

70 YEARS' EVOLUTION OF THE RURAL FINANCIAL SYSTEM OF THE PEOPLE'S REPUBLIC OF CHINA[1]

Tongquan Sun, Xingyuan Feng and Chong Dong

In the 70 years since the People's Republic of China was founded, its rural financial system has experienced great historical changes, from its establishment at the beginning to the reform and development in the late 1970s. In the early days of the founding of the PRC, in order to adapt to the strategic goal of restoring the economy and developing production as soon as possible, China established a rural financial system dominated by state-owned banks, supplemented by credit cooperation and informal lending. With the completion of the socialist transformation and the establishment of the public ownership system, the PRC's rural financial system has gradually changed into an integrated planning system of state-owned banks. After the reform and opening up, the rural financial system has experienced two changes: one is the reform, that is, the reform of the existing rural financial institutions; The second is the development, that is, the formation and development of new rural financial institutions. Along these two main lines, The PRC's rural financial system had been developing with its reform, and being reformed with its development, with different emphases in different periods.

On the whole, the development of the PRC's rural financial system can be divided into two stages, that is, taking reform and opening up as the watershed. Before the reform and opening up, the PRC's rural financial system was initially established, and its changes can be divided into two phases: first, at the beginning of the founding of the PRC, the state banks were the main components, supplemented by rural credit cooperative organizations, allowing the development of informal lending; The second is the phase of the integration into state-owned banks. After the reform and opening up, The PRC's rural financial system entered the stage of reform and development. Its reform can be divided into four phases: the first is the predominance of specialized banks; the second is the commercialization of specialized banks; the third is the opening up of rural financial market; and the fourth is the building of rural inclusive finance. The emphasis of the first two phases of the rural financial system reform is reforming the existing rural financial institutions. The emphasis of the third phase is adding up new rural financial institutions and some non-deposit financial institutions such as microloan companies. The emphasis of the fourth phase is building rural inclusive financial systems.

DOI: 10.4324/9781003369776-2

1. The Establishment of Rural Financial System and the Formation of State Banking Institutions

1.1 Strategy and Objectives

Before the reform and opening up, The PRC's rural financial system can be divided into two stages. First, from the early days of the founding of the PRC to the completion of socialist transformation, and second, after the establishment of the planned economic system. In the first stage, the country just left behind long-lasting wars. Rural areas need to restore agricultural production as soon as possible, and solving the problem of capital supply in rural areas has become an urgent task for the new government. However, in the early days after the founding of the PRC, the government stipulated that all the debts owed by farmers and other working people to landlords before their liberation should be abolished and vigorously promoted rent and interest reduction and land reform. At one time, informal lending in rural areas stagnated, resulting in a serious shortage of rural capital supply. Therefore, governments at all levels actively advocated free informal lending on the one hand and increased state agricultural loans on the other (Chen et al., 2009). In 1953, China began to implement the first five-year plan with the strategy of giving priority to the development of heavy industry. The funds were tight, and the agricultural surplus was the main source of the accumulation of national industrial development funds. It was impossible to allocate too many funds to support agricultural production. Therefore, while issuing agricultural loans, the government placed special emphasis on mobilizing and utilizing social capital, making full use of rural informal loans and promoting rural development through all forms of rural credit cooperative development (Chen et al., 2009), building the rural service network of the state-banks while promoting the establishment of rural credit cooperative organizations. Therefore, during this period, the strategic goal and guiding ideology of taking the state banks as the main body, encouraging the development of credit cooperatives supplemented by informal lending, was formed.

1.2 Progress

1.2.1 Establishment and Cancellation of the Agricultural Bank of China (ABC)

In 1951, the Agricultural Cooperative Bank (ACB) was established. As one of the specialized banks of the central bank, the People's Bank of China's main tasks were to implement investment allocation and handle long-term loans to the agricultural, water conservancy, forestry and land reclamation cooperatives according to the national budget and the credit plan; to prepare short-term credit plans for agricultural cooperation and carry out credit business; and to organize and lead rural financial work (Xu, 1996). At that time, the ACB only had the head office, which adopted the practice of "one institution with two brands" for the external brand of the ACB and the internal brand of the Rural Financial Administration Bureau under the PBC, without branches (Shi, 1992). However, even though the ACB was established, it did little business in rural areas. Instead, the grassroots rural financial business was still managed by the branches of the PBC at all administrative levels. ACB failed to play its due role and was abolished in 1952; that means the Rural Financial Administration of the PBC is still in charge of the rural financial work (Chen and Liu, 2009).

In March 1955, the Agricultural Bank of China (ABC) was established. Its main task is to handle fiscal allocation for agriculture and agricultural loans. Other rural financial businesses were still handled directly by the PBC. In April 1957, the State Council decided to merge the ABC into the PBC again (Shi, 1992). Subsequently, in 1963, the ABC was separated from the PBC and then merged into the PBC again in 1965 (Wu, 2000).

During the ten-year "Cultural Revolution", financial business was seriously damaged. In September 1972, the PBC held a national banking conference and set up a separate Rural Financial Bureau, which made a turnaround in financial administration and restored some reasonable rules and regulations (Hu and Wu, 2001).

1.2.2 The Establishment and Development of the Rural Credit Cooperatives

The first batch of rural credit cooperatives (RCCs) was established in 1951. In May of that year, the PBC held the first national rural finance work conference and decided to vigorously develop the RCCs. During this period, there were three kinds of organizational forms of the pilot rural credit cooperatives: rural credit mutual-help groups, credit units affiliated to the supply and marketing cooperatives (hereafter referred to as SMCs), and RCCs. In December 1951, the PBC issued *Standard Rules for the Articles of the Rural Credit Cooperatives (Draft)* and the *Convention on Rural Credit Mutual-help Group (Draft)*, so there would be rules to follow for the development of credit cooperatives in rural China (Zhan, 1991).

By the end of 1957, the RCCs had been developed in most parts of the country, with a total number of 88 368 (Shi, 1992). During this period, RCCs' capital was invested by farmers, and the managers were elected by their members. They served the production and living of the members through credit activities. RCCs basically maintained the nature of cooperatives and played an important role in supporting farmers' living and agricultural production.

However, similar to the fate of the ABC, RCCs also experienced several ups and downs. At the end of 1958, RCCs were incorporated into the people's communes as a business division and were also merged into banking offices as "credit units", which seriously affected the development of RCCs (Yang et al., 2013). In April 1959, the central government delegated the administration of RCCs to the production brigades in rural areas, where RCCs became "credit divisions" (Shi, 1992). In 1963, the central government summed up the previous experience and lessons and decided to take over the PBC RCCs for comprehensive and thorough vertical leadership in order to restore the nature and task of RCCs as independent credit cooperatives and endow RCCs with business autonomy (Shi, 1992). In November 1977, the State Council issued *Several Provisions on Rectifying and Strengthening Banking Works*, which pointed out:

> RCCs are collective financial organizations and grassroots institutions of the state bank in rural areas. . . . The funds of RCCs should be included in the national credit plan, the staffing should be included in the county collective labor wage plan, and the treatment of employees should be basically consistent with that of the PBC.

RCCs once again became "government-run" institutions.

1.3 Achievements and Deficiencies

Before the reform and opening up, although the rural financial system of the PRC had twists and turns under the influence of political movements and ideological changes in economic development, a relatively complete rural financial system had been established on the basis of nothing, which taking state-owned banks as the core and foundation, being supplemented by RCCs, and restricting informal lending. The establishment and development of the ABC and RCCs expanded various rural financial businesses, accelerated the development of rural credit cooperation, strengthened the rural capital force, and supported the recovery of agricultural production in the early days after the founding of the PRC and the subsequent rural socialist construction.

The national banking system, which integrated rural finance under the planned economic system, has seriously inhibited the development and growth of rural endogenous financial systems. At the same time, formal financial institutions did not fully serve the development of the agricultural and rural economy and the needs of farmers' living. Wen and Wang (2005) believed that the PRC's rural formal finance was exogenous at the beginning because after the founding of the PRC, in the face of "the pressure jointly formed by international political, military competition and harsh external economic environment", China implemented the national catch-up strategy and had to "at the expense of economic efficiency, choose the political centralization system, economic planned control, state monopoly in property rights and strategic heavy industrialization" to "consolidate and develop the emerging socialist regime". Therefore, finance

> has completely become a tool for the state to mobilize economic resources and economic surplus to invest in heavy industry and establish a relatively complete industrial system as soon as possible to independently deal with the threat of external competition

and the informal finance generated in the PRC's rural economy is either constantly formalized or constantly suppressed by the government.

2. The Establishment of a Specialized Banking System and the Initial Formation of a Rural Financial Market

2.1 Reform Strategy and Objectives

In December 1978, the Third Plenary Session of the Eleventh Central Committee of the Communist Party of China clearly put forward "restoring the ABC and vigorously developing rural credit businesses" in the *Decision of the Central Committee of the Communist Party of China on Several Issues Concerning Accelerating Agricultural Development (Draft)*. In February 1979, the State Council officially issued a notice on restoring the ABC, which became a specialized bank focusing on agricultural lending. In August 1984, the State Council approved the *Report on Reforming the Management System of RCCs* drafted by the ABC and required to turn RCCs into real cooperative financial organizations, as the grassroots branches of the ABC, providing loans to township and village enterprises (TVEs).

2.2 Main Reforms and Implementations

2.2.1 Recovery and Development of the ABC

In 1979, the State Council restored the ABC as an institution directly under the State Council, which was administrated by the PBC and independently performed its functions and business. Its main task was to uniformly manage the funds for supporting agriculture, centrally handle rural credit, lead RCCs and develop rural finance. In this way, the ABC became a specialized bank serving agriculture and the rural economy. In March 1979, the ABC took over the rural financial business of the central bank. According to the guideline of vigorously supporting rural commodity production, the target groups of credit businesses were gradually adjusted from collective economic organizations to farmers. In 1985, the ABC established a reform plan to transform itself into a real economic entity.

2.2.2 The Independent Operation of RCCs

According to the *Notice on Restoring the Agricultural Bank of China* issued by the State Council in 1979, RCCs were managed by the ABC as its subordinate institutions. But at the same time, the reform of RCCs was started.

In 1984, the No. 1 Document of the Central Committee of the CPC titled The *Central Committee's Notice on Rural Work in 1984* pointed out that RCCs should be reformed and become the real cooperative financial groups of the masses. Under the guidance of the thought of

> restoring and strengthen the mass character in organization of credit cooperatives, democracy in their management and flexibility in their operation, letting them implement independent operation, conduct independent accounting, and take sole responsibility for profits and losses, and giving full play to the role of informal lending,

county-level associations of RCCs were created, which was an important symbol of RCCs to become entities conducting complete self-management and independent development.

2.2.3 The Development of Rural Cooperative Foundations

After the implementation of the rural household contract responsibility system, peasant households and TVEs became the main body with rural financing demands, and the financing demands were also diversified, reflecting the diversification of industries. In 1983, some areas began to use the funds of village collective economic organizations to establish rural cooperative foundations (nongcun hezuo jijinhui) to provide financing for the economic and social activities of their own townships or villages and mitigate the contradiction between supply and demand of rural funds.

The rural cooperative foundations were highly valued and strongly supported by the central government. In 1986, when approving and forwarding the "Opinions on Clearing Up Rural Collective Property", the General Office of the CPC Central Committee and the General Office of the State Council pointed out that:

> Some rural cooperative economic organizations voluntarily concentrate the collective idle funds and adopt the method of paid use to support the township and village cooperative economic organizations and farmers to develop commodity production. This method should be allowed to be tried out as long as it does not absorb deposits from outside and only finance each other internally.

The Decision on Further Strengthening Agricultural and Rural Work adopted at the Eighth Plenary Session of the 13th Central Committee of the Communist Party of China in 1991 stressed that "continue to run the rural cooperative foundations well".

2.3 Achievements and Deficiencies

2.3.1 Achievements

In the period of specialized banking systems, the PBC did not directly provide loans to farmers; only RCCs provided a small number of loans to farmers. After the recovery of the ABC, it began to issue loans to rural collective economic organizations and farmers, and the availability of rural credit has been significantly improved. In 1980, farmers' loans increased by 57% over the previous year, and in the following years, they almost maintained a growth rate of more than 70%. Taking 1980 as the base period, from 1980 to 1993, the loans from the ABC and RCCs increased by 15.6 times, with an average annual growth rate of 24.1%, and the total rural social output value increased by 12.3 times, with an average annual growth rate of 22.1%, indicating that the growth of rural credit services was basically synchronized with the growth of the rural economy during this period (Chen et al., 2009).

The development of rural cooperative foundations supported and promoted the all-round development of the whole rural economy and society and was conducive to managing and using collective funds well and maintaining and increasing the value of collective funds. Driven by the central policy and the affirmation and active support of local governments and relevant departments, the rural cooperative foundations developed rapidly throughout the country. By the end of 1992, 17,400 townships and towns had established rural cooperative foundations, accounting for 36.7% of the total number of townships and towns in China; 112,500 villages (teams) have established such foundations, accounting for 15.4% of the total number of villages. The amount raised through these foundations increased from 5.66 billion yuan in 1988 to 16.49 billion yuan in 1992 (Zhou, 2010).

2.3.2 Deficiencies

Although the rural financial reform in the period of specialized banking systems has achieved remarkable achievements, its shortcomings are also obvious.

First, as a specialized bank, the ABC had the functions and tasks of both a commercial bank and a policy bank, which seriously affected its operation and management as an independent enterprise. Second, the rural financial system led by the specialized banking system was a financial institutional arrangement established around the needs of urban industrial and commercial development. This means that rural financial supply does little to meet rural financial demand; the degree of commercialization of specialized banks was very low, so agricultural loans were often issued intended by the government according to administrative orders and financial allocation: state-owned economic organizations and collective economic organizations were often easier to get loans, while private economic organizations had difficulties getting loans. Therefore, the financial supply and demand of the rural agricultural sector were unbalanced in terms of total amount and structure. The shortage of supply in the PRC's rural financial market became the norm. The "distancing of funds from agriculture" has led to a long-term dilemma of lack of funds in rural areas, lack of investment in agriculture and difficulty in farmers' access to loans (Zhou, 2010). Third, although the rural cooperative foundations had a high degree of commercialization, due to the lack of effective supervision, in some places, the problem of chaotic management gradually appeared.

3. The Formation of Rural Financial System in Which Different-type Institutions Working Together

3.1 Reform Strategy and Objectives

In December 1993, the *Decision of the State Council on Financial System Reform* (hereinafter referred to as the *1993 Decision*) declared the objectives of the PRC's financial system reform: establishing a system of financial institutions in which policy-oriented finance is separated from commercial finance; state-owned commercial banks will be the main body and a variety of financial institutions coexist; establishing a unified, open, and strictly managed financial market system with orderly competition. Under the guidance of this policy, the *Decision of the State Council on Rural Financial System Reform* issued in August 1996 put forward a new round of rural financial system reform plan, put forward the goal of establishing and improving the rural financial system that was to take cooperative finance as a basis, promoting the collaboration of commercial finance and policy-oriented finance, with emphasis on the restoration of the cooperative nature of RCCs, the enhancement of the functions of policy-oriented finance, and leading role of the state-owned commercial banks.

According to the above-mentioned policies and guidelines, the ABC started its commercialization, or transition toward a state-owned commercial bank, and RCCs became independent from the ABC and started the commercialization process. The Agricultural Development Bank of China and the Postal Savings Bank of China were established successively. Thus, a rural financial system with the characteristic of collaboration of commercial, policy-oriented and cooperative financial institutions took shape gradually. At the same time, rural cooperative foundations were banned.

3.2 Main Reform Contents and Implementations

3.2.1 The Commercialization and Restructuring of the ABC and Its Partial Withdrawal from Counties

3.2.1.1 Commercialization and Restructuring of the ABC

The original intention of the commercialization and restructuring of the ABC was to support the production and sales of agricultural products. Most of its loans were issued to state-owned agricultural operating institutions such as food bureaus and supply and marketing cooperatives (SMCs), and township industrial enterprises. It ran business with both commercial and political features. With the continuous strengthening of the demand for the commercial operation of specialized banks, the *1993 Decision* put forward that the ABC should be transformed into a state-owned commercial bank. In 1995, the *Law of the PRC on Commercial Banks* was promulgated and implemented, and the ABC began to gradually explore the operation mechanisms of a modern commercial bank. Then, according to the *Decision on the Reform of Rural Financial System* issued by the State Council in 1996, the function of leading and administrating RCCs was removed from the ABC. In 1997, the ABC basically completed its historical mission as a national specialized bank and began to transform into a state-owned commercial bank.

3.2.1.2 Partial Withdrawal of the ABC from Counties

The National Conference on Financial Work in 1997 determined a basic strategy of "all commercial banks reduce county-level (and below) institutions, develop small and medium-sized financial institutions to support local economic development". State-owned commercial banks, including the ABC, withdrew some of their branches from counties or below the county level. Accordingly, the ABC had branches previously in almost all townships and towns in China, about 50,000 branches in total, ranking first among the four major state-owned banks. After this round of commercialization reform, by 2007, the ABC had only 24,900 branches in China, and the number of branches had been reduced by half in ten years (Miao, 2007).

3.2.2 Reform of RCCs

3.2.2.1 Restoration and Regulation of the Rural Cooperative Financial System

At this stage, RCCs were firstly regulated as cooperative institutions, and then some of them were transformed into commercialized institutions. In August 1996, the State Council Inter-Department Coordination Group for Rural Financial System Reform issued the *Notice on the Implementation Plan for Separating RCCs from the ABC*, which officially announced the decoupling of RCCs from the ABC. Since September of that year, more than 50,000 RCCs and more than 2400 county-level Rural Credit Cooperative Associations (RCCAs) have gradually decoupled from the ABC (*China Cooperation Times*, 2018).

In February 1997, the National Working Conference on the Reform of RCCs Administration determined to regulate RCCs according to the principle of a cooperative system and turn RCCs into real cooperative financial organizations.

In the same year, the Bureau of Rural Cooperative Financial Supervision and Administration of the PBC was established and promulgated the *Regulations on the Administration of RCCs*, the *Regulations on the Administration of RCCs at the County Level*, the *Articles of a Rural Credit Cooperative (Model)* and the *Articles of a Rural Credit Cooperative Association at the County Level (Model)*. These regulatory documents put the administration of RCCs in accordance with the principle of a cooperative system.

3.2.2.2 Formation of Provincial-level Rural Credit Cooperative Associations

At the end of November 1999, the first batch of provincial-level rural credit cooperative associations with the function of self-regulation of their member RCCs was established as pilots in five provinces (Heilongjiang, Shaanxi, Sichuan, Zhejiang and Fujian), and the provincial government's functions of administrating RCCs were gradually transferred to these provincial industrial associations. Therefore, the PBC realized in the reform the separation of the responsibility of administration and supervision of RCCs. RCCs started to be regulated by their industrial associations.

3.2.2.3 Restructuring and Commercialization of RCCs

There were serious mismanagement and losses when the RCCs separated from the ABC. In this context, the PBC gradually launched the reform of RCCs and introduced new property rights models of RCCs.

On the basis of individual pilot reforms of several RCCs beforehand, the State Council began the Pilot Plan for Deepening the Reform of RCCs in 2003. Eight provinces and cities, such as Zhejiang and Shandong, took the lead in carrying out the reform pilot in the property right and management of RCCs. The pilot reform produced a number of county-level RCCs (as a unified legal person entity within the respective county-level jurisdiction, with a legal form of a cooperative), rural cooperative banks (with a legal form of a shareholding cooperative) and rural commercial banks (with a legal form of a shareholding company). The emergence of rural commercial banks marks the beginning of the commercialization and restructuring of the PRC's RCC system.

3.2.3 Establishment of Agricultural Development Bank of China

In order to improve the efficiency of resource allocation and to separate policy-oriented finance and commercial finance, the Agricultural Development Bank of China (ADBC) was established in 1994. The business scope of the ADBC included: handling national special loans for the reservation of major agricultural and sideline products such as grain, cotton, oil, pork and sugar; handling loans for the purchase of agricultural and sideline products such as grain, cotton, oil and meat, and loans for the marketing and wholesale of grain and oil; handling loans for enterprises undertaking policy-oriented processing tasks of national grain, oil and other products as well as loans for cotton primary processing enterprises in the cotton hemp system; handling various subsidized loans for poverty alleviation, comprehensive agricultural development loans and other subsidized agricultural loans; handling loans for small-scale agriculture, forestry, animal husbandry and water conservancy capital construction and technological transformation; handling the agency allocation of financial support for agriculture funds of the central and provincial governments; and opening special accounts for the food risk funds established by governments at all levels and allocate them as agents.

By 2013, the ADBC had formed a "one body and two wings" business development pattern with grain, cotton and oil purchase credit as the main body, agribusiness credit as one wing and medium and long-term credit for agricultural and rural infrastructure construction and ecological agriculture construction as the other wing, establishing an initial modern banking framework.

3.2.4 Establishment of the Postal Savings Bank of China

After the founding of the PRC, China established the Ministry of Posts and Telecommunications, which once carried out postal savings business. But the business stopped in 1953. In 1986, the Ministry of Posts and Telecommunications and the PBC jointly issued the *Joint Notice on the Agreement on the Establishment of Postal Savings*, which fully opened the postal savings business. Since then, the postal savings business has been officially resumed. In 2004, the China Banking Regulatory Commission (CBRC) issued the *Interim Measures for the Postal Savings Institutions in Business Management*, which clearly required that postal savings and postal business should be "separated in finance and operation". In the same year, these *Interim Measures* were implemented, and postal financial business was regulated as the banking business. In 2005, the State Council issued the *Postal System Reform Plan* and decided to establish a postal savings bank. In 2007, the Postal Savings Bank of China (PSBC) was officially established.

3.2.5 The Ban on Rural Cooperative Foundations

Rural cooperative foundations (RCFs) were mutual funding organizations in rural communities which were limited to the service for their member shareholders. The government also planned to develop them into regulated rural cooperative financial organizations. However, some RCFs had broken through these limitations, absorbing a large amount of deposit savings from the public in the name of share offering, while the shareholders neither participated in management nor bore risks and were interfered seriously with administrative control. The management is chaotic, and the problems of loss and misappropriation of funds are more serious. In particular, loans issued to the township and village enterprises and local governments had become the main part of non-performing loans.

In 1999, the General Office of the State Council released the *Notice of Transmitting the Work Plan of the Working Group for the Rectification of Rural Cooperative Foundations to Rectify Rural Cooperative Foundations*, requiring to ban RCFs throughout the country. By the end of 2000, all RCFs nationwide were either closed or merged into rural credit cooperatives in the relevant counties or county-level cities.

3.3 Achievements and Deficiencies

3.3.1 Achievements

With the commercialization of the ABC, the establishment of the PSBC and ADBC and the provincial self-discipline management system of RCCs, a rural financial system with division and cooperation of commercial, policy-oriented and cooperative financial institutions have gradually formed. The vigorous development of rural cooperative foundations had fully mobilized and effectively utilized the funds of rural collective economic organizations and farmers, filled the gap of insufficient financial supply of the ABC and RCCs, and supported the development of township and village enterprises and the financing demands of farmers to generate income and get rich.

3.3.2 Deficiencies

First, problems arose from the restructuring of the Agricultural Bank of China. The ABC's business outlets and businesses were largely withdrawn from the county-level jurisdictions or below, which greatly increased the cost of providing financial services to scattered small and medium-sized farmers and township and village enterprises. Second, the centralization of loan approval authority also affected the enthusiasm of branches to issue agricultural credit. Many county-level branches operated only deposit businesses but not lending businesses, and the county-level business shrank on a large scale. Third, with such a development, rural credit cooperatives were made a monopoly force in the rural financial market. With the restructuring and commercialization of rural credit cooperatives, their nature of credit cooperative finances got lost, and their strength of serving agriculture, rural areas and farmers began to weaken.

Second, the cooperation mechanism of the ADBC and other institutions in serving "agriculture, rural areas and farmers" was not perfect. First, the positioning of the agricultural development bank was not accurate enough, it lacked complementarity with commercial and cooperative financial institutions and there was a problem of crowding out some commercial and cooperative finance. Second, the postal savings bank absorbs a large amount of savings from rural areas every year, and the agricultural loans put in by it were very limited.

4. The Further Open-up of the Rural Financial Market and the Formation of a Modern Rural Financial System

4.1 Reform Strategy and Objectives

The restructuring of the ABC and RCCs led to the formation of the monopoly position of RCC institutions (RCCs, rural commercial banks and rural cooperative banks) in the rural financial market and exacerbated the tensions between the supply and demand of rural finance. They did not only increase the effective supply of rural financial services but led to a large reduction of rural financial service outlets and a large outflow of rural funds. Therefore, increasing the supply of rural financial services and breaking the monopolization of RCCs were of great strategic significance in promoting the development of a rural economy.

In 2004, *No. 1 Document* of the Central Committee of the CPC pointed out that China was to "accelerate reform and innovation of rural financial system, actively set up various financial institutions to develop agriculture, the countryside and farmers". *No. 1 Document* of the Central Committee of the CPC in 2005 required that

> in order to foster rural competitive financial market, relevant departments should put more efforts to make regulation on the entry and supervision for new rural multi ownership financial institutions. In some suitable places, we may explore to establish some microfinance organizations being initiated by natural persons or enterprises, which can closely serve farmers and meet rural demands.

The *No. 1 Document* of the Central Committee of the CPC in 2006 stressed:

> On the premise of ensuring sufficient capital, strict financial supervision and establishing a reasonable and effective exit mechanism, we encourage the establishment of community financial institutions with various ownership systems in counties, allowing private and foreign

capital to participate in shares. We encourage the creation of microfinance organizations initiated by natural persons, enterprises or associations. The relevant departments should speed up the formulation of regulations. Farmers should be introduced to develop financial mutual aid organizations.

Under this background, the Chinese government carried out incremental reform of the rural financial market, that is, to increase new rural financial institutions, including village and town banks (cunzhen yinhang), loan companies (daikuan gongsi), rural mutual fund associations (nongcun zijin huzhu she) and quasi financial institutions such as microloan companies, and to support the operation of internal mutual funds carried out by farmers' cooperatives.

4.2 Main Reform Contents and Implementations

4.2.1 Establishment of the New Rural Financial Institutions

In December 2006, the CBRC issued *Several Opinions on Adjusting and Relaxing the Access Policies for Banking Financial Institutions in Rural Areas to Better Support the Construction of New Socialist Countryside*, proposing to set up village banks, Loan Companies and Rural Mutual Fund Associations in rural areas to solve the problems of low coverage, insufficient supply and inadequate competition of financial services.

In 2007, the CBRC issued the *Interim Provisions on the Administration of Village Banks*, the *Interim Provisions on the Administration of Loan Companies* and the *Interim Provisions on the Administration of Rural Mutual Fund Associations*. According to the above documents: village banks refer to those being established in rural areas by domestic and foreign financial institutions, domestic non-financial institutions, enterprises or domestic natural persons, providing financial services for agricultural and rural economic development; the loan companies refer to non-banking financial institutions established by domestic commercial banks or rural cooperative banks to be specialized in providing loan services for farmers, agriculture and rural economic development within counties or county-level cities, which should be full subsidiaries of and fully funded by the initiating bank; rural mutual fund associations refer to community mutual aid banking financial institutions jointly owned by farmers and small enterprises in townships (towns) and administrative villages, which service members with deposits, loans, settlement and other businesses.

4.2.2 Development of Microloan Companies

In order to regulate the wide-spread non-governmental finance institutions and promote the economy of counties, in 2005, the PBC selected one county (district) each in one province (Shanxi, Sichuan, Guizhou, Shaanxi and Inner Mongolia Autonomous Region) to start there the pilot of microloan companies (MLCs). In 2008, the *Guidance on the Pilot of Microloan Companies* jointly issued by the CBRC and PBC expanded the pilot area and stipulated that MLCs should be established by private capital which can only give loans without absorbing public deposits. The document clarified the regulatory responsibility of local governments. Since then, MLCs have developed rapidly all over the country.

4.2.3 Support Farmers' Mutual Funds

After 2006, in addition to rural mutual fund associations, a large number of mutual funds were spontaneously established by farmers, and farmers' specialized cooperatives carrying out operations of internal mutual funds emerged in China. The rapid development of farmers' mutual financial assistance appeared under the background of the continuous introduction of relevant policies by the central government. In 2006, the *No. 1 Document* of the Central Committee of the CPC provided that the government guide the development of mutual fund organizations for farmers. In 2008, the Third Plenary Session of the 17th CPC Central Committee further confirmed that qualified farmers' specialized cooperatives were allowed to carry out credit cooperation. The *No. 1 Document of the Central Committee* in 2010~2017 put forward the support and regulation of farmers' specialized cooperatives to carry out credit cooperation and put forward the responsibility of local government for supervision of their operations with credit cooperation. Among them, the *No. 1 Document* the Central Committee of 2014 puts forward four principles of the operations of farmers' mutual funds: "adhering to the membership system, closeness, no external deposit and loan, and no fixed return".

In order to improve the farmers' abilities of self-development, mutual funding assistance and cooperation, and then enhance the ability of poor farmers to get rid of poverty and enter the upward development track, the Poverty Alleviation Office of the State Council and the Ministry of Finance issued in 2006 the *Notice on Carrying out the Pilot Work of Establishing "Mutual Aid Fund for Development of Poor Villages"*, and then launched the pilot of "mutual aid fund [huzhu zijin] for development of poor villages" in 14 provinces (autonomous regions), establish "mutual funds" in some poor villages that implement the promotion of the whole villages with a certain amount of fiscal poverty alleviation funds (caizheng fupin zijin). At the same time, the farmers in the villages can expand the scale of mutual funds by investing in their own capital, and villagers can use in rotation "mutual funds" by borrowing to develop production. By the end of 2013, a total of 19,397 poverty-stricken villages had carried out pilots of mutual funds.

4.2.4 Standardizing Rural Internet Finance (FinTech)

After 2013, The PRC's Internet finance (FinTech) developed rapidly and gradually extended to the field of "agriculture, rural areas and farmers". Nationwide, the government's regulation of the whole internet finance was initially vacant and lagging behind, which provided space for the emergence and development of internet finance. Although it has only been a few years since entering the era of internet finance, a variety of internet finance models of serving "agriculture, rural areas and farmers" have emerged in China. Specifically, it includes: "internet finance for e-commerce platform dealing with agricultural products", "P2P lending platform for serving agriculture, rural area and farmers", "Online lending services provided by banks and RCCs", "crowdfunding for projects servicing the agriculture, rural area and farmers", "online insurance for the agriculture, rural area and farmers", "online wealth management for agriculture, rural area and farmers", "internet finance plus agricultural supply chain", "online payment platform servicing the agriculture, rural area and farmers" and other models.

4.2.5 Transforming the Agricultural Bank of China and the Postal Savings Bank of China into Banks with Shareholding System

In 2008, the Executive Meeting of the State Council deliberated and principally approved the *Overall Implementation Plan for the Shareholding Reform of the Agricultural Bank of China*. In 2009, the Agricultural Bank of China Co., Ltd. was established and launched its IPO in 2010, which was listed in Shanghai and Hong Kong stock markets, respectively.

The Postal Savings Bank of China Ltd. (PSBC) was established in 2007. Its provincial branches were set up afterwards. It began to handle the company's self-operated loan business in 2009 and then carried out the transformation of the entire bank into a shareholding system. In 2016, the PSBC was successfully listed on the main board of the Hong Kong Stock Exchange (HKSE).

4.2.6 *Establishing New Management System for RCC Institutions and Transforming Them into Shareholding Financial Institutions*

From 2003 to 2007, the pilot reform of rural credit cooperatives continued to expand. The then CBRC gradually delegated some industry management functions and responsibilities of controlling the risks related to the RCC system to the provincial government for the provinces where the reform pilot area was located and established a management framework with the provincial rural credit cooperative associations as the main body taking charge of management and supervising RCCs. Since rural cooperative banks and RCCs have basically lost the nature of cooperative finance, the CBRC issued the *Guiding Opinions on Accelerating the Equity Transformation of Rural Cooperative Financial Institutions* in 2010 to strongly push forward their commercialization and the adaptation of a shareholding system for all of them. According to the aforementioned *Guiding Opinions*, no matter what types of names these Rural Cooperative Banks or RCCs still would bear, they should all be transformed into entities with shareholding systems. According to the statistics of the CBRC, by the end of 2016, there were 1114 rural commercial banks, 40 rural cooperative banks and 1125 RCCs in China.

4.3 Achievements and Deficiencies

4.3.1 Achievements

The emergence and development of three new types of rural financial institutions and microloan companies and the penetration of Internet finance into rural areas have greatly increased the supply of rural financial services, enhanced the degree of market competition, improved the tense situation of rural financial supply to a great extent, and showed the positive effect of incremental reform. At the same time, the restructuring of the ABC, PSBC, rural cooperative banks and rural credit cooperatives into shareholding banking financial institutions has promoted the formation of a modern rural financial system. By the end of 2017, a total of 1,587 village banks (cunzhen yinhang) had been established in China, with the county and county-level city coverage rate reaching 67%. Among these counties and county-level cities, there were 416 national-level poverty-stricken counties (pinkun xian) or counties and county-level cities within contiguous poverty-stricken areas (lianpian tekun diqu) in China. By the end of September 2015, there were 8,965 microloan companies in China, with a loan balance of 950.8 billion yuan.

Farmers' mutual funds kept rural financial resources in the countryside; provided convenient services such as deposit, financing and money management for member farmers; provided conditions for farmers to start businesses; generated income and improved their lives so as to promote the all-round development of rural areas; and enhanced farmers as the principal parts in development.

4.3.2 Deficiencies

First, the commercialization and restructuring of large state-owned banks had accelerated their "escape" from rural areas. The core of their commercialization and restructuring was to reduce costs and increase benefits. The restructuring of the ABC and PSBC into shareholding banks and the commercialization and restructuring of all RCCs and rural cooperative banks into shareholding banking financial institutions had increased the centrifugal force for these financial institutions to break away from the rural financial market.

Second, the high cost of rural financial operation and management and the difficulties in increasing profit made most rural financial institutions unable to expand and deliver steadfast services in the countryside. For example, there are seven provinces in which the county and county-level city coverage of village banks in China was less than 50% by the end of 2016, and six of them were in central and western regions (poorer areas of China). By the end of 2016, there were only 13 loan companies in China, which had only 13 business outlets and 104 employees. Rural mutual fund associations have not been widely developed. By the end of 2016, there were only 48 rural mutual fund associations in China with 589 employees (Rural Financial Service Research Group of the PBC, 2017).

Third, financial supervision needs to be improved and strengthened. The business of MLCs is limited to mainly providing services for "agriculture, rural areas and farmers" and small and micro enterprises. However, because they do not have a license in finance, it is difficult for them to enjoy the preferential policies in this respect from the government. There has been some chaos in the development of farmers' mutual funds. Some individual farmers' mutual funds were transformed into illegal fund-raising organizations, which seriously affected the rural economic and social stability. In the face of a large number of farmers' mutual funds with wide coverage, the existing single supervision system is difficult to deal with.

5. Construction of a Rural Inclusive Financial System

5.1 Reform Strategy and Objectives

In 2017, General Secretary Xi Jinping put forward in the *Report of 19th National Congress of the Communist Party of China* that the main contradiction of the PRC's society now is transformed into the contradiction between people's growing needs and the imbalanced development. Developing inclusive finance is the way to solve this contradiction. In November 2013, the Third Plenary Session of the 18th CPC Central Committee put forward the goal of "developing inclusive finance". In December 2015, the State Council issued the *Plan for Promoting Inclusive Finance (2016–2020)*, which pointed out that we should provide appropriate and effective financial services to all social strata and groups at an affordable cost based on the requirements of equal opportunities and the principle of commercial sustainability. Let all market players share financial services, encourage mass entrepreneurship and innovation, enhance social equity and social harmony, and promote the building of a well-off society in an all-round way.

The development of inclusive finance in China can be traced back to the special poverty alleviation loans in the early stage of reform and opening up, which is followed by the Poverty-alleviation Subsidized Loans and Microfinance (in the following of this part, just name them as "Subsidized Loans" and "Microfinance"). The PRC's poverty alleviation and development practice has proved that the fundamental solution to the problem of poverty depends on economic development so that the poor can get fair development opportunities and share the fruits of development. Therefore, while continuing to promote the direct provision of credit services to poor groups, China has made greater efforts to build an inclusive financial system that improves the availability and convenience of financial services at all levels of society. In addition to opening up the rural financial market and introducing more financial service providers, large state-owned banks are also encouraged and supported to set up financial departments dedicated to poverty alleviation and serving "agriculture, rural areas and farmers" and small and micro enterprises. Also, capital markets, futures markets and insurance markets provided a good environment for developing poor areas.

5.2 Main Reform Contents and Implementations

5.2.1 Establishment of Specialized Loans and Subsidized Loans for Poverty Reduction

5.2.1.1 Specialized Loans for Poverty Reduction

In the early stage of reform and opening up, in order to meet the needs of financial system reform and national economic development, in accordance with the needs of economic development in different regions and periods, the PBC set up some specialized loan projects, which adopted preferential interest rates to support poor counties to develop regional leading backbone projects with less investment and quick results, such as planting and breeding, agricultural processing and small mining. These loans have been a way to enhance the ability of self-reliance of poor counties, increase the economic strength of poor counties to get rid of poverty and achieve the goal of solving the problem of shortage of food and clothing in poor counties. From 1983 to 1986, the PBC successively set up Specialized Loans, including "Loans for Ethnic Minority Areas", "Loans for Old, Minority, Frontier and Poor Areas" and "Loans for County-level Government Run Industrial Enterprises in Poor Counties".

5.2.1.2 Subsidized Loans

In 1986, the PBC and ABC jointly promulgated the *Interim Measures for the Administration of Specialized Interest-Subsidized Loans in Poor Areas* and began to issue interest-subsidized loans for poverty alleviation in the counties on the government priority poverty relief list for the production projects which could supply food and clothing to people as soon as possible. The subsidized loan policy has been implemented up to now. It is the most important, largest and longest-lasting financial vehicle for poverty alleviation in China.

The management system of Subsidized Loans has changed several times. When it was just established, it was operated and managed by the ABC. In 1994, it was administrated by the ADBC. Later, because the ACBC had no branches at the grassroots level, it was transferred to the ABC again. In 2008, the Poverty Alleviation Office of the State Council and four other departments issued the *Notice on Comprehensively Reforming the Management System of Subsidized Poverty Alleviation Loans*, which decided to delegate the management authority to local governments. The local governments should be responsible for the management, use and efficiency of Specialized Loans and subsidies. The document encouraged commercial banks to voluntarily participate in Specialized Loans issuance work according to commercial principles in open and fair competition. The issuing entities of Subsidized Loans are open to all commercial banks.

The credit fund of Subsidized Loans initially came from the PBC and later came from the refinancing from both the ABC and PBC. After the delegate of the operating authority in 2008, the credit funds were raised by the lending institutions themselves, and the PBC only provided re-loans. The preferential interest rate has been applied to the Subsidized Loans, and the interest is subsidized by the financial departments.

During the development of Subsidized Loans, the key objects and purposes of the loans have been adjusted several times.

5.2.2 Development of Microfinance

During the Seven-Year Priority Poverty Alleviation Program (starting from 1994), poverty alleviation to households was an important strategy in which offering credit funds directly to poor households was essential. Since 1993, the Rural Development Institute of the Chinese Academy of Social Sciences, in collaboration with many institutions domestic and abroad, has established many microfinance institutions in the form of non-governmental organizations in many parts of China. They learned from the microfinance poverty alleviation model of the Grameen Bank of Bangladesh and conducted wide experiments. These activities really sent funds to households, with good effects such as "real poverty alleviation, helping real poor" and with high repayment rates. These microfinance models are later called "public-interest microfinance". After 1998, the Chinese government adopted the poverty alleviation model of public-interest microfinance, which was widely practiced by the Poverty Alleviation Office and the RCC system.

In 2014, the Poverty Alleviation Office of the State Council and five other ministries and commissions jointly issued the *Guiding Opinions on the Innovative Development of Poverty Alleviation Microcredit*. According to the above document, the registered poor households were provided credit loans of less than 50,000 yuan with a term of less than 3 years. To borrowers who could meet the related requirement, they could get full interest subsidy from the Specialized Loans.

5.2.3 Establishment of Business Unit of Poverty Alleviation, "Agriculture, Rural Areas and Farmers" or Inclusive Finance

The Third National Financial Work Conference in 2007 clearly proposed that the ABC should provide services for "agriculture, rural areas and farmers" while "overall restructuring, commercializing and selecting a good time to get listing". In 2008, in accordance with the *Requirements of the Overall Implementation Plan for the Joint-stock Reform of the ABC* issued by the State Council, the ABC launched the pilot reform of the financial business division of agriculture, rural areas and farmers. Subsequently, the ABC incorporated 2,097 County sub-branches in 1,875 counties and 128 municipal districts into the Financial Business Division for Serving the "Agriculture, Rural Areas and Farmers" and put them under the latter's management, effectively enhancing the ability to serve "agriculture, rural areas and farmers".

Since 2004, *No. 1 Document of the Central Committee of the CPC* has continuously proposed to prevent the outflow of rural capital, guide capital return to the countryside and increase the credit for projects related to agriculture, rural areas and farmers. In 2016, the PSBC established the Financial Division for Serving the "Agriculture, Rural Areas and Farmers" and set up a microcredit team dedicated to supporting agriculture, rural area and farmers at the county level. In the same year, the Agricultural Development Bank (ADB) and China Development Bank (CDB) successively established the financial business department for poverty alleviation, in which the Agricultural Development Bank achieved full coverage of 832 national, poverty-stricken counties in China. Subsequently, in 2017, the five major state-owned commercial banks, including the Industrial and Commercial Bank of China (ICBC), die ABC, Bank of China (BOC), China Construction Bank (CCB, Bank of Communications), all responded to the call and set up Inclusive Finance Division at their headquarters.

5.2.4 Introduction of Other Poverty Alleviation Measures Such as Futures and Insurance

In 2016, PBC and seven other ministries and commissions issued the *Implementation Opinions on Financial Assistance in Poverty Alleviation*, supporting financial institutions such as securities, futures and insurance to set up branches in poor areas. The document encourages and supports qualified enterprises in poor areas to raise funds through the Main Board, Growth Enterprise Market (GEM), National SME Share Transfer System, regional equity trading markets and issuing debt financing instruments such as enterprise bonds, corporate bonds, short-term financing bonds, medium-term notes, project income notes and regional collective SME bonds with credit enhancing by regional government (quyu jiyou zhai). The document supports making price insurance for special agricultural products in poor areas, improving and promoting small loan guarantee insurance and expanding the density and depth of agricultural insurance.

5.2.5 Strengthening Supervision of Informal Finance

Informal finance is an important supplement to formal financial services, an important source of financing for ordinary farmers and a natural part of inclusive finance. Rural informal finance generally refers to financial organizations or activities that are not supervised by financial authorities, both of which lack legal basis. For a long time, rural non-governmental financial organizations and activities mainly involve free informal lending (with or without interest) of various individuals and units, informal lenders, informal money brokers, economic service departments and financial service departments of some cooperative institutions dealing with informal lending, rotating savings and credit associations (RoSCAs), various cooperatives running mutual funds, underground banks or money exchanges, p2p platforms, pawnshops and informal bill discounting, traders' loans and trade credit, etc. Fundraising fraud and "illegal absorption of public deposits" are the most common crimes in informal finance in rural areas.

First, the government regulates informal lending by restricting interest rates. The interpretation of the Supreme Court in 2015 provides:

> If the annual interest rate agreed between the borrower and the lender is less than 24%, and the lender requests the borrower to pay interest at the agreed rate as above, the court shall support it. If the annual interest rate agreed between the borrower and the lender exceeds 36%, the excess part is invalid. If the borrower requests the lender to return the interest being paid in excess of 36%, the court shall support it.

This judicial interpretation relaxed the interest rate ceiling of informal lending and catered to the calls of society to relax this restriction.

Secondly, a strict examination and approval system was implemented for the establishment of financial institutions and organizations or financial business activities. In 1998 and 2018, it was stipulated that without the approval of the competent authority according to law, no unit or individual shall set up an institution engaged in or mainly engaged in the business of granting loans or take the granting of loans as its daily business activities.

5.3 Achievements and Deficiencies

5.3.1 Achievements

With the strong promotion of the central government, China made great progress in the development of an inclusive financial system. From 1986 to 2013, China issued 471.767 billion yuan of Specialized Loans. From 2001 to 2013, the central government subsidized 7.105 billion yuan to Specialized Loans. The central government's funds leveraged large funding from banks. The exploration of public-interest microfinance and farmers' mutual funds have played a good experimental and exemplary role in improving the way of financial poverty alleviation in China.

The construction of the rural finance division and financial division for poverty alleviation of large state-owned banks has also promoted the development of inclusive finance in China and increased loans related to agriculture, rural area and farmers. By the end of 2016, the loan balance serving the agriculture, rural area and farm households of the ABC's Financial Division for Serving the Agriculture, Rural Areas and Farmers reached 2.76 trillion yuan, an increase of 71.6% over the end of 2011, and the growth rate for many consecutive years was higher than the average of bank total loan balance; By the end of 2016, the balance of loans serving agriculture, rural area and farmers of the PSBC reached 917.445 billion yuan, a year-on-year increase of 22.67% from 2011 (Zhang et al., 2017).

In terms of capital market and futures market, as of March 2018, 12 enterprises in poor counties had been listed through the green channel, raising more than 3 billion yuan, 63 enterprises have started to go through the procedure of getting listed and 82 companies had been listed on the new third board. On December 22, 2017, the futures of apple contracts were officially listed and traded in the Zhengzhou Commodity Exchange, which helped to promote the development of the apple industry.

5.3.2 Deficiencies

The PRC's rural inclusive financial system is still far from perfect. The problem with lack of legal status and deficiencies with the supervision of public-interest microfinance institutions and farmers' mutual funds serving low-income farmers and new rural business entities has not been solved. The supervision system of microloan companies needs to be improved. The inclusive financial service strategies and measures of large state-owned banks have not been fully implemented; the capital market, futures market and agricultural insurance market for agricultural and rural economic development are seriously underdeveloped.

6. Outlook of the Reform and Development of the Chinese Rural Financial System

6.1 Continue to Adopt the Principle and Direction of Marketization and Market Opening to Promote the Reform of the Rural Financial System

As a part of the overall financial system, China's rural financial system is constantly changing with the reform of the economic system. The main axis of these changes is the marketization of rural financial institutions and the continuous opening of rural financial markets. The market-oriented reform has brought about great vitality to rural financial institutions. Market opening has enriched rural financial institutions and thus strengthened the main body of rural financial supply, enhanced the supply and competitiveness of rural financial markets and promoted the formation of a multi-level, wide-coverage and sustainable rural financial system. In the future, we should continue the principles and policies of marketization and market opening to make the rural financial market more dynamic.

6.2 Continue to Construct Rural Financial System Suitable for Serving the "Agriculture, Rural Areas and Farmers"

The National Financial Work Conference in 2007 put forward the goal of establishing and improving a multi-level, wide-coverage and sustainable rural financial system suitable for serving "agriculture, rural areas and farmers" and required to give full play to the role of commercial finance, policy-oriented finance, and cooperative finance. The current rural financial system has not fully achieved this goal.

First of all, rural cooperative finance, in its authentic sense, should be supplemented as soon as possible. In terms of mechanisms, China should learn from Germany or Japan to adopt the mechanisms of a rural cooperative financial system. At present, with the encouragement of the government, farmers' mutual funds are rising and developing in rural China. The government should establish an effective supervision system as soon as possible to provide institutional guarantee for the real development of these organizations into a new type of rural cooperative finance in its authentic sense.

Secondly, internet finance or digital finance of FinTech is helpful in overcoming the difficulties of traditional rural financial services and should be vigorously developed. The wide and rapid application of information technologies such as the internet, big data and artificial intelligence in the financial field helps to solve the problems of high cost and high risk of rural finance to a great extent. At present, two development trends of internet finance coexist in rural China: on the one hand, the innovation and development of internet finance for agriculture, rural areas and farmers of non-financial institutions as leaders of the internet finance industry are accelerating; On the other hand, the digital transformation of financial institutions, who are followers in the internet finance industry, and their introduction of internet finance are also accelerating. Of course, the risk of internet finance cannot be underestimated. Generally, the government needs to implement appropriate supervision rather than excessive or insufficient supervision.

Thirdly, improve the incentive mechanism of rural commercial financial institutions and guide them to effectively serve the implementation of the Rural Revitalization, especially the agricultural and rural economic development. The divisions for serving agriculture, rural areas and farmers of the ABC and PSBC should make full use of their business and network advantages to strengthen the credit extension to new agricultural business entities, to key areas such as agricultural and rural infrastructure construction and new business forms of rural economy. The PSBC needs to establish an effective mechanism to return their fund to rural areas and carry out the capital wholesale business to the existing small and medium-sized rural financial institutions. Rural commercial banks, rural cooperative banks and RCCs should break the shackles of administrative regions and be allowed to run business in larger economic areas encompassing both the administrative regions where they are based and the surrounding regions. Regarding village banks, the government should adjust their regulatory policies: They should be treated as small rural community banks and regulated properly. The government should promote the pilot work of "one village bank is allowed to cover and cross multiple counties" and of investment management type of village bank (which has the normal village bank functions and further functions such as investing in other village banks and managing such investment) to improve the development and service capacity of village banks.

6.3 Further Strengthen the Construction of Rural Inclusive Financial System

Rural inclusive finance is the weakest link in the PRC's inclusive financial system and faces many problems and challenges. For example, the development of rural financial institutions in rural areas, especially in remote and poor areas, is uneven, and the problems with difficult and expensive access of small and micro enterprises and vulnerable groups to loans are prevailing. The macro-level policies need to be adjusted and improved. The construction of financial infrastructure needs to be strengthened. The direct financing market lags behind. The function of policy-oriented financial institutions has not been fully brought into play. There are problems with the sustainability of Subsidized Loans. The problem of the "digital gap" is prevailing. The commercial sustainability of inclusive finance needs to be improved, and so on. Tackling these problems should be the main direction and focus of striving to improve the development level of inclusive finance in future rural China.

At the meso level of the inclusive financial system, the supporting systems of rural financial market need to be further improved, including the credit guarantee system, the insurance system (agricultural insurance, life insurance and credit insurance), the credit rating system and the agricultural and rural data statistical system.

6.4 Accelerate to Complete Rural Financial Legislation

The perfection and development of the rural financial market must be guaranteed by constructing a system of rural financial policies, laws and regulations. At present, the PRC's laws and regulations on public-interest microfinance institutions and farmers' mutual funds are absent, the laws on micro-loan companies and Internet finance are not perfect, and the legislation of agricultural insurance and informal finance law also need to be improved. These have become the bottleneck restricting rural finance, especially the development of inclusive finance and rural financial innovation.

Note

1 Source: Tongquan Sun, Xingyuan Feng, Zhang Yuhuan, and Chong Dong, 2019. 70 Years' Evolution of the Rural Financial System of the People's Republic of China, Rural Finance Research, No. 10.

References

Chen Fei, Liu Feipeng. *Review of China's Rural Credit Cooperatives in 60 Years*. China Finance, No. 19, 2009.

Chen Xiwen, Zhao Yang, Chen Jianbo, Luo Dan. *60 Years of Institutional Change in China's Rural Areas*. People's Publishing House, 2009.

China Cooperation Times. *Remember History and Continue Glory*. December 28, 2018, www.zh-hz.com/Item/403565.aspx

Hu Hai'ou, Wu Guoxiang. *Theory and Practice of China's Financial Reform*. Fudan University Press, 2001.

Miao Yan. *The Branches of Agricultural Bank of China are Basically in Place and Employees Will not be Distributed on a Large Scale*. China's Securities Net – Shanghai Securities News, 2007, http://finance.sina.com.cn/money/bank/bank_hydt/20070202/03543305558.shtml

Rural Financial Services Research Group of the People's Bank of China. *Report on Rural Financial Services in China 2016*. China Finance Press, 2017.

Shi Danlin (Ed.). *A Brief History of Rural Finance*. Beijing Agricultural University Press, 1992.

Wen Tao, Wang Yuyu. *The Economic Effect of Government-led Agricultural Credit and Financial Support for Agriculture: Based on the Experience of China from 1952 to 2002*. Chinese Rural Economy, No. 10, 2005.

Wu Chengji (Ed.). *History of Agricultural Bank of China*. Economic Science Press, 2000.

Xu Tangling. *History of China's Rural Finance*. China Finance Publishing House, 1996.

Yang Ximing et al. *Research on The Development of Rural Credit Cooperatives*. Hubei Science and Technology Press, 2013.

Zhan Yurong. *History of China's Rural Finance*. Beijing Agricultural University Press, 1991.

Zhang Chenghui, Pan Guangwei et al. *China Rural Financial Development Report 2016*. China Development Press, November 2017.

Zhou Li. *China's Rural Finance: Market System and Practice Investigation*. China Agricultural Science and Technology Press, 2010.

3

FARM HOUSEHOLDS' DEMAND FOR AND ACCESS TO LOANS IN RURAL CHINA

Guangwen He, Jing He and Pei Guo

1. The Problem Statements

Farmers can change their initial endowment, expand the scale of production, and increase their income through credit (Feder et al., 1990), but rural financial markets in developing countries suffer from severe information asymmetries (Hoff and Stiglitz, 1990), which increase transaction costs, and coupled with the lack of collateral and credit history of a larger number of farmers, farm credit constraints are particularly pronounced (Banerjee and Newman, 1993). In this way, the problem of difficulty in obtaining loans for farmers has been more prominent. Alleviating or mitigating the problem has been the focus of the government policy of deepening financial inclusion in rural China, and the status of farmers' credit demand and the accessibility of formal credit have been the focus of rural finance theory, policy and practice. In a survey of farmers organized by the author (He, 1999), it was found that 60.96% of farmers' borrowing behavior occurred within the informal financial sector; in 2005, the Rural Economic Research Department of the Development Research Center of the State Council conducted a survey of farmers in 29 provinces (municipalities and autonomous regions) nationwide, which showed that 60.6% of farmers had loan demands, but only 52.6% of farmers with borrowing demands could obtain funds from formal financial institutions. A survey of 20,040 farm households in 10 provinces conducted by the People's Bank of China and the National Bureau of Statistics in 2007 also showed that 46.1% of farm households demanded to borrow money, and the formal financial coverage rate was only 31.67% (People's Bank of China Farmers' Credit Situation Questionnaire Survey, 2009).

In order to alleviate the problem of farmers' difficulties with access to loans since the reform and opening up, the Chinese government and financial institutions have adopted a series of reform measures and methods to improve the delivery of financial services to farmers, and, especially after entering the 21st century, the efforts to tackle financial exclusion have been continuously strengthened, firstly, to promote business innovation to guide financial institutions to carry out innovative microcredit. The most typical one is the "Guiding Opinions on the Management of Small Credit Loans to Farmers by Rural Credit Cooperatives" issued by the People's Bank of China in 2001, and the "Guiding Opinions on the Vigorous Development of Rural Microfinance Business by Banking Financial Institutions" issued by the China Banking Regulatory Commission in 2007; secondly, financial and tax benefits are given to the improvement of rural financial services. In 2010, the Ministry of Finance and the General Administration of Taxation issued the Notice on Tax Policies Relating to Rural Finance, which exempted the interest income of financial institutions from

DOI: 10.4324/9781003369776-3

business tax and reduced the amount of income tax paid on small loans to farmers. In June 2017, the Ministry of Finance and the General Administration of Taxation issued the Notice on the Continuation of Tax Policies Relating to the Support of the Development of Rural Finance, the interest income of financial institutions from a single small loan or a total small loan balance for farmers amounting to 100,000 yuan or less is exempt from VAT, and 90% of its value is included in the total income base when calculating taxable income; third, monetary policy tools are used to promote financial institutions to improve the delivery of rural financial services. In order to support financial institutions in developing inclusive finance business, the People's Bank issued the Notice on the Implementation of Targeted Reserve Rate Reduction for Inclusive Finance in September 2017, which provides that, regarding the borrowers who are granted by the commercial banks a single credit line of less than 5 million Yuan, their small enterprise loans, micro enterprise loans, business loans for individual households in industry and commerce (geti gongshang hu), business loans for owners of small and micro enterprises, farmer production and operation loans, guaranteed business start-up (for the laid-off and unemployed) loans, consumer loans for the poor and student loans, a targeted reserve ratio reduction policy can apply, if the increase of such loans or balance of such loans reaches a certain percentage of the total loan increase or balance, respectively.[1] Fourthly, to relax the access policy of banking financial institutions in rural areas and promote the diversification of financial institutions, especially the diversification of small financial institutions. At the end of 2006, the CBRC issued "Several Opinions on Adjusting and Relaxing the Access Policy of Banking Financial Institutions in Rural Areas to Better Support the Construction of New Socialist Countryside", allowing domestic and foreign bank capital, industrial capital and private capital to invest in rural areas, acquire, set up new village banks to provide financial services for local farmers, establish community-based credit cooperatives to serve their members who paid contributions for their shares and set up wholly-owned subsidiaries of commercial banks specializing in lending business. In May 2008, it also issued the "Guiding Opinions on the Piloting of Microfinance Companies" to promote the "lending without deposit" piloting of microfinance companies. At the end of 2015, the State Council issued the "Plan for Promoting the Development of Inclusive Finance (2016–2020)", which includes financial services for farmers as a key target of inclusive financial services.

Theoretical studies have argued that bank concentration has a direct negative impact on economic growth (Rajan and Zingales, 1998), thus demonstrating that financial development centered on the diversification of financial institutions, especially small institutions, is conducive to the deepening of financial inclusion. First, such financial development can improve access to financial services for low- and middle-income groups and micro and medium-sized enterprises (Beck et al., 2007) and alleviate underemployment and inefficient technological production in areas where financial development lags (Conroy, 2005). Secondly, the development of micro and small financial institutions is beneficial to meet the credit demands of small-scale production and operators. A study by Goldberg and White (1998) found a significant inverse relationship between the size of banks and their efforts to lend to small businesses (as a percentage of bank assets). Thus, it is demonstrated that the development of small institutions facilitates the deepening of financial inclusion. It has also been shown that large banks with complex structures are less likely to lend to small businesses (Berger and Udall, 1996) and that newly established banks lend more to small businesses than established banks of the same size (Shull, 1999). It can also be argued that the theoretical findings support the Chinese government's policy of promoting the diversification of MFIs and the promotion of the issuance of micro and small credit by financial institutions.

So, after years of rural reform and development, deepening and practice of rural inclusive financial reform, what is the status of meeting the inclusive financial demands of farmers? Has it changed? Has the accessibility of credit improved? This is an empirical question worthy of in-depth study. The answer to this question is of great importance for the improvement of China's inclusive finance policy. Therefore, the purpose of this study is to explain the evolution pattern of financial service demand of rural households, credit availability, and satisfaction channels during this period of structural transformation of the rural economy.

2. The Source of Data and the Basic Situation of the Sample Farmers

2.1 Data Source and Sample Description

The data in this paper come from the database of the "China Rural Inclusive Finance Survey" conducted by the School of Economics and Management of the China Agricultural University in July 2017. The survey adopts a stratified random sampling method, in which Shandong rovince, Henan rovince and Guangxi Zhuang Autonomous Region are selected, with each province representing one macro region, i.e., the Eastern Region, Central Region and Western Region, respectively. And three counties are selected within each province using GDP per capita as a proxy variable, stratified according to the level of economic development, and three townships are selected in each county according to the level of economic development, and two natural villages are randomly selected in each township, with the population of the village generally in the range of 30–50 households, to conduct a census by means of household interviews on basic conditions (individual characteristics; household conditions; business activities; and consumption, income and expenditure levels; etc.), farm households' financial demands and financial behaviors (deposits, investment and wealth management, borrowing from formal financial institutions and borrowing willingness, borrowing from informal financial institutions, and lending of funds by farmers). With this effort, the survey team obtained information on household production and financial situation of 2,093 farm households in 2016, of which 1,730 were valid sample farm households, and the valid sample rate was 82.67%.

Valid sample statistics show that 60.8% of the respondents are male, the youngest is 21 years old, the oldest is 75 years old, the average age is 45.08 years old, the average years of education is 7.74 years, between elementary school graduation and junior high school graduation; the average size of the household is 4.59 people, 58.5% of which are working people aged 18–60. Among the farm households interviewed, 52% had one or more laborers working outside the hometown, 18.2% had college students, 13.5% were poor households, and 2% had their family members, relatives or friends acting as county, township or village level cadres.

In all the sample counties, there are rural credit cooperatives (rural commercial banks or rural cooperative banks), agricultural banks, postal savings banks, industrial and commercial banks, construction banks, and agricultural development banks, respectively. In addition, there are also branches of the Bank of China, village banks, branches of regional urban commercial banks, microfinance companies, and some branches and services of some FinTech institutions in these sample counties, so it can be said that the financial supply has been largely diversified.

2.2 Farmers' Production and Operation and Income Characteristics

Firstly, the diversification of farm households' economic activities is obvious, and more farmers have abandoned Philip C. Huang's "crutch logic" of non-farm household income (Huang, 2000a, 2000b). More farmers are no longer engaged in traditional farm production activities but in other industries on a part-time basis. Although this is generally consistent with the findings of Han et al. (2007) and the People's Bank of China Farmers' Credit Situation Questionnaire Survey and Analysis Group (2009), the authors find that some Chinese farmers can already rely on urban workers for survival, and that income from urban work is no longer a supplement to family farm income, moving away from Huang's "small farmer proposition". Therefore, instead of broadly dividing farm households into agricultural and non-farm sectors, we divide farm households in detail into those engaged in farm production, such as farming, those engaged in commercial and industrial operations such as small stores, and those engaged in peripheral and other activities at home. We classify farm households into three types: those engaged in farm production, such as farming; those engaged in commercial and industrial operations, such as small shops; and those working outside the home and in other areas. From the surveyed sample, only 33.7% of the surveyed farm households are simply engaged in traditional farm production and operation, and more farm households are engaged in farm production and other industries at the same time, among which the number of farm households engaged in agriculture and working outside at the same time is the largest, accounting for 38.38% of the total sample; farm households engaged in farm production and industrial and commercial operation at the same time, accounting for 5.95%; households engaged in three production and operation activities at the same time The proportion of households engaged in three production and business activities at the same time was 3.53%. In 10.64% of the households, they had completely abandoned farm production, and all of their household income came from working outside the home; 2.49% of the households were engaged in industrial and commercial operations only, such as running small stores and supermarkets, acting as agricultural brokers, opening farmhouses, and selling seeds and fertilizers; 1.04% of the households worked and engaged in industrial and commercial production at the same time. Furthermore, 4.28% of the interviewed farming households are no longer engaged in any production or operation and mainly receive income through land transfer rent, children's support and government relief, etc. This part is mainly composed of aging rural households and sick and weak households.

Secondly, the income of combining farming and industrial and commercial farming households was significantly higher than that of other types of farming households. The average annual income of the sample farm households was about 66,400 Yuan, among which those engaged in farm production and operating industrial and commercial businesses had the highest income (Table 3.1), followed by farm households with the greatest diversification of economic activities, i.e., those engaged in farm production, operating industrial and commercial businesses, and having members working outside the home; and thirdly, those specializing in industrial and commercial businesses. Those households without any productive activities had the lowest income, only 17,200 Yuan.

TABLE 3.1 Farmers' production and operation types and income status

Type	Number of households	Proportion %	Average annual income 10,000 Yuan	Cultivating land Acres	Percentage of land transferred	Average household land transfer (mu)
Farm production	583	33.70	6.33	12.05	15.27	9.76
Working outside	184	10.64	5.13	0.16	0.00	0.00
Industrial and commercial operations	43	2.49	10.44	0.19	0.00	0.00
Farm production + commercial and industrial operations	103	5.95	15.94	14.80	19.42	37.33
Farm production + outside work	664	38.38	5.74	7.63	10.24	10.64
Business and industrial operation + outside work	18	1.04	7.56	0.00	0.00	0.00
No production activities	74	4.28	1.72	0.26	0.00	0.00
Farm + business + outside work	61	3.53	11.26	9.20	6.56	6.50
Total	1730	100.00	6.64	8.21	10.46	13.06

Again, the degree of scale farm production is generally low. This is the same finding as that of Han et al. (2007) and the People's Bank of China Farmers' Credit Situation Questionnaire Analysis Group (2009). The average cultivation area of farm households specializing in farm production is only 12.05 mu, and the cultivation area of farm households whose farm production is also engaged in industrial and commercial operations reaches 14.80 mu, while the actual cultivation area of other households not engaged in farm production is less than 1 mu on average. At the same time, the proportion of land transfer is not high; the average proportion of land transfer in the interviewed sample is only 10.46%, and the land transfer area is only 13.06 mu, mainly on a moderate scale.

3. Evolution of Farmers' Credit Demand and Credit Accessibility

3.1 Farmers' Credit Demand Remains Strong and Formal Credit Satisfaction Rate is Still Low

In 2005, the Rural Economic Research Department of the Development Research Center of the State Council conducted a survey of rural households in 29 provinces (municipalities and autonomous regions) nationwide, which showed that 60.6% of rural households had a demand for credit (Han et al., 2007). A 2007 survey of 20,040 farm households in 10 provinces conducted by the People's Bank of China in collaboration with the National Bureau of Statistics also showed that 46.1% of farm households demanded to borrow money (People's Bank of China Farm Household Credit Survey Analysis Group, 2009).

The analysis of credit demand and credit satisfaction in this paper focuses on a series of eliciting questions to find the existence of credit demand and its satisfaction level among farmers. The demand for credit and its satisfaction level are examined through the following two questions.

Question 1: Have you ever received a loan from a bank or rural credit cooperative?

Question 2: What is the reason for selecting "No application"?

If the interviewed farmer answered that he had not received any loans from banks or the rural credit cooperative and the reason was "no need", then we believe that he does not have a demand for credit, and if not, then he has a demand for credit.

Among farmers with credit demands, we measure the credit satisfaction of farmers by credit rationing. If the farmer answers "I can obtain bank loans" in question 1 or "I can borrow money from other places" in question 2, it is considered that the credit demand can be met through formal or informal channels, and there is no credit constraint. If the farmer answered, "I applied but was rejected" in question 1, or "I did not apply" in question 1 and "did not know how to apply", "no collateral", "no guarantor", "I don't know anyone at the bank or rural credit cooperative", "It took too long to apply", "The interest rate is too high", "Too short application period", "Worried about not being able to repay", etc. in question 2, we believe that there are credit constraints.

Of the 1,730 farm households interviewed, 705 have credit demands, accounting for 40.75% of the total sample. Farmers' credit demands remain relatively strong, consistent with the findings of Han (2007) and the People's Bank of China Farmers' Credit Situation Questionnaire Analysis Group (2009). Outside of formal and informal borrowing, there are still 220 farm households with financial demands but unable to obtain financial support from any channel, and the credit rationing rate is 31.21%, indicating that after years of inclusive financial mechanism construction, the percentage of credit-constrained farm households is still high.

In short, farmers' credit demand remains strong, but the formal credit satisfaction rate is still low, and credit rationing for farmers is still serious.

3.2 Informal Credit is Still the Main Channel for Farmers to Meet their Credit Demands

A diversified and competitive commercial banking system with declining bank concentration not only increases the likelihood that farmers will use formal borrowing but also helps to achieve an effective shift in farmers' financing preferences from informal to formal borrowing and increase the proportion of farmers' formal borrowing to total financing (He et al., 2017). More established studies have consistently shown that formal credit availability of farm households is low, mainly satisfied by borrowing from relatives, friends and private financial organizations, etc., and formal credit rationing is serious (Han et al., 2007; People's Bank of China Farm Household Credit Situation Questionnaire Analysis Group, 2009; Turvey et al., 2012). 2003–2009 Ministry of Agriculture Rural Fixed Observation Point A study conducted by the Development Research Center of the State Council in 2005 showed that the proportion of borrowing from informal channels was as high as 47.4%, and only 52.6% of farmers with borrowing needs could obtain funds from formal financial institutions (Han et al., 2007), and a joint study by the People's Bank of China and National Statistics in 2007 also showed that formal financial coverage was only 26.6%. In 2007, a joint study by the People's Bank of China and national statistics also showed that the formal financial coverage rate was only 26.3% (People's Bank of China Farmers' Credit Survey Analysis Group, 2009).

So, what is the situation regarding the availability of formal credit to farmers? In analyzing the access of farmers to credit, we consider them to have access to formal credit if they get it from financial institutions such as rural credit cooperatives, rural commercial banks, rural cooperative banks and other commercial banks and access to informal credit if they get it from relatives and friends and informal financial organizations. Among the sample of 705 households with credit demands, 485 can be satisfied through formal and informal channels, and the informal credit channels are mainly borrowing from relatives and friends, etc. Only a very small number of farmers turn to informal financial organizations with higher interest rates. Among the 485 households with credit support, only 165 households (34.02% of the households without credit rationing) received a sufficient amount of credit support from formal financial institutions, 60 households could obtain formal credit support, but their borrowing amount could not meet their financial demands and needed to be supplemented by informal credit, while 260 households could not obtain formal credit support and relied entirely on informal credit. This indicates that after years of inclusive financial

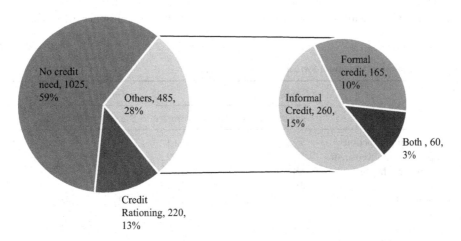

FIGURE 3.1   Farmers' Credit Demands and Their Satisfaction Level and Channels

development, the service capacity of formal finance still needs to be improved, and many farmers still cannot obtain financial support through formal credit channels, which is still consistent with the findings of Han (2007) and the People's Bank of China (People's Bank of China Farmers' Credit Questionnaire Analysis Group, 2009).

At the same time, we examined the behavior of borrowing through financing methods such as P2P and crowdfunding on the Internet (Figure 3.1). Only six farm households in the full sample had tried borrowing on the Internet, and most of them obtained consumer credit through the Ants Credit Pay (Huabei) of the Ant Financial Group, provided on the Taobao platform, indicating that the development of digital inclusive finance still needs to be improved and the penetration rate needs to be strengthened. The role of new financial institutions, such as microfinance companies, which have been added to the rural financial reform since 2007, in meeting farmers' credit demands is not reflected in the sample area.

In short, informal credit is still the main channel for farmers to meet their credit demands, and formal credit services need to be strengthened.

3.3 The Degree of Formal Financial Satisfaction of Farmers' Productive Credit Demands Has Increased

There is a significant difference between the borrowing purposes of formal and informal credit for farmers (Table 3.2). 43.61% of formal credit is mainly used to support farm production and investment, and 13.22% of formal credit is used to support non-farm production and investment, which together indicates that more than half of the formal financial institutions' borrowing is productive borrowing and supports the production and operation of farmers; 29.96% of formal credit is used to support farmers to buy apartments and building houses, with the development of urbanization, more and more farmers choose to buy apartments in towns through a mortgage, which is the second largest demand of farmers' borrowing. Borrowing for shopping and consumption, medical care, children's education and repayment of existing loans accounts for a relatively small share.

In contrast to the use of formal credit, informal borrowing is mainly used for consumer spending, with the largest percentage of 36.33% for medical care and children's education, followed by 22.93% for buying and building houses, and only 19.29% and 2.89% for agricultural and non-farm production respectively, which is much lower than the percentage of formal credit. The problem of difficulty in accessing medical care and schooling still exists.

In short, the degree of formal financial satisfaction of farmers' productive lending demands has increased, but farmers mainly rely on informal finance to meet their consumer demands.

TABLE 3.2 Analysis of formal and informal credit use by farmers

	Formal Credit		Informal Credit	
	Number of households	Percentage	Number of households	Percentage
Investment in farm production	99	43.61	60	19.29
Non-farm production investment	30	13.22	9	2.89
Buying or building a house	68	29.96	71	22.83
Shopping cost	16	7.05	38	12.22
Medical care and children's education	10	4.41	113	36.33
Repayment of loans	4	1.76	2	0.64
Wedding and funeral fees	0	0.00	18	5.79
Total	227	100.00	311	100.00

3.4 Collateral and Guarantee Are Still the Main Ways for Farmers to Obtain Formal Credit

In the modern commercial credit market, the lack of legally acceptable collateral for farmers has been the biggest barrier to their access to the formal credit market, as evidenced by Clarke et al. (2006), who argue that financial markets primarily direct funds to the wealthy and those with good social networks because they can provide collateral and have less risk of default. Financial development provides better quality financial services to wealthy households, while low- and middle-income groups, such as farmers, are excluded from the formal financial system because they cannot provide collateral. Therefore, innovative loan risk management methods to enhance the availability of formal credit for farm households are important elements of the Chinese government's efforts to deepen inclusive financial services, and what is their performance? This is also an important issue examined in this study.

As can be seen from Table 3.3, in terms of the way farmers obtain loans from banking financial institutions, the percentage of farmers who obtain credit loans is the highest, at 36.89%, but the average household credit loan is only 84,800 yuan[2]; followed by loans obtained through guarantees (the majority of farmers' guarantors are other farmers in the same village), and the average household amount of guaranteed loans is 129,200 Yuan, higher than that of credit loans. 16.44% of the farmers obtained loans through joint guarantees by three or five households; only 17.33% of the farmers obtained loans through collateral, mainly for families with purchased urban apartments. Although the pilot scheme of "two rights" secured loans has been carried out, very few farmers in the research sample obtained loans through the secured with land management rights, rural residential land using rights and attached properties, indicating that the pilot scheme of "two rights" secured loans needs to be deepened. A small number of farmers obtained loans through innovative models such as "government + insurance + bank", "agricultural guarantee company + farmers" and "leading enterprise + cooperative + farmers". At the same time, their average loan amount is also the highest, which is reflected in the other items in Table 3.3.

It can be seen that the percentage of farmers who rely on their own creditworthiness to obtain formal loans is relatively low, which is close to the finding of Gan and Li (2014)[3] that the level of formal credit availability is 27.6%, and the threshold of formal credit for farmers is still high, and its availability still needs to continue to be improved.

In short, collateral and guarantee are still the main ways for farmers to obtain formal credit, and the availability of formal credit for farmers is still low.

3.5 The Degree of Self-exclusion of Financial Services for Farmers is Still High

When we analyzed the causes of farmers' credit constraints, we found that, in line with the previous findings, demand-based rationing was a factor that triggered farmers' credit constraints. 41.34% of farmers who were unable to obtain formal credit support (see Table 3.4) said they "did not know

TABLE 3.3 Analysis of formal credit lending methods and amounts for farmers

Lending method	Mortgage	Guarantee	Credit	Co-insured loans	Others
Number of households	39	49	83	37	17
total households receiving formal credit %	17.33	21.78	36.89	16.44	7.56
Average amount of household borrowing (million yuan)	18.06	12.92	8.48	9.09	22.03

TABLE 3.4 Analysis of the causes of credit rationing and constraints of farm households

Type	Number of households	Percentage
Don't know how to apply	148	41.34
Application process is too long	18	5.03
The interest rate is too high	47	13.13
Worry about not being able to pay back	27	7.54
Overly complex process	5	1.40
Banks don't know responsible persons	25	6.98
Lack of collateral	49	13.69
Lack of guarantor	35	9.78
Short term	4	1.12
Total	358	100.00

how to apply", indicating a lack of understanding of bank borrowing and the existence of the percentage of farmers who felt that the interest rate was too high was 13.13%, followed by 5.03% who felt that the application process was too long, 7.54% who were worried about not being able to repay, and 1.4% who thought the process was too complicated. Credit rationing and constraints on the supply side of financial institutions accounted for a relatively small percentage, with only 13.69% and 9.78% of farmers citing lack of collateral and guarantees as the reason for the unavailability of credit, which echoes the previous credit loans as the main way of bank lending. 6.98% of farmers suggested that banks did not know people, which caused difficulties in obtaining bank loans, and only 1.12% of farmers pointed out that the loan terms of formal financial institutions were too short.

4. The Hierarchical and Structural Characteristics of Farmers' Credit Demand

4.1 Demands of Farmers with Different Production and Operation Modes Are Still Relatively Strong

Although there are significant differences in the demands for credit and the degree of satisfaction among farmers with different production and operation modes, the demands are still relatively strong.

Some studies show (Zhang and Yang, 2011) that farmers with different production and operation modes have different capital needs, farmers with mainly non-farm income have a relatively more stable income and a lower level of capital needs and farmers with more non-farm income are less likely to generate credit rationing. However, its analysis does not distinguish the occupational differences of nonfarm practitioners. This paper differentiates farm households' occupations from three perspectives: farm production, industrial and commercial operations and outworking and examines the credit demands and satisfaction of farm households with different production and operation combinations (Table 3.5).

Overall, the percentage of farmers with credit demands was as high as 40.75%, and the percentage of farmers with credit demands was relatively high for all types of farmers. Among them: (1) commercial and industrial farmers, whether they are engaged in commercial and industrial business alone or in commercial and industrial business, the proportion of farmers with credit demands is higher, accounting for 53.49%; however, the degree of credit rationing for these farmers is relatively low, with 21.74% of farmers engaged in commercial and industrial business alone suffering credit rationing; those commercial and industrial farmers with relatively stable cash flow due to

TABLE 3.5 Credit demand of farm households and their credit rationing in the perspective of production diversification

Type	Households with no credit needs	Households with credit needs	Percentage with credit needs	Of which no credit rationing households	Of which with credit rationing	Credit rationing as %	Total
Farm production	365	218	37.39	149	69	31.65	583
Working outside	98	86	46.74	48	38	44.19	184
Industrial and commercial operations	20	23	53.49	18	5	21.74	43
Farm production + commercial and industrial operations	53	50	48.54	44	6	12.00	103
Farm production + outside work	401	263	39.61	178	85	32.32	664
Business and industrial operation + outside work	10	8	44.44	7	1	12.50	18
Not engaged in any production activities	45	29	39.19	18	11	37.93	74
Farm + business + outside work	33	28	45.90	23	5	17.86	61
Overall	1025	705	40.75	485	220	31.21	1730

Note: The percentage of having credit demand = having credit demand/(having credit demand + no credit demand)*100%. Credit rationing ratio = with credit rationing/with credit demand * 100%. Same as below.

their labor force working outside the hometown are only 12.5% of those suffering credit rationing. The proportion of households suffering credit rationing is only 12.5% for those commercial and industrial households with relatively stable cash flow. (2) The degree of credit rationing is higher for non-commercial farmers who are engaged in farm production, whether professionally or part-time. The proportion of those who have engaged in farm production alone or work outside the hometown while engaging in farm production is more than 30%, and the credit rationing of these farmers is also high, with the proportion of those who suffer from credit rationing being about one-third, i.e., about one-third of farm production farmers are unable to obtain credit support. (3) Farmers who work outside their hometown also have a high demand for credit, and the satisfaction rate is low. The percentage of those with credit demands is 46.74%, and 44.19% of farmers with credit demands have difficulty obtaining formal and informal credit support. (4) The proportion of farmers with credit demands who are not engaged in any production activities is higher, and it is more difficult to obtain financing. The percentage of farmers with credit demands in this category is 39.19%, and it is more difficult to obtain financing due to the lack of business foundation, and those who are subject to credit rationing is 37.93%.

4.2 All Types of Farmers' Borrowing Still Rely Heavily on Informal Financial Channels

Table 3.6 analyzes the sources of borrowing for farmers with credit demands that are met in the context of diversified production operations. It can be seen that, in general, regardless of the type of farmers, the satisfaction of their borrowing demands relies heavily on informal credit channels, and 66% of the farmers who obtained loans met their demands only through informal credit channels. Among them, as many as 53.61% relied purely on informal credit channels to meet their demands. Among the farmers who are solely engaged in farm production and those who are solely engaged in outside work, 49% and 66.67% of them rely solely on informal credit channels to meet their demands, respectively.

4.3 Farmers at All Levels of Income Have Relatively High Credit Demand

We divided the total income of farm households into five quintiles and examined the credit demands of farm households in different quintiles and their degree of satisfaction, respectively (Table 3.7), and we found that.

(1) In general, the proportion of those with credit demands is relatively high among farmers of different income levels, which is different from the findings of existing studies and does not show a U-shaped distribution as shown in the studies (Han, 2007; People's Bank of China Farmers' Credit Situation Questionnaire Survey, 2009).[4] On the contrary, the proportion of those with credit demands is higher in the group of farmers with moderate to low income, while the proportion of those with credit demands is not very different among farmers of different income groups. The difference in the percentage of those who have credit demands is not too great.

(2) The degree of credit rationing is significantly higher for farmers with lower incomes. Overall, a higher percentage of farm households suffered credit rationing, 33.48%, i.e., one-third of farm households suffered credit rationing. Among them, the rate of credit rationing for farmers in the low-income bracket was as high as 48.87%. Low-income farmers, being closer to subsistence small farmers, have a lower ability to provide legally recognized collateral and face quantitative rationing by financial institutions and self-rationing of loans (Zhang and Yang, 2011), thus the availability of formal credit is lower, and credit demand is mainly met through special instruments such as policy-oriented finance (He, 2001), indicating that poor farmers' credit demand is met to a lesser extent, and is a group that needs to be focused on for financial inclusion.

TABLE 3.6 Analysis of farmers' borrowing sources under production and business diversification

Borrowing source	Formal Credit		Informal Credit		Both Formal and Informal		% of those with informal credit
	Number of households	Percentage	Number of households	Percentage	Number of households	Percentage	
Farm production	57	38.26	73	48.99	19	12.75	61.74
Working outside	11	22.92	32	66.67	5	10.42	77.09
Industrial and commercial operations	11	61.11	5	27.78	2	11.11	38.89
Farm production + commercial and industrial operations	28	63.64	12	27.27	4	9.09	36.36
Farm production + outside work	47	26.40	110	61.80	21	11.80	73.6
Business and industrial operation + outside work	1	14.29	4	57.14	2	28.57	85.71
Not engaged in any production activities	3	16.67	11	61.11	4	22.22	83.33
Agriculture + business + outside work	7	30.43	13	56.52	3	13.04	69.56
Total	165	34.02	260	53.61	60	12.37	65.98

TABLE 3.7 Status of credit demand, credit rationing and its channel to meet the demand of farm households with different incomes

Income (X) Level (million Yuan)		X≤1.36	1.36<X≤3	3<X≤4.8	4.8<X≤8	X>8	Overall
Credit Demand and Credit Rationing Status	No credit needs	213	243	144	215	210	1025
	Have a credit need	133	200	107	143	122	705
	those in need %	38.44	45.15	42.63	39.94	36.75	40.75
	No credit rationing	68	128	77	90	106	469
	Credit rationing available	65	72	30	53	16	236
	With rationing %	48.87	36.00	28.04	37.06	13.11	33.48
	Total number of farm households	346	443	251	358	332	1730
Formal and Informal Credit Access	Obtain Formal Number of households	12	29	23	31	70	165
	Farm households in the group %	17.65	22.66	29.87	34.44	66.04	34.02
	Get Informal Number of households	48	92	48	47	25	260
	Farm households in the group %	70.59	71.88	62.34	52.22	23.58	53.61
	There are Both Formal and Informal Number of households	8	7	6	18	21	60
	Farm households in the group %	11.76	5.47	7.79	20.00	19.81	12.37
	Total credit received	68	128	77	96	116	485

(3) The lower the income of farm households, the lower the formal credit satisfaction rate. Observing the borrowing channels of farmers at different income levels, we find that formal credit mainly serves farmers with higher income levels, and the percentage of farmers who obtain formal credit increases as their income increases, from 17.65% in the lowest income group to 66.04% in the highest income group, correspondingly. Farmers with lower income can only obtain informal credit. More than 70% of the farmers in the two lowest-income groups obtained their loans from informal credit channels. This is inconsistent with the findings of Peng et al. (2017). According to Peng Keqiang et al., because high-income farmers, similar to rational smallholder farmers, increased income enhances formal credit availability. However, for relatively high-income farmers' credit, scholars have different findings, some scholars (Zhu et al., 2009; Liu et al., 2014) believe that high-income farmers have easier access to formal credit support, but some scholars (Zhang and Yang, 2011) believe that high-income farmers will still be granted credit products such as microfinance, although they have larger credit demand. Such credit products are difficult to fully meet their demands, which implies that they suffer quantitative rationing.

4.4 The Credit Demand of Small-scale Farmers Remains Relatively Strong

Land is a basic factor of production and an important factor influencing the credit demand of farm households (Huang and Zou, 2015; Huang et al., 2015). The transfer of agricultural land and land scale will lead to an increase in credit demand, and in areas with larger land scale per farmer, the credit demand of farmers is significantly higher than that in areas with smaller land scale; for example, the research for Heilongjiang in 2011 showed that the percentage of farmers with loan demand in Heilongjiang was 53.83%, but in areas with smaller land scale, such as in Chongqing, only 38.38%. The reason for this is that some scholars believe that agricultural scale operation increases the demand for capital (Huang and Zou, 2015), while others believe that land rights transactions will stimulate the transfer of land out of the hand of farmers so that such farmers will engage in non-agricultural industries and start their own businesses, increasing their demand for credit. The upscaling of agricultural land will also slow down the degree of credit constraints of farm households (Huang et al., 2016).

China is a vast country with great differences in natural conditions and economic and social development levels, so it is difficult to propose a universally applicable standard for agricultural scale operation. In this paper, we refer to the "Opinions on Guiding the Orderly Transfer of Rural Land Management Rights and Developing Moderate Scale Agricultural Operations" issued by the General Office of the State Council in November 2014, which proposed that "at this stage, key support should be given to those whose land management scale is equivalent to 10 to 15 times the average contracted land area of local households and whose income from farming is equivalent to the income from local secondary and tertiary industries". Therefore, we differentiate the average local farming scale by the county-level administrative division and consider farmers whose land cultivation area is greater than 10 times the average to be farmers operating on a large scale. At the same time, we exclude farmers with an actual cultivated area of zero and divide the rest of the farmers into large-scale operation farmers and ordinary farmers to study the impact of different land operation scales on credit demand and satisfaction.

Through the division of land scale (Table 3.8), we found that the survey sample accounted for a relatively small number of farmers operating on a large scale, only 8 households, and the lowest planting scale among farmers operating on a large scale was 44 mu, and the highest was 300 mu. Although the sample was small, the credit demand was strong, with 6 out of 8 households having credit demand, and at the same time, farmers operating on a large scale did not have credit rationing and were able to meet their credit demand through various channels. In terms of loan channels (Table 3.8), half of the large-scale farmers received funds from formal financial institutions, and half received financial support from informal financial institutions.

TABLE 3.8 Analysis of credit demand, credit rationing and their borrowing channels of farmers with different land cultivation scale

Land Cultivation Scale Categorized Farmers			General farmers	Farmers operating on a large scale	Overall
Credit demand and credit rationing		No credit needs	844	2	846
		Have a credit need	542	6	548
		Those in need of all farmers %	39.11	75.00	39.31
		No credit rationing	366	6	372
		Credit rationing available	176	0	176
		With rationing all farm households %	32.47	0.00	32.12
		Total number of farm households	1,386	8	1394
Formal and informal credit access	Access to formal credit	Number of households	130	3	133
		this category of farmers %	35.52	50.00	35.75
	Access to informal credit	Number of households	204	3	207
		this category of farmers %	55.74	50.00	55.65
	There are both formal and informal	Number of households	32	0	32
		this category of farmers %	8.74	0.00	8.60
	Total number of farmers receiving credit		366	6	372

5. Countermeasures for Deepening Credit Services for Farmers

From the theoretical analysis of this paper, it can be seen that, objectively speaking, the diversification of financial institutions in counties, especially the existence of local banks and non-bank financial institutions with legal person status, such as rural commercial banks (rural cooperative banks, rural credit cooperatives), village banks, microfinance companies, and rural capital mutual societies, is conducive to enhancing credit accessibility for farmers and micro and small enterprises. To this end, the authors argue that in order to enhance credit accessibility for farmers, it is necessary to further deregulate market access from the financial supply perspective, integrate county-level financial supervision, enforce special financial institutional arrangements that are conducive to enhancing credit services for farmers and small and mini enterprises, and make structural adjustments from the demand side, such as enhancing the financial literacy of farmers and increasing the scale of their operations, etc.

1. **Further deregulate the access to the rural financial market; promote the diversification of micro and small financial institutions, such as rural mutual fund associations, village banks and loan companies; and improve the structure of rural financial institutions.** The change in financial structure is an important factor causing economic growth and development. The financial structure is jointly determined by financial instruments and financial institutions. The number and type of financial institutions in the financial structure is a concentrated expression of financial deepening, and if financial institutions are lacking or underdeveloped, it is also an important characteristic of financial inhibition in a country (Goldsmith, 1969). There are significant differences in financial systems between developed and developing countries. The financial systems of industrialized countries are both more complex and sophisticated than those

of developing countries, resulting in a higher degree of ease of intermediation (Gurley and Shaw, 1955). Small-scale financial institutions, which can take advantage of decentralized but rich local knowledge and more complete information, are the only ones that can more easily issue small loans to meet the loan demands of farmers and SMEs, as evidenced by the history of small and medium-sized financial institutions in the United States. A study of the banking situation in the United States in the mid-1990s found that the smaller the bank, the larger its microloans as a proportion of total loans and the higher the proportion of microloans to total assets. Domestic small business loans accounted for 8.9% of total assets in banks with less than $100 million in assets, compared to 2.9% in banks with more than $5 billion in assets (Federal Reserve Bank of New York, 1995). The reason why the diversification of microfinance institutions is beneficial to the financing of farmers and microenterprises is that the main dilemma of the credit market for farmers and microenterprises is information asymmetry, which can be alleviated by promoting competition from the diversity of micro and small institutions. The best utilizers of decentralized local knowledge are those cooperative financial institutions, local small and medium-sized commercial financial institutions, microfinance institutions and so on, which have grown up with an eye on serving local economic agents. The existence of competition among these financial organizations is crucial to the efficiency of the rural financial system and the optimal allocation of financial resources (Feng et al., 2004). Innovation and competition among institutions will ultimately lead to higher efficiency in the functional performance of the financial system (Bodie et al., 2017: 28).

2. Integrate the regulatory mechanism of MFIs in Chinese counties. These micro and small financial institutions operating in Chinese counties are supervised by different regulatory bodies. While banks are regulated by the formal regulatory body, non-bank financial institutions are actually subject to informal regulation. For this reason, first, there may exist regulatory competition, and the regulation might become increasingly too strict; second, although these institutions realistically serve micro and small economic entities in their respective counties, it is difficult to be treated fairly in terms of monetary policy and fiscal policy, for example, the People's Bank issued the Notice on the Implementation of Targeted Reserve Rate Reduction for Financial Inclusion in September 2017, which is only for bank financial institutions; third, those stronger non-bank financial institutions, who play an important role in local economic development, may use their "captured" local informal government regulators to influence the latter one's decisions and compete unfairly with their competitors, and thus increase the vulnerability of these institutions. Nobel Prize–winning economist Sargent has noted, "I would prefer a complete consolidation of all financial regulators into one, single agency regulation" (Wu, 2017).

3. Construct a structured monetary policy which promotes inclusive financial services and is based on a combination of simultaneous functional and institutional promotion. Therefore, in terms of the monetary policy tools of the Central Bank of China to promote rural inclusive finance, the tools to provide liquidity structurally are pluralizing, targeting a reduction in the cost of funds for financial institutions and guiding them to focus on the provision of inclusive financial services such as farmers and small and micro enterprises through product and business innovation, rather than at promoting a certain type of financial institutions to carry out services for the support of the development of agriculture, rural area and farmers and small and micro enterprises. According to American financiers Bodie et al. (2017: 28), an analysis should be done from a functional perspective rather than with a focus on discussing the optimization of the financial institutional structure by looking at the established financial institutions and organizations. Therefore, the authors believe that it is correct to look at institutional functions and operations, not institutions, as the general direction of the basis of the Central Bank's adjustment of its structural monetary policy promoting financial inclusion. However, the authors also believe that in this period of supply-side structural reform and agricultural transformation and upgrading, it is difficult to strengthen and upgrade agricultural financing functions by relying only on self-organization mechanisms in the financial market. Special, transitional, non-market factor financial system arrangements are needed, such as the construction of professional and policy-oriented agricultural guarantee mechanisms, policy-oriented agricultural insurance mechanisms, etc. In addition, institutional promotion policies in favor of financial institutions are also needed.

4. Structural adjustment focusing on the demand side, such as strengthening farmers' financial education, improving farmers' financial literacy, reducing farmers' financial self-exclusion, promoting farmers' non-farm entrepreneurship and advancing the degree of the scale of their operations. Structural adjustments on the financial supply side, especially the diversification of financial institutions, the integration of regulatory mechanisms for small and medium-sized financial institutions in counties, and the construction of a structured, inclusive finance promotion monetary policy based on a combination of simultaneous promotion of functions and institutions, are undoubtedly conducive to the improvement of farmers' credit accessibility. However, to fundamentally change the financial constraint of farmers, it is necessary to restructure the demand side; strengthen financial publicity, education and guidance; improve the financial knowledge and awareness of farmers; strengthen the knowledge of FinTech; and reduce farmers' self-rationing. Meanwhile, as seen in the previous study, the credit rationing of farmers with diversified business operations and large-scale farmers is relatively low. Therefore, promoting non-farm entrepreneurship and increasing the scale of farmers' operations through land transfer are conducive to improving the availability of credit to farmers.

Notes

1 Starting from 2018, the deposit reserve ratio may be reduced by 0.5 percentage points from the benchmark grade announced by the People's Bank of China for commercial banks with the above-mentioned loan balance or incremental share of 1.5% in the previous year, and by 1 percentage point from the first grade for commercial banks with the above-mentioned loan balance or incremental share of 10% in the previous year, in accordance with the progressive principle. The above measures will be implemented from 2018 onwards.
2 To avoid the effect of extreme values, this paper winsor the loan amount at the 5% level.
3 In 2013, the Agricultural Bank of China and Southwest University of Finance and Economics jointly conducted the "China Household Finance Survey", interviewing more than 28,000 sample households in 29 provinces (autonomous regions and municipalities directly under the Central Government), which is a typical research with a larger sample in recent years.
4 Both Han et al. (2007) and the People's Bank of China (2010) showed that the effect of income on the propensity of farmers to borrow was "U" shaped, with the demand of low-income and high-income farmers being stronger and the demand of middle-income farmers being lower.

References

Banerjee, A.V. and Newman, A.F. Occupational Choice and the Progress of Development. *Journal of Political Economy* 1993, 101: 274–298.

Beck, T., Demirguc-Kunt, A., and Peria, M.S.M. Reaching Out: Access to and Use of Banking Services Across Countries. *Journal of Financial Economics* 2007, 85(1): 234–266.

Berger, Allen and Gregory Udall. Universal Banking and the Future of Small Business Lending. In Saunders, Anthony and Walters, Ingo (eds.). *Universal Banking: Financial System Design Reconsidered*. Irwin Professional Publishing Co., 1996.

Bodie, Z., Merton, R.C., and Cleeton, D.L. *Finance* (2nd ed.). People's University of China Press 2017.

Clarke, G., Xu, L.C., and Heng-fu, Z. Finance and Income Inequality: What Do the Data Tell Us? *Southern Economic* 2006, (72): 578–596.

Conroy, J. APEC and Financial Exclusion: Missed Opportunities for Collective Action? *Asia Pacific Development Journal* 2005, 12(1): 53–80.

Feder, G., Lau, L.J., Lin, J.Y., and Luo, X. The Relationship between Credit and Productivity in Chinese Agriculture: A Microeconomic Model of Disequilibrium. *American Journal of Agricultural Economics* 1990, 72: 1151–1157.

Federal Reserve Bank of New York. Current Issues in Economics and Finance, June 1995.

Feng, Xinyuan, He Mengpen (German), and He Guangwen. A Trial on the Diversification of China's Rural Financial Organizations. *China Rural Observer* 2004, (5): 17–29.

Gan, Li and Li Yun, eds. *China Rural Household Finance Development Report.* Southwest University of Finance and Economics Press, 2014.

Goldberg, Lawrence and Lawrence J. White. De Novo Banks and Lending to Small Businesses: An Exploratory Analysis. *Journal of Banking & Finance* 1998, 22(6–8): 851–867.

Goldsmith, Raymond W. *Financial Structure and Development.* Yale University Press, 1969.

Gurley, J.G. and Shaw, E.S. Financial Aspects of Economic Development. *American Economic Review* 1955, 45: 515–538.

Han, J., Luo, D., and Cheng, Y. An Empirical Study of Farmers' Borrowing Demand Behavior Under Credit Constraints. *Agricultural Economics* 2007, (2): 44–52.

He, Guangwen. Rural Financial Inhibition and Financial Deepening from Rural Residents' Money Borrowing Behavior. *China Rural Economy* 1999, (10): 42–28.

He, Guangwen. Characteristics of Supply and Demand in Chinese Rural Finance and the Path Choice of Equilibrium Supply and Demand. *China Rural Economy* 2001, (10): 40–45.

He, Guangwen and Wang Liheng, The Impact of Structural Changes in the Banking Industry on the Financing Channel Selection Behavior of Farm Households-Based on Farm Household Survey Data from 18 Counties in 7 Provinces in China. *Journal of South China Normal University* (Social Science Edition) 2017, (1): 86–93.

Hoff, K. and Stiglitz, J.E. Introduction: Imperfect Information and Rural Credit Markets: Puzzles and Policy Perspectives. *World Bank Economic Review* 1990, 4(3): 235–250.

Huang, Huichun, Xu, Zhangxing, and Qi, Yan. Do Farmland Transfer and Large-Scale Management Alleviate Farmers' Credit Constraints? -Empirical Evidence from Jiangsu. *Journal of Nanjing Agricultural University* (Social Science Edition) 2016, 16(6): 109–120.

Huang, Linxiu and Zou, Xinyang. Farm Household Characteristics, Financial Demand for Farmland and Agricultural Development-an Empirical Analysis based on Two Locations in Heilongjiang and Chongqing. *Agricultural Technology Economics* 2015, (5): 114–121.

Huang, P.C. The Small Farmer Economy and Social Change in North China, Beijing, China Bookstore, 2000a.

Huang, P.C. Small Farmers' Economy and Rural Development in the Yangtze River Delta, Beijing, China Book Bureau, 2000b.

Liu, Xichuan, Chen Lihui, and Yang Qiming. Farmers' Formal Credit Demand and Interest Rates: An Empirical Examination based on the Tobit III Model. *Management World* 2014, (3): 75–91.

Peng, Keqiang, Zhang Lin, and Qiu Yan. Does Farmers' Income Increase the Availability of Formal Credit to Farmers – and the Economic Attributes of Farmers in China's Grain-Producing Regions. *Finance and Trade Economics* 2017, (6): 49–65.

People's Bank of China Farmers' Credit Situation Questionnaire Survey and Analysis Group. *Analysis Report of Questionnaire Survey on Farmers' Borrowing and Lending.* Economic Science Press, 2009.

Rajan, R.G. and Zingales, L. Financial Dependence and Growth. *American Economic Review* 1998, 88: 559–586.

Shull, Bernad. *The Separation of Banking and Commerce in the United States: An Examination of Principle Issues.* Financial Markets, Institutions & Instruments, May, 1999, 1–55.

Turvey, C.G., He, G., Jiujie, M.A., Kong, R., and Meagher, P. Farm Credit and Credit Demand Elasticities in Shanxi and Gansu. *China Economic Review* 2012, 23(4): 1020–1035.

Wu, Si. Nobel Laureate Sargent: Financial System Fragility Stems from Institutional Design. *China Economic Report* 2017, (9): 12–13.

Zhang, Longyao and Yang, Jun. A Study on Farmland Mortgage and Credit Accessibility of Farm Households. *Economic Dynamics* 2011, (11): 60–64.

Zhu, X., Ma, X.Q., and Shi, Q.H. Credit, Wealth and Rural Credit Rationing – A Study on the Supply Behavior of Different Rural Financial Institutions in Less Developed Areas. *Journal of Financial Research* 2009, (8): 4–14.

4

OWNERSHIP, GOVERNANCE AND INTERESTS OF FINANCIAL INSTITUTIONS WITHIN THE RURAL CREDIT COOPERATIVE SYSTEM[1]

Xingyuan Feng

Since 2003, reforms of rural credit cooperatives (RCCs) in China have resulted in the creation of county-level single legal persons of rural credit cooperatives, rural cooperative banks and rural commercial banks. Many governmental institutions use the term "rural cooperative financial institutions" to refer to RCCs as well as these two types of banks. This is clearly an expedience because rural commercial banks are by nature not cooperatives and are unrelated to rural cooperative financial institutions. Many problems related to the ownership and governance of these three types of rural financial institutions remain, many of which can be attributed to repressive government financial policies. In addition, RCCs and rural cooperative banks have an unusually large number of shareholders, which makes it difficult for them to operate as cooperatives and results in unavoidable commercialization. Oppressive financial policies and problems of ownership and governance of these three types of rural financial institutions have resulted in a distortion of the relationship of rights, responsibilities and interests of internal and external shareholders. These problems must be investigated in detail.

1. An Overview of the Reform Process

The first rural credit cooperative of post-1949 China was founded in 1950. The problems of distorted incentive structures and interests among RCCs have been long-standing ones and are directly related to distortions in their ownership and governance structures. Prior to reforms that began in 2003, RCCs were plagued with problems, including unclear ownership structures, large numbers of employee shareholders, scattered and fragmented equity, shareholders not exercising their powers, serious "internal control" by managers and "external control" by government regulators, historical financial burdens, poor asset quality and considerable hidden risks (Feng et al., 2015).

China began reforms of the rural credit cooperatives in 2003 as outlined in the State Council Notice on Issuing Pilot Program Plans for Deepening Reform of Rural Credit Cooperatives, which resulted in a group of rural credit cooperative associations registered as unified legal person entities within respective counties, rural cooperative banks and rural commercial banks. Prior to this, several regions already began reforms of their own in support of the People's Bank of China. Examples of these include the Zhangjiagang Rural Credit Cooperative, which began reforms in 2001 to become the first rural commercial bank under a shareholding model, the Yinzhou Rural Credit Cooperative, which began reforms in 2003 and reappeared as the Yinzhou Cooperative Bank (Yinzhou Bank), using a shareholding cooperative model, and the Danyang Rural Credit Cooperative

DOI: 10.4324/9781003369776-4

Association, which completed reforms and merged the county-level association and township-level primary credit cooperatives into one legal person entity in 2001 to become a county-registered institution with members at the county and township levels, adopting a cooperative model.

After 2003, RCCs that initially did not meet reform requirements gradually carried out reforms to meet these requirements. For example, in 2008, the Ninghai Rural Credit Cooperative Association and township-level primary credit cooperative merged to form the Ninghai Rural Credit Cooperative Association, registered as a county-level legal person entity. Starting from April 28, 2003, the China Banking Regulatory Commission (CBRC) took on responsibilities for the supervision and regulation of rural credit cooperatives, with some industry regulation and risk responsibilities being delegated to local governments in provinces where reforms were being carried out. This resulted in a comprehensive regulatory framework based on the provincial credit cooperative associations. A total of 25 provincial credit cooperative associations were established with rural commercial banks established in Beijing, Shanghai, Chongqing and Ningxia, along with rural cooperative banks in Tianjin (Jiang, 2009). Main prefecture-level cities also created regional offices for provincial credit cooperative associations. In recent years, the CBRC has been implementing reforms of provincial credit cooperative associations, starting with the reform of these "regional offices of provincial credit cooperative associations", later changing the name of some of these offices to "regional auditing centers". The People's Bank of China (PBoC), responsible for China's monetary policy, was also made responsible for administrating rural credit cooperatives through monetary policy (for instance, allowing a lower deposit reserve ratio). In recent years, local governments have gradually established financial offices. In actual practice, these government agencies and "industry self-regulatory bodies" have strong administrative control over financial institutions within the RCC system. This has clearly increased the level of "oversight" of rural credit cooperatives, rural cooperative banks and rural commercial banks since 2003, with more and more regulatory and supervisory channels.

Reforms since 2003 no longer emphasized restoring the "three characteristics" of rural credit cooperatives, namely "mass-oriented organization", "democratic management" and "flexible business operations" as required by the Head Office of the Agricultural Bank of China at the Fourth National Branch Governors' Meeting of Agricultural Bank of China, which was held on January 3–15, 1983 in Beijing.

Of course, rural commercial banks can stray by their definition from these "three characteristics". The problem is that both the rural cooperative banks and rural credit cooperatives became commercial-oriented, drifting far away from such requirements, claiming to be "cooperative finance" or "shareholding cooperative" institutions in name while operating commercially. This is not to say that commercialization is at all inappropriate since economic entities have the right to choose their own operational direction and model, but this practice is a deviation of the financial institutions within the rural credit cooperative system that have chosen a cooperative or shareholding cooperative system from acting as cooperatives.

In 2011, the CBRC went a step further, requiring county-level rural credit cooperative associations and rural cooperative banks to restructure and become rural commercial banks. For example, in 2015, the Ninghai Rural Credit Cooperative Association was restructured to become the Ninghai Rural Commercial Bank. This policy provided further evidence of officially pushing forward the commercialization of the rural credit cooperative system and helped to improve ownership structures, management structures and performance of financial institutions within the rural credit cooperative system.

Gradual reforms of rural credit cooperatives since 2003 resulted in overall improvement of ownership and management structures within the rural credit cooperative system. Compared with the considerable losses that rural credit cooperatives across China faced prior to 2003, asset holdings grew, and economic indicators greatly improved. As of the end of 2015, of the 2,303 financial institutions in China's rural credit cooperative system (rural commercial banks, rural cooperative banks and rural credit cooperatives), 839 obtained official licenses of rural commercial banks, while the number in the process of application for transforming into rural commercial banks reached 107. The total assets of financial institutions within China's rural credit cooperative system reached RMB 25.81 trillion with RMB 223.3 billion in profits (Qiao, 2016). The capital adequacy ratio reached 11.6%, while the percentage of non-performing loans stood at 4.3% (People's Bank of China, 2016).

However, problems remained in terms of how regulatory and governmental agencies carried out their duties. A fundamental principle in the regulation of rural credit cooperatives, rural cooperative banks and rural commercial banks is the integration of responsibilities, rights and interests, which should be expressed in all aspects of their operations, but this has not been the case. As a supervisory body, the supervision and direct regulation carried out by the CBRC is categorized as external regulation. This type of external regulation still retains many elements of China's previously planned economy and administrative bias. This can be seen in the *Guiding Opinions on Accelerating the Restructuring of the Ownership System of the Rural Cooperative Financial Institutions* released by CBRC on November 9, 2018, which provides that the government requests financial institutions within the RCC system should speed up the transformation of qualification shares and eliminate the qualification shares before the end of 2015. Rural credit cooperatives and rural cooperative banks that meet the requirements for becoming rural commercial banks can be directly transformed into rural commercial banks. For those rural financial cooperatives which do not meet the requirements for the time being, all the qualified shares should be converted into investment shares as soon as possible, and these rural credit cooperatives should be restructured into shareholding entities. At present, the shareholding reform of rural credit cooperatives is still in progress. Clearly, the CBRC is making decisions that should be reserved for members of rural credit cooperatives and shareholders of rural cooperative banks. Only the members of rural credit cooperatives can decide to give up qualifying shares, and only shareholders of rural cooperative banks can decide to carry out restructuring to become a rural commercial bank. This is not to say that reducing the number of member-shareholders or that reform of rural cooperative banks is not necessary, but the choice to restructure or how to restructure should be reserved for the members or shareholders of said financial institutions. The fact that the CBRC has made this decision supports the general position of academics that have analyzed rural credit cooperatives and rural cooperative banks. Even former Director of the CBRC's Cooperative Financial Institution Supervisory Department Jiang Liming stated that rural credit cooperatives had not been "cooperatives" for a long time.

In fact, the members, shareholders or managers of financial institutions within the rural credit cooperative system tend to prefer transiting to a rural commercial bank structure. This can clearly be seen in reforms after 2003, with the vast majority of rural credit cooperatives hoping to qualify to become rural commercial banks, while those that couldn't settled for second best and became rural cooperative banks if approved by the CBRC. Very few rural credit cooperatives actually wanted to continue operating as rural credit cooperatives. There were huge benefits to both members/shareholders and management to transit to either rural commercial banks or rural cooperative banks. The drive to become rural commercial banks could be termed as rash, but it was, without a doubt, a decision based on reason. However, the decision of which institutions could become rural commercial banks and which could become rural cooperative banks rested with the CBRC. The 2011 decision regarding transforming all rural credit cooperatives with a unified legal person entity status within respective counties and all rural cooperative banks to rural commercial banks can be interpreted as an admission that during the 2003 reform, the differentiation between three types of financial institutions that RCCs were to be transformed into was unnecessary. From the perspective of researchers, the CBRC should have given the right to choose the appropriate type of financial institution to rural credit cooperatives from the very beginning. Similarly, the continued stronghold that the CBRC has in the reform of financial institutions within the RCC system is in and of itself a problem. From the perspective of rent-seeking, some Public Choice School economists might regard this as a kind of "rent creating" exercised by some regulators and an opportunity to provide extra benefits (Tullock, 1993). If it is the case, rural credit cooperatives must provide various resources to "seek rent" and take advantage of these benefits. Where there are controls, there will always be rent seekers, but the real problem lies in those who do "rent creating".

2. Policy Impacts: Advantages and Disadvantages

Government policies on rural credit cooperatives can be beneficial or detrimental to their development. For instance, 2003 reforms issued by the State Council required rural credit cooperatives to provide uncollateralized and unguaranteed microcredit to farmers, which was not being pushed very strongly. The outcome of following this requirement was generally positive for financial institutions of the RCC system. Huaxi Rural Commercial Bank in the city of Guiyang is a perfect example. The bank initially transited from a rural credit cooperative to a rural cooperative bank, then later into a rural commercial bank. It pushed such microcredit for small farm households from a very early stage and benefitted quickly in terms of realizing profits from its microcredit business.

Government policies may benefit all financial institutions within the rural credit cooperative system, but they may also only benefit some. For instance, the 2003 restructuring requirements only allowed an extremely small number of rural credit cooperatives to become rural commercial banks. To rural credit cooperatives with similar qualifications, this was unfair. Requirements in 2011 for all rural credit cooperatives with a unified legal person entity status within respective counties and all rural cooperative banks to become rural commercial banks benefitted all institutions.

In some areas, government policy may be beneficial to rural credit cooperatives, but it may also be detrimental. Reform plans issued by the State Council in 2003 called for "local government to be responsible the management of credit cooperatives", requiring pilot areas to establish provincial credit cooperative associations or other provincial-level management institutions. Under the leadership of the provincial people's governments, these institutions were to be responsible for the management, guidance, coordination and servicing of financial institutions within the RCC system within their administrative area. After their establishment, provincial credit cooperative associations were able to provide financial institutions within the rural credit cooperative system with services that included card issuance, technical support, new product development, capital operations, settlement services and training programs, but they also became supervisors of these financial institutions within the province. The result was overly strong management and weak service support, which resulted in strong dissatisfaction among these financial institutions in terms of daily operations.

The CBRC continues to set a service goal for financial institutions within the RCC system, which is serving rural, agricultural and farm households' development. This has some earmarks of traditional top-down commanding practices. However, financial institutions within the rural credit cooperative system will set in reality their own goals based on their own interests. While serving rural, agricultural and farm households' development is one way to fulfill their goals, this generally is not enough to meet their ultimate goal. Even if these financial institutions were to follow the requirement of pursuing the government-set goal of serving rural, agricultural and farm households' development, they would take second place to goals suited to their own interests. In fact, in most rural areas, even if the government does not place emphasis on such a goal, the result is generally the same. These financial institutions mainly serve rural markets, downscaling branches and their services in order to better serve farmers and rural small and medium enterprises and generate returns from them, which is, in fact, in their own interest.

Furthermore, urbanization efforts have resulted in many of the areas served by financial institutions within the RCC system becoming urbanized. The number of actual farm households in these areas is very low or extremely low, but the government continues to require financial institutions to serve rural, agricultural and farm households' development. This has created an obvious disparity between actual target groups and the required ones. The fact that these institutions are also forced to include the word "rural" within their name is also not in line with actual levels of local socioeconomic development in almost completely urbanized city districts.

3. Current Ownership Structures of RCCs and Rural Cooperative Banks are Detrimental to Operations

The ownership structures of RCCs and rural cooperative banks are detrimental to their operations, and restructuring into a shareholding system from their cooperative and shareholding cooperative system is the best choice. With the 2003 reform, financial institutions within the RCC system could be divided into three categories: shareholding, shareholding cooperative and cooperative structures. If these structures were to be implemented fully, they must meet certain criteria. Shareholding companies must make profitability their primary goal. They must demonstrate that ownership and equity holdings lie with investors, who, in turn, take financial responsibility based on their level of investment. Shareholders have decision-making powers regarding major issues based on the amount of equity they hold. The benefit of a shareholding model is that ownership and operations can remain independent, and the institution can continue to grow and expand. Shareholding systems are the most commercially oriented of the three and can incorporate a large or small number of shareholders. One example of this is the Zhangjiagang Rural Commercial Bank, which reduced its number of shareholders from 29,651 when it was a rural credit cooperative to 1,700 after it became a rural commercial bank (see Table 4.1). Increases or decreases in the number of shareholders do not affect the commercial nature of the institution. The shareholding cooperative model integrates elements of shareholding and cooperative structures, distinguishing between qualifying shares and investor shares. Qualifying shares use a one-vote per member-share principle, while investment shares are eligible for dividends and a number of votes based on the level of investment. After Yinzhou Rural Cooperative became Yinzhou Rural Cooperative Bank in 2003, investor share votes were based on one vote per 100,000 shares (RMB 100,000). Financial institutions that choose a cooperative model should follow four major principles: voluntary participation, mutual cooperation, non-profit operation and democratic management (Han et al., 2009). Following these principles is the only way to protect the interests of members, but the management and organization of rural credit cooperatives were unable to uphold these principles. This often had to do with the number of members in individual primary credit cooperatives. Under the cooperative model, levels of information asymmetry increase as the number of members increases. This made it difficult to meet the criteria of a cooperative model and increased the trend toward commercialization. One example of this is the Danyang Rural Credit Cooperative Association in Jiangsu province, which restructured in 2000 (as a pilot reform) to transit from county/township-level dual legal person entity status to a county-level single legal person entity status (this institution is currently a rural commercial bank). The number of members was reduced from 110,459 before restructuring to 3,119 after restructuring. It is difficult for this type of county-level single legal person credit cooperative association with such a large number of members to ensure one vote per member, which makes it difficult to ensure democratic voting, decision-making, management and supervision. In actual operation, this type of situation can very easily lead to commercialization.

Clearly, the three ownership structures mentioned above have the potential to fall victim to "external control" by government or provincial credit cooperative associations and "internal control" by management. Furthermore, shareholding systems also face the possibility of control by large shareholders,[2] which, strictly speaking, can be interpreted as a type of "internal control". This is why a comprehensive incentive mechanism based on the principle-agent theory is necessary to effectively empower shareholders and balance the power of upper management. Under the principle-agent theory, information asymmetry can result in the owners of an enterprise (or bank)

TABLE 4.1 Comparison of different pilot restructuring models – Zhangjiagang, Yinzhou and Danyang

Type of reform	Rural commercial bank (shareholding model)	Rural cooperative bank (shareholding cooperative model)	County-level single legal person entity (cooperative model)
Example	Zhangjiagang Rural Commercial Bank (Jiangsu province)	Yinzhou Rural Cooperative Bank (Zhejiang province)	Danyang Credit Cooperative Association (Jiangsu province)
Date of Restructuring	November 12, 2001	April 8, 2003	End of 2000
Number of Members/Shareholders	– Before restructuring: 29,651 members – After restructuring: member-shareholders reduced to 1,700 (1,688 natural persons, 12 legal entities)	– Before restructuring: 6,645 members – After restructuring: 11,996 member-shareholders (11,258 natural persons, 738 legal entities)	– Before restructuring: 110,459 members (632 internal employee-members, 109,827 external members) – After restructuring: 3,119 members (632 original employee-members, 702 external members [remaining 109,125 shares liquidated] and 1,785 new members [including 55 legal entities])
Shareholding Structure	– Before restructuring: 12 million RMB in equity capital – After restructuring: 88 million RMB in equity capital (16 million RMB [18.18%] held by 12 legal entities with the largest shareholder holding 4.2 million RMB [4.77%] in equity; 72 million RMB [81.82%] held by natural persons including bank employees holding 21.6 million RMB in equity)	– Before restructuring: 7.68 million RMB in equity capital – After restructuring: 220.6 million RMB in equity capital (128.87 million RMB [58.4%] held by natural persons, including 53.68 million RMB [24.3%] held by bank employees with the largest shareholder holding 1 million RMB [0.45%]; 91.79 million RMB [41.6%] held by legal entities with the largest shareholder holding 5.01 million RMB [2.27%]; 135.33 million RMB [61.3%] in qualifying shares and 85.33 million RMB [38.7%] in investor shares)	– Before restructuring: 5.64 million RMB in employee shares held by 632 employee-members; 7.31 million RMB in external shares held by 109,827 external members. – After restructuring: 5.64 million RMB in employee shares held by 632 employee-members; 192,000 RMB in external shares held by 702 original external members; 42.09 million RMB in additional capital held by 1,785 further external members. Total: 47.92 million RMB.

(*Continued*)

TABLE 4.1 (Continued)

Type of reform	Rural commercial bank (shareholding model)	Rural cooperative bank (shareholding cooperative model)	County-level single legal person entity (cooperative model)
Shareholder Rights	Equal rights for equal shares. Includes employee shares.	Differentiation between qualifying shares and investor shares – investor shares receive one vote per person with dividends based on the level of investment, with an additional vote for each additional 100,000 RMB in investment. Includes employee shares.	One vote per person regardless of level of investment. Includes employee shares.
Operational Characteristics	– The large number of shareholders makes it difficult to hold a full vote, and a representative committee is used to make decisions, which gives power to the Board of Directors, making it difficult for small investors to participate in decision-making. The shareholding model makes control by large shareholders and "internal management" more likely. – The existence of employee shareholders may lead to conflict between labor benefits and maximizing shareholder value. – Direct interference by regulators and local government, esp. in the selection of a chairman and bank president (external control).	– The large number of shareholders means that the balance between shareholder and cooperative elements can easily change, and the integrative "one vote per person" element is difficult to maintain, hence the selection of a Board of Directors and Board of Supervisors through a representative committee, which gives easily decision making power to the Board of Directors. – Possibility of "internal management control" under the shareholding cooperative model. – The existence of employee shareholders may lead to conflict between labor benefits and maximizing shareholder value. – Direct interference by regulators and local government, esp. in the selection of a chairman and bank president (external control).	– The large number of members makes it difficult to maintain a "one vote per person" system with democratic selection, decision-making, management and supervision, which is carried out by a representative committee. – Possibility of "internal management control" under the cooperative model. – The existence of employee shareholders may lead to conflict between labor benefits and maximizing shareholder value. – Direct interference by regulators and local government, esp. in the selection of a chairman and director (external control).

– Government requirements to provide services oriented to rural, agricultural and farm households' development might restrict operations.
– Under the shareholding model, the bank can be more directly commercial and set profit targets.

– Government requirements to provide services oriented to rural, agricultural and farm households' development might restrict operations.
– Stability is limited under the shareholding cooperative model, tending more toward shareholding or cooperative elements. Especially in the course of growth when business volume or shareholding increases occur, cooperative elements nearly always give way to shareholding elements. This trend toward commercialization is not essentially wrong.

– Government requirements to provide services oriented to rural, agricultural and farm households' development might restrict operations.
– Under the cooperative model, information asymmetry increases as the number of members increases, making it difficult to meet the requirements of a cooperative model and resulting in unavoidable commercialization.

Source: China Business Times, April 16, 2002; China Economic Times, April 8, 2002; survey results.

being unable to fully supervise the actions of management, which enables management to seek their own interests while ignoring those of shareholders. This type of information asymmetry is often the result of private information exchanges or information advantages that are held by the agent and beyond the control of the principal (Laffont and David, 2002). The issue here is whether the agent has made a "reliable commitment" (Anderson, 2002). Often, the principal must pay a much higher price than the agent to obtain highly detailed information.

The above analysis shows that the 2010 decision of the central government to restructure all of the RCCs and rural cooperative banks into a shareholding system is necessary. Anyhow, their cooperative system or shareholding cooperative system couldn't work well, and they worked, in fact, in a way similar to rural commercial banks.

4. Distribution of Responsibility, Rights and Interests of Financial Institutions within the RCC System

Original capital equity in RCCs before the 2003 reform came mainly as membership contributions from members. Part of capital equity was non-voluntary equity because the goal of such members who paid in such membership contributions was to take loans issued by the RCCs. In this sense, RCCs before the 2003 reform were commercialized entities. The same phenomena of non-voluntary equity existed among many of the three types of RCC institutions after the 2003 reform, which implies that such RCC institutions have been actually commercialized entities and haven't complied with cooperative principles (Figure 4.1).

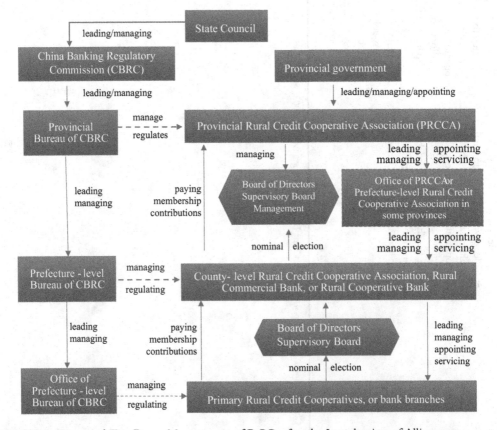

FIGURE 4.1 Increased Top-Down Management of RCCs after the Introduction of Alliances

Source: Feng, Xingyuan; He, Guangwen; Du, Zhixiong: Research on Innovations in the Organizational Structure of Rural Company Financing and Homegrown Grassroots Finance in China, Shanxi Economic Press, Taiyuan, 2006.

The dispersed distribution of membership shares in RCC institutions has been too dispersed, and there has been a lack of supervision of the board directors and management by members or their representatives or the board of supervisors. The power that the board of directors and management have over operations and decision-making can result in an "insider control" problem.[3] However, in terms of operation, "external control" problems are very noticeable. The qualifications of the chairpersons of the board of directors and board of supervisors and presidents of RCC institutions are not chosen by members or shareholders; they are nominated by the provincial credit cooperative associations, which, in general, also choose them. This might create channels for direct or indirect control of the RCC, resulting in "outsider control" or government interference. These practices

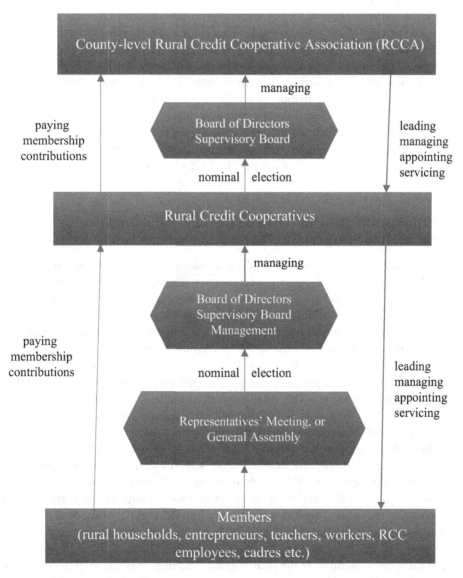

FIGURE 4.2 Organizational Structure of Rural Credit Cooperative Associations with Their Primary Rural Credit Cooperatives within Chinese Counties or County-level Cities

Notes: 1. Rural commercial banks and rural cooperative banks are not included. 2. Since the 2003 reform, A part of RCCAs have a unified legal person entity status, while other RCCAs and their RCCs have separate legal person entity statuses.

Source: The authors.

deviate from the original principles of the cooperative, shareholding cooperative or shareholding system.

The fact that RCCs are cooperative financial institutions means that they must obey the basic principles of a cooperative model, one of which is that they are not-for-profit organizations that work for the mutual benefit of their members. If RCCs incorporate "cooperative" into their name, they should also put this concept into practice. However, because in the past RCCs gathered large numbers of members at the township and town level, when the control of RCCs was at the hand of the county level, the rights of these members were set aside, and management exercised "insider control" (Figure 4.2). This resulted in an operational trend toward commercialization and not mutually beneficial cooperation. In addition to this, supervision by financial regulators and administration by local parties and governmental agencies, as well as the provincial association, also resulted in a certain level of "outsider control". This created gaps in both internal and external management structures. The practice of the government is to avoid the cooperative element of RCCs, simply calling RCCS or RCCAs "rural credit associations" (nongcun xinyongshe), avoiding the awkwardness of admitting a practical lack of cooperative elements. The move by CBRC in 2010 to transition all RCCs to rural commercial banks has decisively ended this awkwardness. There is no longer a need to object to the commercialization of RCCs. As long as their members, or "shareholders", agree to commercialization, there is nothing stopping them. The only requirement is that these organizations no longer call themselves "credit cooperatives", which at the same time also makes room for real credit cooperatives that may spring up if government policy is favorable to such a development. The use of the word "cooperative" by RCCs has resulted in a lack of true rural credit cooperatives in China.

5. Opportunities Remain for New and Genuine Rural Credit Cooperatives to Prosper

Genuine rural credit cooperatives that fulfill the principles of cooperative finance should be established and developed, but this requires a respect for the willingness and independence of economic entities to establish such credit cooperatives. The term "rural credit cooperative" has been abused, but new and genuine cooperative financial institutions can differentiate themselves from the existing RCCs if they are able to continue using this nomenclature by adding a non-localized title in front of the RCC's name. The name of existing RCCs consists of the full name of the administrative jurisdiction and the term "rural credit cooperative" or "rural credit cooperative association". Once a new and genuine cooperative financial institution is established, it must fundamentally follow the principles of cooperative finance. The government need not limit the entry of new and genuine rural credit cooperatives. By simply establishing and maintaining a competitive environment, they can allow new and existing organizations to enter and compete naturally.

Let us first examine the internal management structure of a standard RCC which should comply with the principle of cooperative finance (Figure 4.3). An ideal RCC requires equity from its members, which, through a general assembly or member representative meeting, elect, criticize and dismiss directors and members of its board of directors or supervisory board, and approve work reports of both boards. This is an expression of four democratic processes: democratic election, decision-making, management and supervision, allowing members to exercise their rights and responsibilities. The power exercised by the Board of Directors and Supervisory Board is given by consent of the general assembly or the representatives' meeting. It is also subject to limitation by members, the general assembly or the representatives' meeting. If this structure is to be successful, there must be a high level of trust and information symmetry among members, which implies that a spirit and a culture of cooperation should exist among their members. Authentic RCCs are

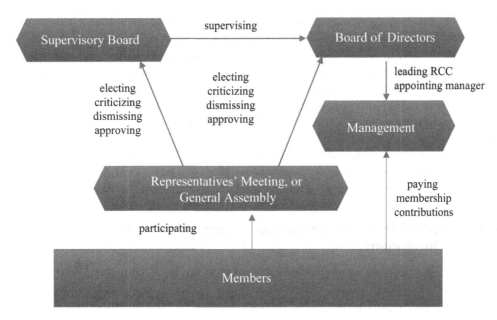

FIGURE 4.3 The Internal Management Structure of a Standard Genuine Rural Credit Cooperative According to the Principle of Cooperative Finance

Source: The authors.

primarily people-centered. They rely first on people's collaboration and then integrate capital. This also means that the size of primary RCCs cannot be too large in terms of the number of members, and their equity must not be dispersed among too many members, or there may be a trend toward commercialization. One of the advantages of authentic RCCs is lower lending rates, thus lower costs of financing primarily among their members. If a commercial model and profit-oriented goals are the basis for the institution, an RCC should take form as a rural commercial bank and not a rural credit cooperative.

A standard authentic RCCA can be formed through cooperation between primary RCCs and serves a purely service-oriented function. This is different from a shareholding system in that grass-roots-level primary credit cooperatives control their higher-level credit cooperative association from the bottom up while the latter provides certain services. This is the model followed by the German or Dutch cooperative financial system.

Similarly, following the introduction of provincial credit cooperative associations, operations within the RCC network also tended toward a bottom-up model as provincial credit coopera-tive associations provided only services and did not have a management function. Whether in terms of enforcing self-discipline within the RCC sector of respective provinces, provincial credit cooperative associations should only serve to convey the interests and requests related to the affairs of member banks or RCCs. Similarly, the role of CBRC should revert to one of a regulatory body.

The transition of RCCs and rural cooperative banks to rural commercial banks, as well as that of provincial credit cooperative associations, has helped to improve both the ownership and adminis-trative structures of financial institutions within the RCC system and strengthened commercializa-tion. On December 22, 2008, the Ningxia Rural Credit Cooperative Association became the first institution to undergo an institutional restructuring and was renamed the Huanghe Rural Com-mercial Bank, indicating one possible direction. However, the reform process was only partially enforced. A 2016 central government document titled "Several Opinions by the CCCPC and State Council on Implementing New Development Concepts to Accelerate Modernization in Agriculture to Fully Achieve the Goal of Little Well-off Society" clearly stated that it would carry out "pilot reforms of provincial credit cooperative associations with gradual decreases in executive administration and strengthening of service functions". This showed that the central government was aware of issues in provincial credit cooperative associations and that the focus of reforms was correct, but there still were issues of excessive executive administration in the way reforms were carried out. RCC institutions have no say in whether they need a provincial association or whether they can choose their own association through a bottom-up approach. Furthermore, there is no national rural credit cooperative association. If there were one, it should be very conducive to the development of the entire RCC system.

6. Downscaling Branches and Services Fit Best the Interests of RCC Institutions

Branches of RCC institutions are usually established in townships or towns along with service stations or representatives in villages. They also carry out regular or ad hoc assessments of personal or village credit ratings. This is why the local knowledge that they can utilize is a huge advantage over other financial institutions. Local knowledge refers to dispersed knowledge of specific circumstances at a specific time and place, scattered among numerous individuals (Hayek, 1937, 1948). It is only by remaining close to rural residents and resorting to market mechanisms (with the government providing an enabling environment) that this local knowledge can be better obtained and utilized.

Surveys carried out by the author show that Yinzhou Bank, a rural commercial bank based in the Yinzhou district of Ningbo city, Zhejiang province, has worked hard to establish service stations to solve the problem with the gap of the last mile for farm households' access to financial services. Since the opening of its first service station on March 31, 2012, it set up 372 service stations in 25 towns within Yinzhou District, Ningbo City. These service stations serviced a total of 9.09 million transactions worth 1.9 billion RMB until the end of 2016. The Ninghai Rural Commercial Bank in Zhejiang province has established 69 service locations throughout Ninghai County to service rural residents. As early as 2011, the bank introduced the concept of "mini-banks" that set up "POS Rural ATMs" in remote and sparsely populated mountainous areas as well as "rural finance service stations" in 363 villages, providing seven services including village representative services, service windows, micro-withdrawals/payments and microloan applications. This has gradually grown to include a range of "terminal services for farm households" to meet the needs for financial payments and settlements for people in remote areas. The bank also proceeded on a principle of "pilot experiments first, and upgrade second" to further improve the services of some of its "micro-banks", which were upgraded to "Prosperity Stations" in areas with greater business volumes and more concentrated customer groups. These introduced payment and top-up services, online purchasing/sales, express package receipt and sending, simple health services and financial consultation that provide more people with a convenient one-stop option for financial and public services. The bank currently had three "Prosperity Stations" that provided excellent rural comprehensive financial services by the end of 2016.

With the rapid digital transformation of the RCC institutions, downscaling branches and businesses are now combined with online loan and transfer services among many RCC institutions. For instance, the Yinzhou Bank uses its own mobile phone app, and the Ninghai Rural Commercial Bank uses an app provided by the Rural Credit Cooperative Association of Zhejiang province to deliver online loan and transfer services.

Notes

1 Further Revision based on Feng, Xingyuan. "Ownership, Governance and Interests of Financial Institutions within the Rural Credit Cooperative System", *Front of Social Sciences*, No. 2, 2017, 31–40.
2 The larger shareholders is a benefit as they can better supervise and support an organization's development. However, it must be ensured that large shareholders do not make decisions unfavorable to smaller shareholders.
3 The author led the CASS Type B key research project "Township and Village Enterprise Financing and Informal Financial Innovations in China" during 1999–2001. During rural surveys, it was found that much of the membership contributions for RCCs originated from a portion taken from loans given out to applicants (i.e., 5%). This was often without the consent of the applicant, but it was necessary for the loan to go through. Several days after the loan was given, applicant could freely withdraw their membership contributions. In some areas, promises of a minimum level of interest, which were termed "guaranteed interest" or "equity in form, deposits in reality", were given to encourage loan applicants to hold equity. The reason for this was that local financial regulators required an increase in equity for every 100 RMB in loans at that time. Here, "members" were subject to "insider control" by management. For more examples of "insider control" and "equity in form, deposits in reality", see: Zhou, Maifu, Ji, Jingtao. "Analysis of Game Theory in Standardization of the Cooperative Model in RCCs", *China Rural Economy*, Vol. 5, 2004, 35–39. The phenomenon of "equity in form, deposits in reality" is still prevailing in rural credit cooperatives or rural credit cooperative associations which are to be restructured. See Li Tongran. "Considerations of Deepening the Reform of Rural Credit Cooperatives", *Sohu Finance and Economy*, December 20, 2017. www.sohu.com/a/211633147_600421.

References

Anderson, Elin. *Transaction Cost Analysis and Marketing*. Shanghai: Shanghai University of Finance and Economics Press, 2002.

Feng, Xingyuan, He, Guangwen, Du, Zhixiong, et al. *Research on Rural Corporate Financing in China and Institutional Innovation in Endogenous Private Financial Institutions*. Taiyuan, Shanxi Publishing Group, Shanxi Economic Publishing House, 2006. PBoC Rural Financial Services Research Group. *Report on Rural Financial Services in China 2014*. Beijing, China Financial Press, 2015.

Han, Jun, et al. *A Survey of Rural Finance in China*. Shanghai: Shanghai Far East Press, 2009, pp. 305–307.

Hayek, Friedrich August von. "Economics and Knowledge". *Economica*, Vol. 4. February 1937, 33–54.

Hayek, Friedrich August von. "The Socialist Calculation II: The State of the Debate". In: Friedrich August von Hayek (Ed.): *Individualism and Economic Order*. Chicago: Chicago University Press, 1948, pp. 148–180.

Jiang, Dingzhi. "The Legal Position of Rural Credit Cooperatives Must be Maintained", Posted on People's Net December 28, 2009.

Laffont, Jean-Jacques, and David Martimort. *The Theory of Incentives. The Principal-Agent Model*. Princeton and Oxford: Princeton University Press, 2002.

People's Bank of China. Executive Report on China's Monetary Policy – 2015 Q4, February 6, 2016.

Qiao, Jinliang. "Reforms of Rural Credit Cooperative Provincial Credit Cooperative Associations Must Be Less "Administrative". *Economic Daily*, April 25, 2016.

Tullock, Gordon. *Rent Seeking (The Shaftesbury Papers, 2)*. Cheltenham: Edward Elgar Pubisher, 1993.

Zhou, Maifu and Ji Jingtao. "Analysis of Game Theory in Standardization of the Cooperative Model in RCCs". *China Rural Economy*, Vol. 5, 2004, 35–39.

5

IMPROVING THE FINANCIAL SUSTAINABILITY OF THE FINANCIAL INSTITUTIONS WITHIN THE RCC SYSTEM

Problems and Policy Options[1]

Xingyuan Feng and Xiang Yan

1. Introduction

Financial institutions within the RCC system (in the following "RCC institutions"), i.e., rural commercial banks, rural cooperative banks and rural credit cooperatives, are the financial institutions with the largest number and the widest coverage in China. They have always been rooted in rural areas, serving "agriculture, rural areas and farmers", and are the main forces of the current rural financial market. Especially with the rural financial reform in the late 1990s, the business withdrawal of state-owned commercial banks from the rural market led to a certain level of financial shortages in rural areas, and RCCs assumed an autonomous and important role in providing rural financial services and mitigating the problems with financial shortages.[2] With the RCC reform introduced in 2003, RCCs were transformed into mainly three types of financial institutions, i.e., rural commercial banks, rural cooperative banks and rural credit cooperatives, which are single legal-person entities within their respective counties or other county-level jurisdictions. With a reform introduced by the China Banking and Insurance Regulatory Commission in 2010, all rural cooperative banks and rural credit cooperatives were transformed into shareholding entities without any element of a cooperative system, which implies that all of the RCC institutions are now shareholding entities without any element of a cooperative system, no matter whether their names are coined with "cooperative". After almost 2 decades of development since the 2003 reform, the asset scale, asset quality and profitability of RCC institutions have significantly improved.

According to the traditional view, because the average asset scale of RCCs is generally small[3] and they are rooted in a rural community and grassroots, the financial risks are generally controllable, not to such an extent as to cause systemic risks affecting the whole country. However, the emergence of systemic financial risk is often an unintended consequence, i.e., that of a "butterfly effect", which is to be traced back to complicated nonlinear interactions of various seen and unseen factors. The bank run of a small financial institution may become the trigger of a financial crisis in the region where it is located, which can be contagious to other regions. In recent years, the central government has been pushing forward the deepening of the structural reform of the financial supply side and preventing and mitigating financial risks. Rural financial institutions are required to better serve the real economy, especially better support the development of agriculture, rural area, farm households and micro and small enterprises. At the same time, they are required to control various financial risks and enhance their own ability of financial sustainability in order to improve their supply of financial services for agricultural and rural modernization and promote the implementation of the Rural Revitalization Strategy.

DOI: 10.4324/9781003369776-5

This chapter is divided into two parts. The first part analyzes the factors affecting the sustainable development of RCC institutions from the aspects of their ownership structure and governance, financial risks and other related aspects of RCC institutions, and analyzes the roots of these problems. The second part puts forward some countermeasures to promote the sustainable development of RCC institutions from the micro, meso and macro level.

2. Factors Affecting the Sustainable Development of the RCC Institutions

2.1 Ownership Structure and Governance of the RCC Institutions

At present, the development of RCC institutions is facing difficulties, which is largely due to the imperfect ownership and governance structure. Reviewing the development of RCC institutions, we can find that the problems with property rights and governance of RCC institutions have a long history. In the initial stage after the founding of the RCCs in the early 1950s, they were, in general, genuine cooperative financial institutions supported by a small number of membership fees paid in by the members from rural society, which reflected the "three characteristics" of a rural credit cooperatives system, namely, the mass nature of the organization (a large number of members), democratic management and flexibility of business operations, and contributed a great deal to the development of agriculture, rural area and farm households in the early stage of their development. Since then, the development of RCCs has experienced ups and downs, twists and turns. The management power of the RCCs has also experienced several changes; their right to independent operations has been withdrawn and then given back later by the government several times, which deviated from the original basic principles of cooperative finance. The 2003 reform of RCCs was a decisive round of commercialization reform which transformed RCCs from cooperative financial institutions to commercial or more commercialized financial institutions, including rural commercial banks, rural cooperative banks and rural credit cooperatives with a status of unified judicial person entities within their respective county-level jurisdictions. This round of reform met the overall needs of the development of RCCs, but it is basically determined by the central government from top to bottom and fails to fully consider the specific preferences, needs and autonomous rights of members of RCCs. With the 2010 reform of RCC institutions, all of them became shareholding entities without any cooperative elements, although the names of rural cooperative banks and rural cooperatives are still branded with the term "cooperative". These two types of RCC institutions were also requested to get transformed into rural commercial banks if their business performances met the requirements of the government. According to the statistics of the People's Bank of China, by the end of 2020, there were 2,207 financial institutions within the RCC system in China, accounting for 47.9% of the total number of legal-person financial institutions in the banking industry of China, including 1,539 rural commercial banks, 27 rural cooperative banks and 641 rural credit cooperatives.

With the above reforms of RCC institutions, the problem of equity fragmentation has been mitigated, but the number of natural-person shareholders is still huge. According to statistics, by the end of December 2017, the total share capital of the RCC institutions in Anhui province reached more than RMB 14 billion, and the number of shareholders had reached 96,000, including 94,000 natural person shareholders, accounting for 97.9% and less than 15%. Finally, for the equity of all the nonlisted rural commercial banks, and all the rural cooperative banks and rural credit cooperatives, there is still no flexible open market for the transfer of their shares, which makes the transfer of such shares very difficult because any deal should go through procedures within the respective RCC institutions. This problem affects the interests of shareholders.

At present, according to the modern corporate governance theory, the RCC institutions have established an internal governance structure consisting of a board of directors, a board of supervisors, shareholders' meetings and senior management, which is a perfect one in the form and doesn't function well in reality in many RCC institutions. Firstly, the problem of "internal control" of senior management is still common. The main reason is that senior management must have "hidden information" and even easy to take "hidden actions" compared with other personnel. Within senior management, the degree of information asymmetry between non-executive directors and executive directors is still very high. Secondly, due to the decentralized ownership of rural credit cooperatives in China, the control of members (shareholders) and members (shareholders) meeting over the board of directors and senior managers is very weak. The voting of the general meeting of members (shareholders) and the representative meeting of members (shareholders) is easy to become a mere formality. Its information source mainly depends on the quarterly, mid-year or annual reports provided by the bank and the decisions of the board of directors (Council). Most shareholders or members lack sufficient information to participate in the voting. They generally keep an attitude of "rational ignorance" and don't express personal opinions on major affairs or specific details of the bank. Thirdly, the current provincial association has too strengthened its management means, seriously deviated from its service function, and intervened too strongly in the micro management of the financial institutions of the RCC institutions. The important personnel of RCC institutions need to be nominated by the Provincial Rural Credit Cooperative Associations, reviewed by the local Party committee, and indirectly decided by the provincial associations. Finally, it is difficult for the board of directors, board of supervisors, the shareholders' meeting and the senior management to realize effective mutual checks and balances, and there is a problem with the "dominance by one person", i.e., by the chairperson of the board of director. The functions and powers of the chairperson of the board of directors and the president of the RCC institutions are not clearly divided, and the chairperson interferes too much in the daily operation of RCC institutions. Supervision by the board of supervisors of the board of directors and the senior management of many RCC institutions is, in general, too weak, which tends to affect the sustainability of these institutions.

2.2 Risk Factors

Like other banks, RCC institutions are facing up with the following types of major financial risks: credit risk, liquidity risk, operational risk, and market and systemic risk.

2.2.1 Credit Risks

Credit risk management is the core element for the survival of most banks. Almost all regulators have set minimum standards in credit risk management. Especially for RCC institutions, their own scale is small, and their ability to resist risks is insufficient. They should be more vigilant to prevent the occurrence of credit risks. At present, the NPL rate of rural credit structure is much higher than that of all other commercial banks (including large commercial banks, joint-stock commercial banks, urban commercial banks, private banks and foreign banks), especially the NPL rate of agriculture-related loans is much higher than that of other industries. According to China's rural financial services report (2018), by the end of 2018, in regard to the loans for agricultural, rural and farmers' development, the non-performing loan rate of rural credit cooperatives reached 10%, that of rural cooperative banks reached 13.3%, and that of rural commercial banks was 4.9%.

The credit risk of the RCC institutions is mainly caused by the following factors: first, the RCC institutions' main businesses are mainly regionally based and are confined to the region where they were founded, while the agricultural sector in the same region is vulnerable to the same natural disasters, diseases and insect pests, so it is easy to bring about more concentrated losses to harvest and thus also more concentrated credit risk. Second, RCC institutions in some central and western regions have a high concentration of loans in some high energy-consuming heavy chemical industries and industries with overcapacity. These industries face the risk of removal, liquidation and restructuring under the background of supply-side structural reform and also accumulate a lot of risks of loss. Third, with the promotion of the Rural Revitalization Strategy, the adjustment of industrial structure and the continuous growth of new agricultural business entities, the large loan risk exposure of RCC institutions to single customers or affiliated groups has increased. Fourth, supply chain finance has developed rapidly in recent years, and the vulnerability of agriculture is easy to lead to the accumulation of systemic risks. The longer and larger the agricultural supply chain, the greater the overall risk of agricultural supply chain finance, which leads to the expansion of the exposure of RCC institutions to the systematic risk from the agricultural supply chain.

2.2.2 Liquidity Risk

Liquidity can be understood as "the ability of a bank to fund increases in assets and meet obligations as they come due, without incurring unacceptable losses" (Basel Committee on Banking Supervision, 2008). Ensuring the unity of liquidity, profitability and security are the three principles of commercial bank operation. With the prevalence of uncertain and risk factors in the current market and operations of RCC institutions, liquidity risk has always been a problem to be faced and solved in the future. In fact, the essence of a bank is to transform the term of its liabilities into different maturities on the asset side in the bank's balance sheet (Greuning and Sonja, 2009: 194). Therefore, the matching of liquidity is one key internal characteristic of a bank. The key question is the extent of liquidity mismatch and whether there is potential instability. In the current context of rural revitalization, the amount of credit demand of new business entities usually is much larger than that of a small farm household. New business entities need more longer-term loans to match their larger and longer-term investment. In addition, the construction and improvement of some rural and agricultural infrastructure also need continuous financial service support from RCC institutions, which poses a challenge to their liquidity management. Furthermore, a few RCC institutions have a high ratio of non-performing loans, which can mean their capital adequacy ratio is very low or even negative in reality. If such hidden information were made known to the public (triggered by some event), such RCC institutions might suffer a problem with bank runs.

2.2.3 Operational Risk

Compared with state-owned commercial banks and joint-stock commercial banks, due to the imperfect corporate governance structure of RCC institutions, the lack of risk awareness of their own personnel and the inadequate internal supervision and management, RCC institutions have always been finding themselves within the high incidence areas of operational risk. It can also be seen from the penalty notices issued by the China Banking and Insurance Regulatory Commission (CBIRC) in the past two years that most of the penalty notices were issued to RCC institutions. The frequent occurrence of operational risks in RCC institutions is mainly caused by a set of factors. First, many RCC institutions rely on an extensive operation and management model. In the daily operation process, many RCC institutions adopt an extensive business model of "emphasizing business development while neglecting compliance management", in which it prevails over the phenomenon of "emphasizing lending while neglecting loan collection and management". In such a model, these RCC institutions neglect post-lending management and lack a set of risk control mechanisms for effective monitoring of loan use and collection. In order to fulfill the tasks and performance requirements set by the PBC, CBIRC and the provincial credit cooperative associations, some RCC institutions even conduct lending businesses and other business operations in violation of laws and regulations. Second, the quality of employees is low. At present, with the rapid development of finance, the innovation ability of the financial industry exceeds the overall ability of the employees to understand and deal properly with relevant risks, especially operational risks. The low qualification of personnel and the lack of ICT personnel imply that these banks might easily offer relevant operational risks (including the so-called "model risk"). Third, financial risks are caused by the fraud of personnel of RCC institutions and non-compliance of institutional operation or personnel operation. These phenomena are easy to occur among RCC institutions. For example, major shareholders or directors obtain or even defraud large loans from RCC institutions, resulting in loan losses (conduct risk in concrete).

2.2.4 Market and Systemic Risk

Market risk is similar to systemic risk, but there are differences. Market risk can be hedged, but systemic risk cannot be completely diversified. For RCC institutions, the sources of market and systemic risk include: First, since the businesses of RCC institutions are heavily concentrated on lending business, and their profit mainly relies on interests generated from that lending business, they suffer easily from market risk which is connected to the decline of local industries or natural disasters or pests which affect the agricultural production. Second, the risk of policies and regulations, that is, the possibility that the change of government policies and regulations will lead to the loss of financial activities of economic subjects. For example, on January 14, 2019, the China Banking and Insurance Regulatory Commission issued "Opinions on Pushing Rural Commercial Banks to Adhere to Their Positioning, and Strengthen Their Governance and Improve Their Financial Service Capacity", requiring rural commercial banks to prudently carry out comprehensive and interregional operations. In principle, they should not leave counties (districts), and their businesses should not cross counties (districts). Although the original intention of this requirement is to enable rural commercial banks to focus on supporting the development of the rural economy and adhere to the positioning as the main force in the rural financial market, under the background of huge market pressure on the current operating performance and weak operation ability of rural commercial banks, the introduction of this policy will have a great impact on the operation of rural commercial banks in the future. Third, the high level of debt of local governments may lead to credit default and may further lead to more serious regional systemic risks.

2.3 Other Factors

2.3.1 Adverse Impact of Overall Economic Growth Downturn

For a long time, China's economy has been growing rapidly, but it will inevitably bring about some bottleneck factors, including excessive reliance on the real estate industry and government investment and serious decoupling between financial operations and the real economy. In recent years, the external economic environment has continued to deteriorate, the internal economic structure is seriously unbalanced, the overall economic growth continues to decline, the pressure of industrial structural adjustment and upgrading is great, and the survival pressure of small, and medium-sized enterprises is great. The operation of many small and medium-sized enterprises is difficult. Recent Sino-US trade disputes have led to increased downward pressure on overall economic growth and further worsened the survival of some small and medium-sized enterprises exporting to the United States. The above factors will also affect the loan quality of small and medium-sized enterprises of RCC institutions.

2.3.2 Intensified Market Competition

In recent years, with the state's enforcement of a national inclusive financial development strategy, more and more banking financial institutions have boosted their rural financial market operations, which has caused great competitive pressure on RCC institutions. In theory, the diversification of the participating financial institutions enhances the market competition in the rural financial market, helps improve the efficiency of the provision of financial services, helps force RCC institutions to improve their operational efficiency and realize their own sustainable development. However, in reality, in order to respond to national policies, some large state-owned commercial banks take advantage of their strong and low-cost deposit absorption capacity and participate in providing rural financial services with low loan interest rates (or even its full cost), which has an impact on the sustainable operation activities of RCC institutions, the main loan supplier in the rural financial market. On one hand, in order to win customers, the RCC institutions have to reduce their own credit interest rate and bear more risk of loss; On the other hand, customers of RCC institutions found that there were more favorable interest rates offered by other banks such as state-controlled commercial banks in the market and turned to these banks for obtaining loans, resulting in the RCC institutions' loss of customers. In practice, in the provision of credit services to new types of agricultural business entities, there are cases in which state-controlled commercial banks first crowded out private commercial financial institutions at lower interest rates, and state-owned policy-oriented banks later crowded out these state-controlled commercial banks at even lower interest rates.

In addition to the competition of traditional banking financial institutions, some Fintech banks or platform companies entered the rural financial market. These institutions, relying on their own FinTech and platform advantage, can effectively control credit risks while reducing service costs. In recent years, Ant Group, JD Finance and Ping An Pratt & Whitney delivered financial services in the rural financial market. Good results have been achieved by them in the field of online microfinance.

2.3.3 Intense Operating Pressure

Although China's money market interest rate was marketized, the deposit and loan interest rate has not been completely marketized. Compared with other banking financial institutions, RCC institutions have a simple business model, focus on lending businesses, and the deposit-loan interest margin is their main source of profit. The Report of Evaluation of the Competitiveness of Rural Commercial Banks released by the Research Center of the Bankers Journal in 2018 analyzed the top five rural commercial banks and major listed rural commercial banks in 2017, and the interest income ratio of the selected 11 rural commercial banks was more than 80%. With the continuous advancement of the interest rate marketization reform, the deposit and loan interest margin of banks will narrow, and the profit pressure of RCC institutions will increase sharply.

In addition, at present, the intermediary business carried out by RCC institutions is basically an extension of traditional business, mainly limited to settlement business, insurance intermediary business and some collection and payment business. The variety is relatively small, and most of them belong to labor-intensive low-end products, which mainly meet the basic financial needs of customers. Due to the small scale of RCC institutions, the lack of independent product R&D talents and the economies of scale in independent product development, the result is that product innovation is insufficient, often based on the imitation of peers, the time of developing new products also lags behind, and it is difficult to develop customized financial products for different customers. Their products were often highly imitated and seriously homogenous. At the same time, the degree of product integration is not high.

2.3.4 Overall Non-performing Loan Ratio is Too High

On the whole, the non-performing rate of RCC institutions is on the high side and shows an upward trend year by year. The non-performing loans of RCC institutions in some areas have been at a high level for a long time. Under the current background of preventing and resolving financial risks, the regulatory policies tend to be stricter than before, and a large number of hidden non-performing loans will be gradually exposed. On March 30, 2018, the Rural Finance Department of the CBIRC issued the "Notice on Further Strengthening the Monitoring, Prevention and Control of Large Risk of Small and Medium-sized Rural Financial Institutions" to further improve the management and monitoring of large risk exposure of rural financial institutions. On April 30, 2019, the CBIRC issued "Interim Measures for Risk Classification of Financial Assets of Commercial Banks" (Exposure Draft), which intends to expand the risk classification objects of commercial banks from loans to all financial assets bearing credit risk. At the same time, it is also clear that claims overdue for more than 90 days should be classified as non-performing loans even if the mortgage guarantee is sufficient. The change in supervision makes the future operation of RCC institutions face greater challenges.

2.3.5 There is a Certain Degree of Financial Repression

At present, there are still some problems in the reform, supervision and management by some relevant government departments of RCC institutions, resulting in a certain degree of financial repression. For example, the reform of RCC institutions adopts a top-down control and a "one size fits all" approach. The *Opinions on Pushing Rural Commercial Banks to Stick to Their Positioning and Improve Their Financial Service Capability* issued by the CBIRC on January 14, 2019, emphasizes that, in principle, rural commercial banks should not go out of the counties (districts) where they are based, and their businesses should not cross counties (districts), they should focus on serving the local area, downscale their services, and the new loanable funds in that year should be mainly used for the local area. This provision strengthens the practice of confining the operation space of rural commercial banks to the county-level jurisdictions where they are based and emphasizes the concept of administrative regions rather than economic regions. In a market economy, we should emphasize economic zones and play down administrative zones. Moreover, this practice puts rural commercial banks at a disadvantageous position in the competition. In addition, after the joint-stock reform of RCC institutions, the regulatory authorities did not issue policies in time to guide some types of real cooperative financial institutions to enter the rural financial market, resulting in the lack of real cooperative financial institutions in the rural financial system after the reform.

3. Countermeasures to Promote the Sustainable Development of RCC Institutions

3.1 Improving the Management and Business Operation of RCC Institutions

3.1.1 Improving the Governance Structure and Strengthening the Internal Supervision of RCC Institutions

Since all RCC institutions are now shareholding entities, it is necessary to further improve the corporate governance structure and realize the unity of rights, responsibilities and interests. Specifically, firstly. RCC institutions should strengthen themselves, strengthen the cultivation of sound corporate culture and promote institutional governance according to the articles of RCC institutions. The board of directors, board of supervisors, shareholders' meeting and senior management need to operate in accordance with the requirements of the articles of RCC institutions and play their respective roles. Secondly, RCC institutions need to build up a corporate governance structure and an internal risk control system which fit the characteristics of these institutions.

3.1.2 Strengthening Training in Internal Control and Compliance

RCC institutions need to regularly carry out internal control and compliance training; establish a sound, reasonable and effective internal control system; build multiple risk defense lines such as internal audit, the appointment of an Accounting Director, business inspection, risk management and audit supervision; and cooperate with performance evaluation and assessment mechanism to strictly enforce reward and punishment discipline. RCC institutions should increase the awareness of compliance operations and cultivate a compliance culture. The so-called "compliance" means that the business activities of RCC institutions are consistent with laws, rules and standards. RCC institutions should constantly strengthen the compliance operation and enhance compliance operation awareness, and turn compliance into a disposition of each manager and employee.

3.1.3 Enhancing the Ability of Sustainable Operation with the FinTech Support

At present, large and medium-sized commercial banks are actively exploring how to innovate their business model and operation mode through the application of FinTech, taking it as a new driving force for enhancing their performance in the future. The RCC institutions should also, according to their own resource endowment and ability, make full use of FinTech to explore digital financial products and service modes suitable for their own development, reduce their own operating costs and improve their risk control ability and efficiency of financial services. RCC institutions should take advantage of combining their online operations with their offline operations and make full use of the local knowledge dispersed among customers and local governments in rural areas, including big data they can generate out of such local knowledge to better serve the diversified customer groups in rural areas.

3.1.4 Strengthening the Innovation of Financial Products and Services

RCC institutions need to give play to their branch density advantages and information advantages to further strengthen the innovation of financial products and services. For example, small credit loans can be issued on the basis of credit evaluation of small farmers and modern agricultural business entities under the condition of risk control. RCC institutions should also actively develop supply chain financial products. They should make full use of the models of "credit + insurance + futures" and "credit + insurance + reinsurance" to realize product innovation through risk sharing. They should also cooperate more than before with the agricultural guarantee companies which are fully owned by the government and provide low-fee guarantees for agricultural loans. Furthermore, RCC institutions should accelerate digital transformation and provide more online lending services.

3.1.5 Learning and Adopting the German "Hausbank" Model

RCC institutions mainly serve the rural financial market and mainly face the difficulties and problems typical in the rural and agricultural economy, such as information asymmetry, high risk connected to natural disasters, diseases and insect pests, high market risk of agricultural production and operation and long time lag for gaining return from agricultural investment. RCC institutions can learn and adopt the German "Hausbank" model and use their own branch density and information advantages to establish a long-term stable and sustainable financing relationship with their customers. Germany's "Hausbank" (house bank) is the bank a local customer keeps their account with, and both the bank and the customer stay loyal to each other. The bank's business is based on the principle of relationship financing, emphasizing mutual trust, mutual support, information symmetry, close relationship, long-term and win–win cooperation between the bank and its customers. The adoption of the "Hausbank" model in rural China can effectively reduce credit risk, meet the financing needs of new agricultural businesses, and help to realize rural revitalization.

3.2 Further Pushing Forward the Reform of the RCC Institutions

3.2.1 Implementing Differentiated Reform Measures and Regulatory Policies in Favor of Different Sub-types of RCC Institutions

The current regulatory authorities often do not distinguish between various sub-types of RCC institutions and adopt one size fits all policies and measures. Although the intention of these policies and measures is very good, their targeting is easy to decline and even is not conducive to some types of RCC institutions. When issuing reform measures and regulatory policies for RCC institutions in the future, regulators should subdivide different sub-types of RCC institutions and implement corresponding and customized reform measures and regulatory policies in a more detailed and accurate classified management method. For example, it is necessary to subdivide the rural commercial banks in counties, county-level cities and municipal districts according to the type of jurisdiction, distinguish the listed and unlisted rural commercial banks according to whether they have been listed, distinguish the rural commercial banks that have carried out more cross-regional operations in compliance with laws and regulations and the rural commercial banks that have carried out more (including not) cross-regional operations but not in compliance with laws and regulations. According to the proportion of the rural population and agricultural added value in the county-level jurisdictions, we can distinguish the RCC institutions with a large proportion of financial services for the development of agriculture, rural areas and farmers from those with a small proportion. These distinctions are crucial for regulators to introduce more detailed and accurate reform measures and regulatory policies.

3.2.2 Encouraging Horizontal Merger Among the RCC Institutions

The government can encourage stronger RCC institutions to participate in horizontal mergers of the RCC institutions with difficult operations and high non-performing loan rates, on the one hand, improve the business scale of RCC institutions, on the other hand. The goal is to solve the development problems of weaker RCC institutions so as to enhance the competitiveness of the remaining RCC institutions. In addition, the downward trend of China's overall economic growth continues. Some RCC institutions with operating difficulties and high non-performing loan ratio are difficult to improve their performance indicators. On the contrary, their operations may continue to deteriorate. We can encourage strong and standardized RCC institutions to voluntarily and spontaneously participate in, control or merge RCC institutions with difficult operations and heavy burden of non-performing loans so as to expand the scale of RCC institutions and help solve the problems of property rights, governance and bad loans of these institutions. After the merger, the business of an enlarged RCC institution in each jurisdiction can still be counted separately, and the assessment of "supporting agriculture and supporting small businesses" can still be carried out separately in each county-level jurisdiction, and the merged RCC institution can even continue to maintain their independent legal person status.

3.2.3 Providing RCC Institutions with a Fair Play Ground

First, RCC institutions, especially rural commercial banks, should be granted more licenses for various financial businesses and be allowed to operate in a larger business scope. In comparison with other banks, RCC institutions are much more restricted in types of financial businesses and in business scope. The government should encourage RCC institutions to introduce more financial products and services and at least give rural commercial banks equal treatment in these aspects, especially those run sound financial businesses and have larger economic strength and provide financial services well for promoting the development of agriculture, rural area, and farmers, and SMEs. Second, local governments should assess the contributions of various banking financial institutions to the lending for the support of the development of agriculture, rural areas, farmers and SMEs and deposit their fiscal funds with these financial institutions according to the latter ones' contributions, which would help the RCC institutions obtain their fair share in this "cake". Third, the government should encourage RCC institutions with cross-regional business supporting the development of agriculture, rural area, farmers and SMEs to set up branches and expand business in surrounding county-level jurisdictions, which would help to break the existing practice of dividing the business scope of RCC institutions according to administrative jurisdictions, and strengthen the concept of encouraging financial institutions' business operations in their economic zones.

3.2.4 Accelerate the Reform of Provincial Credit Cooperative Associations and Strengthen its Service Function

The contradictions between the two functions of provincial credit cooperative associations, that of administrative management and that of providing service, became an increasingly serious problem, especially after some rural commercial banks got listed in the stock exchanges. The provincial associations' service functions are too weak while also intervening too much in the micro-management of RCC institutions. Therefore, the reform of provincial associations has become an urgent problem to be solved. For the first time, the annual *Central Committee Document No. 1*, in three consecutive years from 2016 to 2018, has stressed the reform of provincial associations. Such a reform will help to straighten out the relationship between the RCC institutions and their Provincial Associations, improve the external governance of these RCC institutions and stimulate their motivation and enhance their ability to participate in market competition. On January 29, 2019, the Central Bank and five other relevant ministries and commissions issued jointly the guidance on financial services for rural revitalization, which clearly defined the relationship between grassroots rural credit cooperatives and provincial cooperatives; emphasized the independent legal person status and operational independence of rural credit cooperatives; weakened the administrative functions of provincial cooperatives in personnel, finance and business; and highlighted the professional service function. Therefore, in the future reform of the Provincial Association, we must adhere to the basic principle of "strengthening the service function of the Provincial Association and weakening the management function of the Provincial Association".

Notes

1 This chapter is based on Xiang Yan and Xingyuan Feng. Problems with Sound Management and Sustainable Development of RCC Institutions and Policy Options, *Rural Finance Research*, 2020 (1), pp. 3–9.
2 RCCs were managed by the Agricultural Bank of China (ABC) since 1979 and were separated from it in 1996. During the 1990s, all the banking financial institutions had huge amount of non-performing loans to township and village enterprises which were collectively owned by township-level government, village collectives, or villagers' groups, or even some local government departments.

3 According to the China Banking Industry Association (2021), the overall asset scale of the RCC institutions took RMB 38.39 trillion in 2020. So the average asset size was RMB 17.4 Billion. The bank with largest asset size is Chongqing Rural Commercial Bank. Its asset size reached RMB 1.13 trillion in 2020. It is a rural commercial bank which merged the former Chongqing RCC Association with the 39 former county-level RCCs within the territory of this municipality directly under the Central Government.

References

Basel Committee on Banking Supervision. Principles for Sound Liquidity Risk Management and Supervision, September 2008.

China Banking Industry Association. *China Rural Medium and Small Banking Financial Institution Development Report 2021*. China Finance Press, 2021.

Greuning, Hennie van, and Sonja Brajovic Bratanovic. *Analyzing Banking Risk. A Framework for Assessing Corporate Governance and Risk Management*. 3rd Edition. The World Bank, 2009.

Rural Financial Services Research Group of the People's Bank of China. *China Rural Financial Services Report*. China Finance Press, 2018.

6

THE DEVELOPMENT OF DIGITAL INCLUSIVE FINANCE IN CHINESE COUNTIES

Index Construction, Measurement and Analysis[1]

Xingyuan Feng, Tongquan Sun, Chong Dong and Xiang Yan

1. Introduction

Since China's launch of reform and opening-up policy in 1978, the supply of financial services for the development of "agriculture, rural areas and farmers" has been greatly improved. However, a large number of low-income groups, farmers and small and micro enterprises in rural areas are still excluded or underserved by the formal financial sector. Moreover, most new agricultural business entities, including large farmers, family farms, farmers' cooperatives and agribusiness companies, also suffer from financial exclusion to some degree when applying for loans because of the lack of collateral acceptable to formal financial institutions. All these excluded or underserved by the formal financial sector are groups that need special attention. They should have access to financial services from rural inclusive financial service providers (Feng et al., 2019). Because of this, the Chinese government has paid more and more attention to the development of rural inclusive finance in recent years. In September 2018, the CPC Central Committee and the State Council issued the "Strategic Plan for Rural Revitalization (2018–2022)", which proposed "developing rural inclusive finance". In February 2019, the People's Bank of China, the China Banking and Insurance Regulatory Commission, the China Securities Regulatory Commission, the Ministry of Finance and the Ministry of Agriculture and Rural Affairs jointly issued the "Guiding Opinions on Financial Services for Rural Revitalization", putting forward the requirements of "effective popularization of digital inclusive finance in rural areas". In 2021, the CPC Central Committee and the State Council's *No. 1 Document*, titled "The CPC Central Committee and the State Council's Opinions on Comprehensively Promoting Rural Revitalization and Speeding up the Modernization of Agriculture and Rural Areas", further put forward the "development of digital rural inclusive finance".

Since 2014, with the emergence of "Yu'E BAO" and the popularity of mobile internet and smartphones in urban and rural areas, large FinTech banks or platform companies have rapidly promoted the innovation of digital inclusive financial services with the help of their FinTech advantages, which has had a great impact on the conventional formal financial sector business. In response, conventional formal financial institutions have followed the move from the other end. In particular, after the G20 summit in Hangzhou in 2016 issued the document "High-level Principles of G20 Digital Financial Inclusion", the development of digital inclusive finance has become the common development direction of FinTech banks and platform companies and conventional formal financial sectors, representing the future of the financial industry. In this context, large FinTech banks and platform companies and many conventional formal financial institutions vigorously pushed forward

DOI: 10.4324/9781003369776-6

the development of digital inclusive finance from both sides. They also continue to strengthen cooperation in developing digital inclusive finance and providing digital inclusive financial services, forming a fierce co-competition situation.

However, the overall development level of China's rural digital inclusive finance is still relatively low, the development level of various regions is still uneven, and there are still their own development obstacles. What is the development level of China's rural digital inclusive finance? How big is the gap between different places? What are the obstacles to development? These questions still need to be studied and clarified. Therefore, it is necessary to build a digital inclusive financial development index system for Chinese counties to systematically and quantitatively measure the index scores of the development level of digital inclusive finance in counties (county-level cities and banners) of China. This will help local governments, FinTech banks and platform companies, financial institutions and local governments understand the progress, problems, advantages and disadvantages of the development of digital inclusive finance in these counties and help find the strengths and weaknesses in such development so as to promote the further development of digital inclusive finance and realize rural revitalization in rural areas of China.

Based on the above considerations, this paper first analyzes the relevant status and problems of the research of indices of digital inclusive financial development in rural China, especially in Chinese counties, then constructs its own index system of digital inclusive finance development in Chinese counties, and puts forward the method of measuring the scores of the index, areas, individual components and sub-components. According to these scores, this paper further analyzes the overall situation and shortcomings of the current digital inclusive financial development in Chinese counties, analyzes the relative process of the digital inclusive financial development in counties of macro regions and different provinces, and puts forward relevant policy considerations.

2. Concept Definition and Literature Review

The concept of digital inclusive finance is the product of the combination of digital technology and the concept of inclusive finance. With the rapid development of the mobile internet, the increasing popularity of smartphones and the rapid digitization of the global economy and finance, governments all over the world have accelerated the development of inclusive finance. People are more and more considering the development of inclusive finance combined with digital technology. The concept and concept of digital inclusive finance came into being. According to the definition of the Consultative Group on Poverty Alleviation of the World Bank (CGAP, 2015), digital financial inclusion (another term for "digital inclusive finance") refers to "digital access to and use of formal financial services by excluded and underserved populations. Such services should be suited to the customers' needs and delivered responsibly, at a cost both affordable to customers and sustainable for providers". Although this definition is relatively concise, there are several problems. First, financial service providers should meet the demands of various financial services, not the needs of financial services. As an economic concept, "demand" here reflects the quantity of products or services that demanders are willing to pay and can pay at a certain price level. It is the demand that is to be met by the supply of financial services, while "need" is not an economic concept and may not necessarily be met by the supply of financial services. Second, digital inclusive finance requires the financial sector to meet the financial service demands of the population through digital means. Although it is emphasized to servicing the population excluded or underserved by the formal financial sector, digital inclusive finance does not only service this part of the population. Third, the definition should include as many inclusive financial features as possible. The above definition only includes the three features of "availability, affordable cost and sustainability", while other features such as "diversity, security, appropriateness and convenience of access to and use of financial services" have not been included (World Bank and People's Bank of China, 2019; Feng et al., 2019). Therefore, this paper defines digital inclusive finance as all the population, especially those excluded or underserved by the formal financial sector, access to and use various financial services through digital means. These services should meet the demands of the above target groups; be provided in a responsible manner; be safe, appropriate, convenient and affordable for the target groups; and be sustainable for providers.

So far, there are still several studies on the inclusive finance index, and most of them do not consider the impact of digital technologies on inclusive finance (Sarma, 2008; Li and Tan, 2018; Cheng and Jiang, 2018; Zhang et al., 2017; Li et al., 2017). A few international organizations and central banks of some countries include some digital inclusive financial indicators when launching or updating the inclusive financial indicator system (The world bank and Bill and Melinda Gates Foundation, 2011; IMF, 2021; GPFI, 2016; Financial Consumer Rights Protection Bureau of the People's Bank of China, 2018). Such systems are used to measure the overall development of inclusive finance in different countries or a country, including the development of digital inclusive finance.

At present, there is only one study in China to comprehensively and systematically measure the development level of digital inclusive finance in all provinces and counties, which is the Digital Inclusive Finance Index released by the research group of the Digital Finance Research Center of Peking University (2017). As the first digital inclusive financial index evaluation system in China, it has many innovations and can be used for reference. It also represents the academic frontier of constructing the digital inclusive financial index system in China. The Digital Inclusive Finance Index measures the development level of China's digital inclusive finance from three primary dimensions: coverage, use depth and digitization degree. However, the index system is not designed to measure specifically the development level of digital inclusive finance in all counties (county-level cities and banners) of China, and the construction of the index system does not include consideration of county economic characteristics (for instance, the GDP or per capita GDP). At the same time, the name and explanations of each level-1 dimension and the setting of subordinate indicators can be further adjusted. For example, the first level dimension, "digitization degree", can be changed to "service quality", and subordinate indicators can be set according to the requirements for the quality of digital inclusive financial services so that they can be consistent with these requirements. In fact, "digitization degree" is not an appropriate first-level dimension name because the other two first-level dimensions, "coverage breadth" and "use depth", should also be the expression of "digitization degree". In addition, the primary dimension, "digitization degree", does not include indicators such as digital loan default rate (which can indicate the affordability of using digital loans) and account security insurance coverage (which can indicate the safety or security of using digital financial services). In view of this, it is necessary to build a digital inclusive financial development index specifically for Chinese counties to make up for the shortcomings of existing relevant research so as to comprehensively and systematically measure the development level of digital inclusive finance in Chinese counties.

3. Construction and Measurement Method of Digital Inclusive Financial Development Index of Chinese Counties

3.1 Compiling Principles of Digital Inclusive Financial Development Index of Chinese Counties

The compilation of the digital inclusive finance development index of Chinese counties needs to follow the following principles: first, one should try to comprehensively and systematically grasp the characteristics of the development of digital inclusive finance in Chinese counties, and measure the development level of digital inclusive finance in each county from the three aspects of breadth, depth and quality of digital inclusive financial services; second, one should consider the actual situation of the socio-economic development of Chinese counties, select some indicators which should accurately reflect the characteristics and level of county digital inclusive finance development as far as possible; third, digital inclusive finance relies more on digital technology to realize financial services, so its online service attribute needs to be emphasized in the selection of indicators; fourth, one should cover different types of digital inclusive financial services of Chinese counties, especially digital loan, digital credit line, digital payment, digital financial management and digital insurance; fifth, one should ensure that the selected indicators are representative, data availability and continuity, meet the basic principle requirements of mathematics, statistics, economics and other disciplines, and ensure that the evaluation results are relatively objective.

3.2 Data Sources

The data used in this paper comes from two sources: one is the large amount of data accumulated by MYBank (Ant Group) in the process of developing digital inclusive finance businesses in Chinese counties (county-level city, banner), and the other is the data in China Counties Statistical Yearbook and the Statistical Bulletin of National Economic and Social Development of each county in relevant years. This paper uses mainly the data accumulated by MYBank to evaluate the overall development of digital inclusive finance in Chinese counties, which is mainly based on three reasons: first, MYBank has been deeply engaged in rural digital finance businesses for many years and has absolute advantages in service types, geographical coverage and digital technology. Second, the Ant Group, with which MYBank is affiliated, is the only large FinTech platform company that set up a special rural financial business division. It has a comprehensive and accurate collection of business data relating to digital inclusive finance in all the Chinese counties (county-level cities and banners), ensuring the availability and integrity of these data; third, the digital inclusive finance business data of Chinese counties accumulated by MYBank for many years has strong representativeness and continuity in reflecting the overall development of digital inclusive finance of Chinese counties and can be used to measure such an overall development.

In terms of sample selection, considering that the economic development level and urbanization level of municipal districts are generally high, many municipal districts have been managed as urban areas, and the statistical data of population and regional GDP of some municipal districts are missing, this paper only uses the digital inclusive financial development data of 1,884 counties (county-level cities and banners) out of 2,851 county-level jurisdictions in China, excluding municipal districts. Specifically, the samples include 1,464 counties, 368 county-level cities and 52 banners. Since Beijing, Shanghai and Tianjin have no counties (county-level cities and banners) but only municipal districts, the three municipalities directly under the central government are not included in all the interprovincial comparisons, and their districts are not included in the samples.

3.3 Construction of the Digital Inclusive Financial Development Index System for Chinese Counties

Based on the above compilation principles and the existing literature, this paper divides the Digital Inclusive Financial Development Index System for Chinese Counties (DIFDICC) into four levels from top to bottom by referring to the method of the construction of the Economic Freedom of the World Index of Fraser Institute of Canada (Gwartney et al., 2020) and of the China Marketization Index of National Economy Research Institute (NERI), Beijing (Fan et al., 2011). These four levels include the overall index, area index, indicators of components and those of subcomponents. The overall index of DIFDICC for each county consists of three area indices: the area index of breadth, depth and quality of digital inclusive financial services in a county, as shown in Table 6.1. Among them, the service breadth involves the coverage of different types of digital

TABLE 6.1 Structure of the digital inclusive financial development index system for chinese counties

Area index	Component indicators	Subcomponents indicators	Notes
Service breadth	Service breadth of digital payment		Number of digital (Alipay) accounts opened per 10,000 residents in the relevant county
	Service breadth of digital credit line		Number of digital (Alipay) accounts that were granted digital credit lines per 10,000 residents in the relevant county
	Service breadth of digital loan		Number of digital (Alipay) accounts that received loans per 10,000 residents in the relevant county
	Service breadth of digital wealth management		Number of digital wealth management accounts per 10,000 residents in the relevant county
	Service breadth of digital insurance		Number of digital insurances accounts opened per 10,000 residents in the relevant counties
Service depth	Service depth of digital payment	Number of digital payments per digital payment account	Average number of digital payments per digital (Alipay) account in the relevant county
		Average amount of digital payments per payment account	Average payment amount per digital (Alipay) account in the relevant county (RMB)
		Proportion of active payment account users	Proportion of number of users with more than 365 transactions a year in the relevant county to number of users with more than 1 transaction a year in that county
	Service depth of digital credit line	Proportion of first-time digital credit line grantees among all grantees	Number of first-time digital credit line grantees as a percentage to all grantees (%)
		Ratio of per payment account digital credit line amount to per capita GDP in the relevant county	Per payment account digital credit line amount as a percentage to per capita GDP (%)
	Service depth of digital loan	Number of digital loans per digital (Alipay) account	Number of loans per digital (Alipay) account within one year
		Average digital loan amount per digital (Alipay) account	Accumulated digital loan amount per digital (Alipay) account within one year (RMB)
		Ratio of number of digital (Alipay) accounts that received digital loans for first time	Number of digital (Alipay) accounts received digital loans for the first time per 10,000 digital (Alipay) accounts within a year
		Ratio of total balance of digital loans to regional GDP in the relevant county	Total balance of digital loans as a percentage of regional GDP in the relevant county (%)

(Continued)

TABLE 6.1 (Continued)

Area index	Component indicators	Subcomponents indicators	Notes
Service quality		Ratio of per account average single digital loan balance to per capita GDP in the relevant county	Average single digital loan balance per account as a percentage to per capita GDP in the relevant county (%)
	Service depth of digital wealth management	Number of digital wealth management transactions per account	Average accumulated number of wealth management transactions per account within one year
		Per account digital wealth management amount	Accumulated wealth management amount per account within one year (RMB)
	Service depth of digital insurance	Number of digital insurances per account	Accumulated number of insurances per account within one year
		Per account digital insurance premium	Accumulated insurance premium per account within one year (RMB)
	Convenience of service use	Density in QR code use	Number of business operators using QR code per 10,000 residents
		Degree of active use of QR code	Number of business operators with more than 365 business transactions using QR code in one year as a percentage to number of business operators with more than 1 business transaction using QR code in one year in the relevant county (%)
		24x7 financial service level	Whether it belongs to "310 loan", round the clock, any amount of loan, and per day interest charge (yes=1, no =0)
	Level of Interest	Digital loan interest rate level	Digital loan interest rate for small and micro enterprises (%)
	Security of service use	Default rate of digital loan	Default rate of digital loans for small and micro enterprises (%)
		Account security insurance coverage	Security insurance coverage of MYBank accounts (%)

inclusive financial services to the population of respective counties, and the service depth involves the depth of the different types of digital inclusive financial services for the served population. The combination of the two can reflect the basic requirements of inclusive finance: not only the inclusion of the excluded or underserved persons but also the improvement of the level or depth of services for them are considered. In addition, service quality is also an important requirement of inclusive finance, including the convenience of using services, interest rate level (i.e., an opposite indicator for affordability requirements) and security of using services. Without a certain level of service quality, it cannot be said that the demands of inclusive financial services have been met; For instance, if a bank requires too complicated of a procedure for loan applications, it might scare off the excluded or underserved customers. Therefore, the evaluation system of the county's digital inclusive financial development index must comprehensively consider three aspects: service breadth, service depth and service quality.

The area index "service breadth" is composed of five indicators: service breadth of digital payment, service breadth of digital credit line, service breadth of digital loan, service breadth of digital wealth management and service breadth of digital insurance. Taking account of the fact that having digital accounts is the premise and foundation of digital payment, the use of the "number of digital (Alipay) accounts opened per 10,000 residents in the relevant county" reflects the specific scoring performance of the component indicator of "service breadth of digital payment". What needs to be explained here is that there are two reasons for choosing this to indicate the service breadth of digital payment in counties (county-level cities and banners) in China. The first reason is that Alipay is one of the most important payment tools in the field of digital payment, and it is representative. By the end of the third quarter of 2019, Alipay's market share in digital payment reached 53.58%, ranking first in the digital payment industry. The second reason is that we should consider the availability of data. This paper only has data on the ratio of opening the Alipay account in all counties of the country.

The area index "service depth" is composed of five component indicators: service depth of digital payment, digital credit line, digital loan, digital wealth management, and digital insurance. Some component indicators here are composed of several subcomponent indicators. The component indicator "depth of digital payment service" consists of three subcomponent indicators: the number of digital payments per digital payment account, the average amount of digital payments per payment account and the proportion of active payment account users. The component indicator "service depth of digital credit line" is composed of two subcomponent indicators: proportion of first-time digital credit line grantees among all grantees and ratio of per payment account digital credit line amount to per capita GDP in the relevant county. The component indicator "service depth of digital loan" consists of five subcomponent indicators, namely number of digital loans per digital (Alipay) account, the average digital loan amount per digital (Alipay) account, the ratio of the number of digital (Alipay) accounts received digital loans for first time, the ratio of the total balance of digital loans to regional GDP in the relevant county and ratio of per account average single digital loan balance to per capita GDP in the relevant county. Among them, "ratio of total balance of digital loans to regional GDP in the relevant county" reflects the total utilization of digital loans in the county, while "ratio of per account average single digital loan balance to per capita GDP in the relevant county" reflects the average utilization per account of digital loans in the county". The component indicator "service depth of digital wealth management" is composed of two subcomponent indicators: the number of digital wealth management transactions per account, and per account digital wealth management amount, which are used to reflect the depth of digital wealth management services for county residents. The component indicator "service depth of digital insurance" is composed of two subcomponent indicators: the number of digital insurances per account and per account digital insurance premium.

The area index "service quality" consists of three component indicators: the convenience of service use, level of interest and security of service use. Convenience is the biggest advantage of digital inclusive finance because it can use digital technology to break through physical and spatial constraints and provide financial services for rural residents. The component indicator "level of interest" measures the cost of use of digital inclusive financial services represented by the interest rate level of digital loans for small and micro enterprises. It is a reverse indicator for affordability: The higher the value of this indicator is, the lower the score of this component indicator will be. This component indicator and the component indicator "digital loan default rate" (see below) are different from all the other indicators at four levels: the index, three indices, all the other component indicators and all the subcomponent indicators. These other indicators are positive indicators: The higher the value of an indicator is, the higher the score of this indicator will be. The component indicator "security of service use" includes two subcomponent indicators: "digital loan default rate" and "account security insurance coverage". As a reverse indicator, the former measures the default risk factor of digital inclusive financial services, while the latter considers the importance of the security of the use of digital financial services. Since digital inclusive financial services face greater technical risks than traditional financial services, the security of using inclusive financial services can be effectively improved through the account security insurance provided by financial service providers.

3.4 Determination of Weights

Since the DIFDICC index system includes multiple and multi-layer indicators, and the importance of these indicators is different from each other, their weights need to be determined when calculating the score of these indicators based on their values. At present, the weighting methods of various development indexes mainly include the following: first, the expert scoring method, in which relevant experts subjectively weight each indicator. This method is highly subjective and easily causes deviation. However, because the utility and importance of different types of financial services are quite different for their demanders, and there is a certain order of different utility and importance between these financial services, it is difficult to determine without resorting to the expert scoring method. For example, the weight of the component indicators "breadth of digital loan services" and "breadth of digital payment services" can only be determined by scoring by experts and even users (to some extent, they are also experts). The existing measurement technology is difficult to better solve this problem. The second is the coefficient of variation method. It belongs to the objective weighting method. Based on the characteristics of the data itself, it uses the coefficient of variation to weight. Because the importance of various types of financial service indicators varies greatly, the simple calculation of the coefficient of variation cannot reflect the difference of importance. Therefore, this objective weighting method is not suitable for the weighting of our index. The third is the analytic hierarchy process, that is, the Analytic Hierarchy Process (AHP) weight construction method. This method arranges a group of complex evaluation objects/indicators into an orderly hierarchical structure, then compares and judges between every two evaluation objects, and calculates the relative importance coefficient of each evaluation object, that is, the weight. The key point of the analytic hierarchy process is to establish a reasonable and consistent judgment matrix and select a good scale. This method still needs to use the expert scoring method to weigh the initial weight of each indicator, and the selection of scale directly affects the rationality of the judgment matrix and finally affects the rationality of the weights of indicators at all levels of the index system. The DIFDICC index system belongs to a multi-layer index system. Each layer of indicators involves different types of financial services. It is difficult to ensure rationality by weighting each layer of indicators with the help of determined scales. On the contrary, it is more reasonable to score each layer of indicators by experts. In addition, there are a critical analysis method and an entropy weight method, which belong to the objective weighting method. The problem is the same as the above variation coefficient method, and they are not suitable for weighting for an index system such as the DIFDICC.

In this paper, a multi-layer expert scoring method for weighting is adopted, and the indicators of each layer are weighted by expert scoring. It is required that the sum of the score weights of all lower-level indicators constituting each upper indicator is one. In this paper, 10 experts are invited to weigh the area indices, component indicators and subcomponent indicators respectively, calculate the simple arithmetic average of the weight value of each indicator, and then determine the final weight by rounding. The final weight is shown in Table 6.2. Generally speaking, as long as the result of weight determination can clearly distinguish the relative importance of different indicators, and after combining the index score calculation method, the final score can clearly reflect the relative and undistorted difference of the scores of all indicators of each region and year in each layer, then the weighting can be considered successful.

TABLE 6.2 Weights for the scores of indicators of the digital inclusive financial development index system for chinese counties

Area index	Weight	Component indicator	In-group weight	Subcomponent indicator	In-group weight
Service breadth	35%	Service breadth of digital payment	20%		
		Service breadth of digital credit line	17.14%		
		Service breadth of digital loan	34.29%		
		Service breadth of digital wealth management	11.43%		
		Service breadth of digital insurance	17.14%		
Service depth	35%	Service depth of digital payment	20%	Number of digital payments per digital payment account	33.3%
				Average amount of digital payments per payment account	33.3%
				Proportion of active payment account users	33.4%
		Service depth of digital credit line	17.14%	Proportion of first-time digital credit line grantees among all grantees	50%
				Ratio of per payment account digital credit line amount to per capita GDP in the relevant county	50%
		Service depth of digital loan	34.29%	Number of digital loans per digital (Alipay) account	25%
				Average digital loan amount per digital (Alipay) account	17%
				Ratio of number of digital (Alipay) accounts that received digital loans for first time	17%
				Ratio of total balance of digital loans to regional GDP in the relevant county	25%
				Ratio of per account average single digital loan balance to per capita GDP in the relevant county	16%
		Service depth of digital wealth management	11.43%	Number of digital wealth management transactions per account	50%
				Per account digital wealth management amount	50%
		Service depth of digital insurance	17.14%	Number of digital insurances per account	50%

(*Continued*)

TABLE 6.2 (Continued)

Area index	Weight	Component indicator	In-group weight	Subcomponent indicator	In-group weight
				Per account digital insurance premium	50%
	30%	Convenience of service use	33.34%	Density in QR code use	33.4%
Service quality					
				Degree of active use of QR code	33.3%
				24x7 financial service level	33.3%
		Level of Interest	33.33%	Digital loan interest rate level	100%
		Security of service use	33.33%	Default rate of digital loan	50%
				Account security insurance coverage	50%

3.5 Measurement Method of Index Score

3.5.1 Nondimensionalization

In order to make the values of the indicators in different units in the DIFDICC index system comparable, before calculating the scores of these indicators, it is necessary to standardize the original data (i.e., the values) of indicators to eliminate their dimensional differences. In order to make the scores of indicators at all levels of the index system comparable across years and counties, the maximum and minimum values of the base year (2017) are uniformly used when standardizing the values of indicators of each year with reference to the methods of Fraser Institute of Canada and National Economy Research Institute (NERI), Beijing. The specific nondimensionalization formula is:

$$\text{Positive indicator}: s_i = \frac{x_{i,t} - m_{i,2017}}{M_{i,2017} - m_{i,2017}} \tag{1}$$

$$\text{Reverse indicator}: s_i = \frac{M_{i,2017} - x_{i,t}}{M_{i,2017} - m_{i,2017}} \tag{2}$$

Here s_i denotes the value of the indicator i after the nondimensionaization of its actual original value, $x_{i,t}$ denotes the actual original value of the indicator i in the year t, $M_{i,2017}$ denotes the maximum value of the indicator i *in the base year of 2017 among all the counties*, $m_{i,2017}$ denotes the minimum value of the indicator i in the base year of 2017 among all the counties.

3.5.2 Measuring the Scores of Indicators After Nondimensionalization and Weighting

After the nondimensionalization of the original data/values of the subcomponent and the component indicators which don't consist of subcomponents, the results will be weighted, from which the scores of these subcomponent and component indicators will be obtained. The following equations apply:

For positive indicators :$d_i = w_i \dfrac{x_{i,t} - m_{i,2017}}{M_{i,2017} - m_{i,2017}} \times 100$ (3)

For reverse indicator :$d_i = w_i \dfrac{M_{i,2017} - x_{i,t}}{M_{i,2017} - m_{i,2017}} \times 100$ (4)

Here, d_i denotes the value, i.e., score obtained from the nondimensionalization and weighting of the value of subcomponent indicator or component indicator (which doesn't consist of subcomponents) i, w_i denotes the in-group weight of the above indicator i which is the weight this indicator has in the corresponding group of indicators that jointly constitute the upper-level indicator (If one higher-level indicator doesn't consist of sub-indicators, this indicator itself can be regarded as a group with a weight of one). According to the above equations, the scores obtained for the above subcomponent or component indicators for each county in the base year 2017 range between 0 and 100.

In this paper, the weighted summation method for scoring is used to calculate the score of indicators. Specifically, the index system includes an overall index, area indices, component indicators and subcomponent indicators, a total of four levels of indicators involving three levels of weights. The calculation step is based on the distance index calculation method, applying weighted summation layer by layer from bottom to top. With this approach, all the scores of indicators at all levels are obtained.

4. Measurement Results and Analysis of Scores of Indicators at All Levels of the Digital Inclusive Financial Development Index System

4.1 The Overall Situation of the Development of County Digital Inclusive Finance in China

According to the above measurement methods and data sources, this paper calculates the scores of various indicators of the DIFDICC index system relating to 1,884 counties (county-level cities and banners) in China from 2017 to 2019. The highest score of the overall index increased from 89.52 in 2017 (Dongyang city, Zhejiang province) to 177.74 in 2019 (Yiwu city, Zhejiang province), and the lowest score increased from 7.51 in 2017 (Shenza county, Tibet) to 34.25 in 2019 (Xinghai county, Qinghai province). It can be seen that the development level of digital inclusive finance in Chinese counties has been greatly improved.

As can be seen from Figure 6.1, the median score of the overall index showed a rapid upward trend from 2017 to 2019, and the median score of the overall index increased from 43.37 in 2017 to 79.59 in 2019. Here, the median score is used as the unit of analysis, which is helpful to reduce the influence of outliers, i.e., extreme values of some indicators of some counties.

Furthermore, the median scores of the three area indices are rising rapidly on the whole, but the growth rates are different, indicating that digital inclusive financial development of Chinese counties has improved in terms of service breadth, service depth and service quality during this period, but there is a problem of unbalanced development. Among them, the median score of the area index "service breadth" increased the fastest, from 38.04 points in 2017 to 102.66 points in 2019, an increase of 169.87%; On the one hand, the median score of the area index "service depth" increased slightly lower than that of "service breadth", from 37.46 points in 2017 to 63.79 points in 2019, an increase of 70.29%. And the median score of the area index

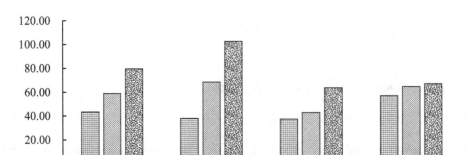

FIGURE 6.1   Median Scores of the Overall Index and Three Area Indices of All Chinese Counties from 2017 to 2019

"service quality" increased relatively slowly, from 57.18 points in 2017 to 67.30 points in 2019, an increase of 17.70%.

Specifically, the median scores of all five component indicators of the area index "service breadth" increased from 2017 to 2019, among which the improvement of the component indicators "service breadth of digital loan" and "service breadth of digital credit line" contributed the most to the improvement of the median scores of this area index. The median score of the component indicator "service breadth of digital credit line" increased from 22.30 points in 2017 to 85.77 points in 2019, an increase of 284.62% (Figure 6.2); The median score of the component indicator "service breadth of digital loan" increased from 17.53 points in 2017 to 105.10 points in 2019, an increase of 499.54%. This shows that China has made significant progress in expanding the coverage of digital credit lines and digital loans in its counties (county-level cities and banners).

From 2017 to 2019, the median scores of the component indicators "service depth of digital loan", "service depth of digital credit line" and "service depth of digital payment" of the area index "service depth" showed an upward trend. Among them, the median score of the component indicator "service depth of digital loan" increased most significantly, from 23.01 in 2017 to 78.14 in 2019, an increase of 239.59% (Figure 6.2). In contrast, the median scores of the component indicators "service depth of digital wealth management" and "service depth of digital insurance" decreased slightly from 2017 to 2018, indicating that the development of digital wealth management and digital insurance in terms of service depth lags behind, and there is more room for improvement.

From 2017 to 2019, the growth rate of the median score of the area index "service quality" of the index obviously lagged behind the area index "service breadth" and "service depth" (Figure 6.2). The reason is mainly related to the low score of the component indicator "interest rate level" and its continuous decline (the rise of credit cost) during this period. With the improvement of the breadth and depth of digital inclusive financial services in the county, the inclusiveness of digital inclusive financial services is also increasing, which means more owners of rural small and mini enterprises who were excluded from financial services of conventional formal financial institutions got included into the groups that are able to obtain financial services, especially digital loans: They were formerly excluded by conventional formal financial institutions due to their low credit level and lack of collateral and are now gradually included in the service target groups of digital inclusive finance, and the risk premium required for these people is relatively high, which led to the rise of overall interest rates instead of falling during this period.

(a) Service breadth

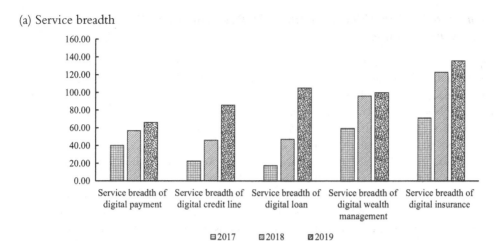

(b) Service Depth

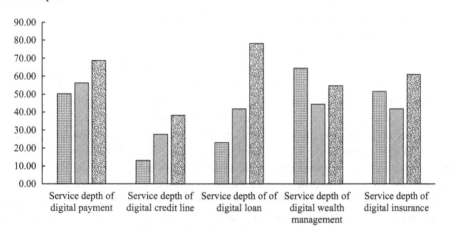

(c) Service Quality

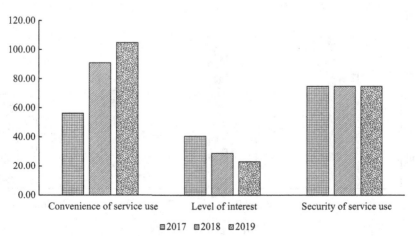

FIGURE 6.2   Median Scores of the Component Indicators of the Three Area Indices in All Chinese Counties from 2017 to 2019

4.2 Comparison of Digital Inclusive Financial Development in Different Regions and Counties

By comparing and analyzing the scores of indicators at all levels of the digital inclusive financial development index system in different macro regions, we can find the development gap of digital inclusive finance between different macro regions. Using the division of national economic regions by the National Bureau of statistics, this paper divides China into four macro regions, i.e., the Eastern Region, Central Region, Western Region and Northeast Region. The median scores of the overall index for all the counties in the Eastern and Central Regions are significantly higher than those in the Western and Northeast Regions. According to the median score of the overall index of all the counties of each region in 2019, the Eastern Region ranks first (108.78 points), the Central Region ranks second (98.78 points), the Western Region ranks third (68.77 points) and the Northeast Region ranks fourth (65.96 points). The median score of the overall index of all counties of the Eastern and Central Region is higher than the median score of the overall index for all counties of the whole country (85.57), and the median score of the Western and Northeast Region is lower than the median score of the overall index of all the counties of the whole country (Figure 6.3).

From the perspective of development trend, the development level of county digital inclusive finance in macro regions in China has significantly improved from 2017 to 2019, and the development gap between regions is also changing (see Table 6.3). Among them, the development level of digital inclusive finance in the Central Region shows a catch-up trend, and the gap with the Eastern Region is significantly narrowed, but the gap between the Western Region, the Northeast Region and the Eastern Region is slowly expanding. It is worth noting that the gap between the Western Region and the Northeast Region is widening in terms of the ratio of the median scores of the overall index of both macro regions from 2017 to 2019: the ratio in 2017 was 0.98, while that in 2019 was 1.04. Nevertheless, the overall development momentum of the western region is good, and the overall development speed is faster than that of the Northeast region. There is a catch-up process here: in 2017, the median score of the overall index in the Western Region was 37.48 points, slightly lower than that in the Northeast Region (38.43 points); In 2019, the median score of the overall index in the Western Region was 68.77, slightly higher than that in the Northeast Region (65.96).

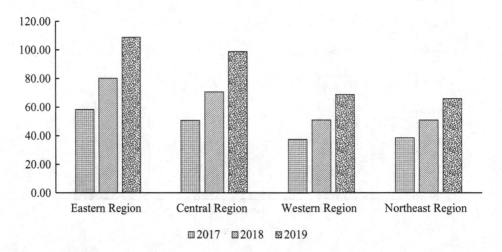

FIGURE 6.3 Median Scores of the Overall Index of Macro Regions of China from 2017 to 2019

TABLE 6.3 Development trend of the median scores of the overall index of different macro regions from 2017 to 2019

	Ratio of the median scores of the overall index of the former macro region to that of the latter macro region in 2017	Ratio of the median scores of the overall index of the former macro region to that of the latter macro region in 2019	Development trend
The gap between the Eastern and Central Region	1.15	1.1	shrinking
The gap between the Eastern and Western Region	1.55	1.58	widening
The gap between the Eastern and Northeastern Region	1.52	1.65	widening
The gap between the Central and Western Region	1.35	1.44	widening
The gap between the Eastern and Northeastern Region	1.32	1.50	widening
The gap between the Western and Northeastern Region	0.98	1.04	widening

4.3 Development of Digital Inclusive Finance in Different Provinces and Counties

According to the median score of the overall index of 28 provinces (municipalities directly under the central government and autonomous regions) in 2019, the development levels of digital inclusive finance of counties can be divided into six gradients, and the corresponding provinces can be divided into six echelons. Among them, Zhejiang province and Fujian province have the highest median scores of the overall index, belonging to the first echelon. Although both belong to the first echelon, there is a large gap in the median scores between both. The median score of the overall index of Zhejiang province was 151.60 points, and that of Fujian province was 129.71 points, with a difference of 21.89 points. Henan, Anhui and Jiangsu provinces ranked in the second echelon, with a median score of about 110 points (Figure 6.4). Shandong, Jiangxi and Shaanxi are ranked in the third echelon, with a median score of 96 to 102 points. Hebei, Hubei, Hunan, Shanxi and Guangdong ranked in the fourth echelon, with a median score of 84 to 90 points; Heilongjiang, Guangxi, Gansu, Hainan, Chongqing, Ningxia, Inner Mongolia, Xinjiang, Jilin, Guizhou and Sichuan ranked in the fifth echelon, with a median score of 59 to 73 points; Liaoning, Yunnan, Tibet and Qinghai ranked in the sixth echelon, with a median score of 48 to 57 points.

As shown in Table 6.4, the median score of the overall index of Zhejiang province and Fujian province ranked first and second for three consecutive years, which is also consistent with the actual development of the digital economy and digital inclusive finance in reality. Zhejiang and Fujian are two developed coastal areas. The economic development is very dynamic and active there, local governments made and implemented a plan for the development of the digital economy earlier than other provinces, and the local digital financial infrastructure is also better than in other provinces. As remote areas in the west, Tibet and Qinghai are relatively backward in the digital economy

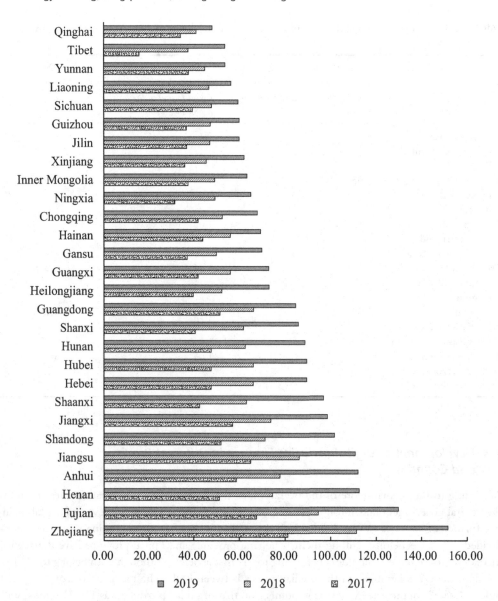

FIGURE 6.4 Median Scores of the Overall Index of Different Provinces from 2017 to 2019

TABLE 6.4 Median scores and ranking of the overall index of different provinces from 2017 to 2019

Province	Overall Index 2017		Overall Index 2018		Overall Index 2019		Change in Ranking from 2017 to 2019
	Median scores	Ranking	Median scores	Ranking	Median scores	Ranking	
Zhejiang	81.18	1	111.26	1	151.60	1	0
Fujian	67.43	2	94.48	2	129.71	2	0
Henan	51.24	8	74.43	5	112.47	3	5
Anhui	58.77	4	77.72	4	111.96	4	0
Jiangsu	65.00	3	86.10	3	110.69	5	-2
Shandong	51.98	6	71.19	7	101.63	6	0

Province	Overall Index 2017		Overall Index 2018		Overall Index 2019		Change in Ranking from 2017 to 2019
	Median scores	Ranking	Median scores	Ranking	Median scores	Ranking	
Jiangxi	57.10	5	73.74	6	98.52	7	-2
Shaanxi	42.64	13	63.11	11	96.79	8	5
Hebei	47.70	10	66.09	10	89.48	9	1
Hubei	47.70	9	66.09	9	89.48	10	-1
Hunan	47.69	11	62.58	12	88.67	11	0
Shanxi	40.67	16	61.87	13	85.74	12	4
Guangdong	51.48	7	66.15	8	84.55	13	-6
Heilongjiang	39.79	17	52.34	17	72.90	14	3
Guangxi	41.94	14	56.06	15	72.84	15	-1
Gansu	37.21	22	49.94	18	69.77	16	6
Hainan	43.96	12	56.08	14	69.25	17	-5
Chongqing	41.91	15	52.52	16	67.83	18	-3
Ningxia	31.73	27	49.33	19	65.02	19	8
Inner Mongolia	37.53	21	49.18	20	63.29	20	1
Xinjiang	36.15	25	45.44	25	62.06	21	4
Jilin	37.01	23	47.06	23	59.94	22	1
Guizhou	36.89	24	47.30	22	59.93	23	1
Sichuan	39.48	18	47.82	21	59.45	24	-6
Liaoning	38.49	19	46.63	24	56.35	25	-6
Yunnan	37.81	20	44.82	26	53.78	26	-6
Tibet	15.81	28	37.63	28	53.67	27	1
Qinghai	34.30	26	41.07	27	48.12	28	-2

and digital financial infrastructure. They have been ranked low from 2017 to 2019 in terms of the median score of the overall index, but the median score has increased.

4.4 Analysis of the Top 100 Counties in the Development of Digital Inclusive Finance of Chinese Counties

According to the median score of the overall index of all counties (county-level cities and banners) in China, the list of the top 100 counties in China can be obtained in the order of scores from high to low, as shown in Table 6.5. Among the top 100 counties in 2019, the counties in the Eastern Region accounted for 65%, the Central Region accounted for 31%, the Western Region accounted for 3%, and the Northeast Region accounted for 1%, and the top 31 are all counties in the Eastern Region. The top 100 counties in 2019 are distributed in 15 provinces in China, of which Zhejiang province and Fujian province are the two provinces with the best performance in the development of digital inclusive finance in their counties. Their number of top 100 counties is 28 and 20, respectively, totaling 48 counties, nearly half of the total number of top 100 counties.

In addition, it is necessary to compare and analyze the gap between the top 100 counties, non-top 100 counties and the last 100 counties regarding the development level of digital inclusive finance in Chinese counties in 2019. As can be seen from Figure 6.5, there is a big gap in the development level of digital inclusive finance among the top 100 counties, non-top 100 counties and the last 100 counties. The median score of the overall index of the top 100 counties was 2.01 times that of the non-top 100 counties and 3.43 times that of the last 100 counties. This gap was mainly caused by the gap in their breadth of services.

TABLE 6.5 Median scores of the overall index and area indices of the top 100 counties in 2019

County (county-level city or banner)	Macro region	Median score of the overall index	Ranking	Median score of service breadth	Median score of service depth	Median score of service quality
Yiwu city, Zhejiang Prov.	Eastern	177.74	1	266.13	148.80	108.37
Dongyang City, Zhejiang Prov.	Eastern	175.7	2	257.42	149.46	110.97
Yunhe County, Zhejiang Prov.	Eastern	175.43	3	259.03	143.65	114.98
Tongxiang City, Zhejiang Prov.	Eastern	175.36	4	265.46	141.31	109.98
Yongkang City, Zhejiang Prov.	Eastern	174.46	5	261.28	149.91	101.79
Pingyang County, Zhejiang Prov.	Eastern	173.5	6	259.24	142.11	110.07
Pinghu City, Zhejiang Prov.	Eastern	172.27	7	266.13	131.41	110.44
Yueqing City, Zhejiang Prov.	Eastern	171.92	8	249.97	151.91	104.22
Sanhe City, Hebei Prov.	Eastern	171.73	9	263.61	137.95	103.93
Anji County, Zhejiang Prov.	Eastern	171.72	10	260.42	139.08	106.32
Haining City, Zhejiang Prov.	Eastern	170.17	11	259.66	138.60	102.59
Cixi City, Zhejiang Prov.	Eastern	168.8	12	258.33	132.99	106.12
Pujiang County, Zhejiang prov.	Eastern	168.65	13	237.22	151.85	108.27
Kunshan City, Jiangsu prov.	Eastern	167.67	14	260.35	133.63	99.24
Rui'an City, Zhejiang Prov.	Eastern	167.49	15	242.34	148.35	102.49
Qingyuan County, Zhejiang Prov.	Eastern	167.04	16	253.74	138.00	99.78
Fuding City, Fujian prov.	Eastern	166.55	17	257.50	135.78	96.33
Wuyi County, Zhejiang Prov.	Eastern	165.86	18	234.67	145.17	109.73
Haiyan County, Zhejiang Prov.	Eastern	165.49	19	258.14	125.88	103.59
Deqing County, Zhejiang Prov.	Eastern	165.44	20	252.06	129.14	106.74
Gaobeidian City, Hebei Prov.	Eastern	165.36	21	233.69	145.38	108.94
Dachang Hui Autonomous County, Hebei Prov.	Eastern	165.27	22	255.88	128.30	102.68
Minhou County, Fujian Prov.	Eastern	165.19	23	238.46	148.19	99.55
Jiashan County, Zhejiang Prov.	Eastern	165.01	24	251.59	133.18	101.14
Yongjia County, Zhejiang Prov.	Eastern	164.99	25	229.80	153.80	102.42
Tonglu County, Zhejiang Prov.	Eastern	164.63	26	251.35	133.18	100.14
Yuyao City, Zhejiang Prov.	Eastern	164.29	27	244.11	135.08	105.26
Wenling City, Zhejiang Prov.	Eastern	163.68	28	234.82	140.87	107.27
Wuyishan City, Fujian Prov.	Eastern	163.47	29	249.12	130.37	102.15
Shishi City, Fujian Prov.	Eastern	163.36	30	239.32	140.46	101.46
Cangnan County, Zhejiang Prov.	Eastern	162.09	31	230.29	144.23	103.35
Changsha County, Hunan Prov.	Central	162.01	32	259.52	114.58	103.58
Houma City, Shanxi Prov.	Central	161.94	33	261.27	125.74	88.28
Nanchang County, Jiangxi Prov.	Central	161.84	34	266.13	114.42	95.50
Zhuji City, Zhejiang Prov.	Eastern	161.69	35	237.35	134.10	105.59
Quanjiao County, Anhui Prov.	Central	161.01	36	249.59	131.90	91.61
Ruili City, Yunnan Prov.	Western	160.28	37	241.31	133.26	97.28
Qinghe County, Hebei Prov.	Eastern	159.83	38	235.82	128.37	107.88
Dehua County, Fujian Prov.	Eastern	159.72	39	236.10	136.31	97.90
Changshu City, Jiangsu Prov.	Eastern	159.54	40	235.81	134.65	99.59
Pingnan County, Fujian Prov.	Eastern	159.39	41	248.55	130.28	89.33
Shuyang County, Jiangsu Prov.	Eastern	159.11	42	246.40	123.27	99.09
Xinzheng City	Central	158.97	43	244.93	120.91	103.08
Zherong County, Fujian Prov.	Eastern	158.36	44	232.23	142.11	91.16
Jinjiang City, Fujian Prov.	Eastern	158.02	45	229.72	134.92	101.34
Huidong County, Guangdong Prov.	Eastern	158.01	46	232.81	133.55	99.28
Xinxiang County, Henan Prov.	Central	156.97	47	252.50	111.07	99.08
Gongqing city of Jiangxi Prov.	Central	156.54	48	240.27	116.41	105.66
Anxi County, Fujian Prov.	Eastern	156.34	49	213.38	143.11	105.23
Hejin City, Shanxi Prov.	Central	156.01	50	259.03	109.83	89.71

County (county-level city or banner)	Macro region	Median score of the overall index	Ranking	Median score of service breadth	Median score of service depth	Median score of service quality
Xiapu County, Fujian Prov.	Eastern	155.71	51	236.47	129.14	92.51
Ninghai County, Zhejiang Prov.	Eastern	155.42	52	233.73	130.11	93.61
Lingchuan County, Guangxi Zhuang Autonomous Region	Western	155.36	53	257.93	107.17	91.92
Xiantao City, Hubei Prov.	Central	154.64	54	249.98	123.31	79.97
Puning City, Guangdong Prov.	Eastern	153.91	55	214.14	134.25	106.57
Haifeng County, Guangdong Prov.	Eastern	153.8	56	218.07	132.48	103.68
Jiyuan City, Henan Prov.	Central	153.72	57	243.09	111.30	98.94
Longhai City, Fujian Prov.	Eastern	153.2	58	241.50	119.17	89.89
Qinyang City, Henan Prov.	Central	152.97	59	251.35	98.74	101.46
Fu'an City, Fujian Prov.	Eastern	152.29	60	226.09	124.44	98.68
Taicang City, Jiangsu Prov.	Eastern	152.19	61	217.05	125.89	107.19
Nan'an City, Fujian Prov.	Eastern	152.07	62	221.84	128.46	98.21
Xiuwu County, Henan Prov.	Central	152.02	63	253.03	99.98	94.88
Longquan City, Zhejiang Prov.	Eastern	151.98	64	211.42	140.33	96.21
Xinyi City, Jiangsu Prov.	Eastern	151.81	65	247.57	107.14	92.22
Shouning County, Fujian Prov.	Eastern	151.81	66	241.21	121.79	82.53
Zhenping County, Henan Prov.	Central	151.63	67	243.49	109.90	93.17
Sihui City, Guangdong Prov.	Eastern	151.36	68	225.14	123.28	98.05
Tiantai County, Zhejiang Prov.	Eastern	151.21	69	211.74	147.77	84.62
Lichuan County, Jiangxi Prov.	Central	150.67	70	234.98	126.84	80.12
Shaowu City, Fujian Prov.	Eastern	150.54	71	245.98	112.64	83.42
Jinzhai County, Anhui Prov.	Central	150.49	72	241.23	121.63	78.31
Dongxing City, Guangxi Zhuang Autonomous Region	Western	150.33	73	230.79	114.87	97.84
Lankao County, Henan Prov.	Central	150.32	74	247.92	102.77	91.92
Yong'an City, Fujian Prov.	Eastern	150.31	75	241.21	113.81	86.84
Pingxiang County, Hebei Prov.	Eastern	150.26	76	195.99	141.62	106.99
BOLUO County, Guangdong Prov.	Eastern	149.97	77	227.54	117.26	97.62
Mengzhou City, Henan Prov.	Central	149.92	78	236.37	104.61	101.91
Susong County, Anhui Prov.	Central	149.85	79	242.73	116.35	80.59
Tongcheng City, Anhui Prov.	Central	149.73	80	220.30	136.42	82.90
Luhe County, Guangdong Prov.	Eastern	149.41	81	227.05	126.67	85.36
Lianjiang county, Fujian Prov.	Eastern	149.2	82	218.74	132.48	87.57
Huaining County, Anhui Prov.	Central	149.12	83	228.33	128.41	80.87
Jing'an County, Jiangxi Prov.	Central	148.99	84	220.83	135.41	81.03
Cao County, Shandong Prov.	Eastern	148.52	85	236.01	109.88	91.53
Changxing County, Zhejiang Prov.	Eastern	148.37	86	226.23	116.60	94.59
Zhongmou County, Henan Prov.	Central	147.82	87	236.70	101.87	97.73
Shaxian County, Fujian Prov.	Eastern	147.82	88	224.52	119.38	91.51
Yi County, Anhui Prov.	Central	147.64	89	205.99	135.19	94.10
Xiaoyi City, Shanxi Prov.	Central	147.53	90	256.61	88.29	89.38
Shangcheng County, Henan Prov.	Central	147.35	91	236.74	116.15	79.45
Neixiang County, Henan Prov.	Central	147.34	92	243.65	104.67	84.78
Xianyou County, Fujian Prov.	Eastern	147.16	93	218.73	124.79	89.74
Yuexi County, Anhui Prov.	Central	147.15	94	227.68	123.11	81.26
Enshi City, Hubei Prov.	Central	147	95	231.36	118.98	81.27
Wuhu County, Anhui Prov.	Central	146.78	96	217.28	123.26	91.98
Ruzhou City, Henan Prov.	Central	146.71	97	243.95	98.25	89.80
Suifenhe City, Heilongjiang Prov.	Northwestern	146.39	98	223.96	108.16	100.50
Liancheng County, Fujian Prov.	Eastern	146.07	99	227.20	114.02	88.82
Tangyin County, Henan Prov.	Central	145.56	100	247.93	89.03	92.08

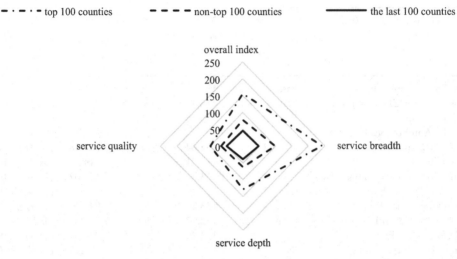

FIGURE 6.5 Comparison of the Median Scores of the Overall Index and Area Indices of Top 100, Non-top 100 and the Last 100 Counties in 2019

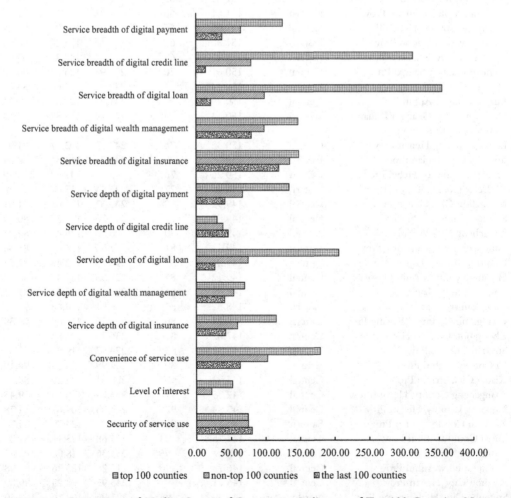

FIGURE 6.6 Comparison of Median Scores of Component Indicators of Top 100 Counties, Non-top 100 Counties and the Last 100 Counties in 2019

From the perspective of component indicators, the gap between the median scores of "service breadth of digital loan", "service breadth of digital credit line", "service depth of digital loan" and "convenience of service use" is the main reason for the huge gap between the top 100 counties, non-top 100 counties and the last 100 counties. It can be seen from Figure 6.6 that the median scores of the component indicators "service breadth of digital loan", "service breadth of digital credit line", "service depth of digital loan" and "convenience of service use" of the top 100 counties in 2019 are 354.75 points, 312.58 points, 205.84 points and 179.43 points respectively, which are 3.60 times, 3.95 times, 2.75 times and 1.75 times of the median scores of the corresponding indicators of the non-top 100 counties, It is 16.91 times, 22.77 times, 7.71 times and 2.85 times of the median score of the corresponding indicators in the last 100 counties. In addition, in terms of the component indicator "level of interest rate", the median score of the top 100 counties is also better than that of the non-top 100 counties and the last 100 counties.

5. Conclusions and Policy Considerations

5.1 Conclusion

This paper constructs the Digital Inclusive Financial Development Index for Chinese Counties (DIFDICC); measures the scores of the overall index, area indices, component indicators and sub-component indicators of 1,884 counties (county-level cities and banners) in 2017–2019; and makes a comparative analysis. The main conclusions are as follows:

First, during this period, the overall development level of the digital inclusive finance of Chinese counties increased rapidly. From the area indices, although the overall scores of the three area indices improve rapidly, there are structural differences in the speed of improvement. Among them, the score of the area index "service breadth" improved the fastest, followed by the score of the area index "service depth", and the score of the area index "service quality" improved relatively slowly.

Second, there is still an imbalance in the development of digital inclusive finance of counties among regions. Among them, the development level of digital inclusive finance of counties in the Eastern Region is the highest, followed by that in the Central Region, and the development level of the Western Region and the Northeastern Region is relatively backward. From the perspective of development trend, thanks to the significant improvement of the score of the breadth and depth of digital inclusive financial services in Chinese counties, the development level of digital inclusive finance in the Central Region shows a catch-up trend, and the gap with the economically developed Eastern Region is significantly narrowed, but the gap between the Western Region and the Northeast region and the economically developed areas is slowly expanding.

Third, there are gradient differences in the development level of county digital inclusive finance among provinces. The 28 provinces (municipalities directly under the central government and autonomous regions) involved in this sample have obvious differences, which can be divided into six gradients. Among them, the median score of the overall index of Zhejiang province with the first gradient (151.60 points) is 3.15 times that of the overall index of the Qinghai province with the sixth gradient (48.12 points).

Fourth, the development space of digital inclusive finance in Chinese counties is still very huge. The absolute levels of "service breadth", "service depth" and "service quality" of all counties (county-level cities and banners) are still not high, and there is still much room for improvement.

Fifthly, among the five main types of digital financial services: digital payment, digital credit line, digital loan, digital wealth management and digital insurance, the service breadth and service depth of digital credit lines and digital loans have been improved faster than those of the other three types of digital financial services, which has also led to a significant overall improvement in the service breadth and service depth of digital inclusive finance. This also means that compared with digital payments, digital credit lines and digital loans, there is still more room for improvement in the breadth and depth of services of digital wealth management and digital insurance.

5.2 Policy Considerations

Based on the above analysis, this paper puts forward some policy considerations to promote the development of digital inclusive financial services in Chinese counties:

5.2.1 One Should Improve the Digital Inclusive Financial Infrastructure and Narrow the "Digital Divide" between Urban and Rural Areas

Although the breadth, depth and quality of digital inclusive financial services in Chinese counties have improved rapidly, the absolute level is still not high enough and there is a lot of room for improvement. This is related to the low internet penetration rate in rural China, which is related to the lagging development of rural digital financial infrastructure in most provinces. In addition, the median score of the overall index of digital inclusive financial development of counties in the Western and Northeastern Regions is lower than that in the Eastern and Central regions, which is related to the generally poor digital financial infrastructure. Therefore, it is necessary to further improve the digital financial infrastructure in rural areas throughout the country, especially in the Western and Northeast regions. Specifically, the following three measures should be taken: first, improve the national communication infrastructure and improve the coverage and accessibility of mobile communication and the internet. Second, optimize the construction of the digital financial service network and its service branches. Third, encourage conventional rural financial institutions to do a good job in the digital credit rating and credit information system of farmers and new agricultural business entities so as to promote the development of their own digital inclusive financial services.

5.2.2 County-level Governments Should Actively Take Practical Policies and Measures to Continue to Improve the Score Performance of Various Indicators Which Already Obtained Higher Scores and Improve the Score Performance of Indicators Which Still Obtained Poorer Scores

Firstly, the county-level government should fully recognize the role of digital inclusive finance in promoting its own local economic development and give policy support for adopting good digital finance practices suitable for local development. Second, county-level governments especially need to maintain open cooperation with qualified FinTech banks and platform companies and conventional financial institutions, allowing them to use, according to law, data on local public affairs and people's livelihood that local governments hold so that these financial institutions and organizations can improve their database and customer profiles for better providing digital inclusive financial services. It is particularly emphasized here that when opening up data on local public affairs and livelihood, county-level governments should maintain an open and cooperative attitude and should not enter into exclusive agreements with any conventional financial institutions or FinTech banks and platform companies. Third, we should improve the status of the financial supervision and administration bureaus or centers affiliated with county-level governments and enrich financial professionals, especially professionals who understand the importance of digital inclusive finance, so that the supervision and administration of the operation of digital inclusive finance in the relevant county can be improved.

5.2.3 The Government Should Continue to Improve the Rural Social Credit Environment and Promote Mutual Competition and Cooperation between FinTech Banks and Platform Enterprises and Conventional Rural Financial Institutions

First, the government should improve the national urban and rural individual and enterprise credit record reporting system and social credit system to improve the rural social credit environment so as to create better conditions for rural digital inclusive financial services of FinTech banks and platform companies and conventional rural financial institutions. Second, the government should effectively promote the diversification of rural financial institutions; promote their mutual competition, including the competition between FinTech banks and platform companies on one side and conventional rural financial institutions on the other side; and promote the formation of a diversified, differentiated and competitive rural inclusive financial system with a rational division of labor between commercial finance, cooperative finance and policy-oriented finance so as to promote the matching between supply and demand of rural digital inclusive financial services. Only in this way can we really improve the breadth, depth and quality of county digital inclusive financial services. Third, the government should provide tax incentives; encourage the diversified, wide coverage and high-quality supply of digital inclusive financial products and services; especially improve the amount of digital credit and digital loans to support the development of agriculture, rural areas and the farmers; and increase the types of digital insurance and their coverage breadth and depth. Fourth, the financial supervising bodies should strengthen the assessment of the performances of inclusive financial businesses of all kinds of financial enterprises and financial institutions to further reduce the cost of digital loans and improve affordability.

5.2.4 The Government Should Further Improve the Digital Inclusive Financial Literacy of the County Population

At present, some people in rural areas do not use the internet, and some internet users do not use or rarely use digital financial services other than "network red packets".[2] In particular, compared with the Eastern and Central Region, the score of the overall index of counties in the Western and Northeast Regions is generally low. These problems are related to the low literacy of digital inclusive finance of the population in relevant counties. Improving the digital inclusive financial literacy of these populations will help activate their digital inclusive financial service demands, and digital inclusive financial service providers can create their own value by first connecting and meeting these demands and creating values for these demanders.

Notes

1 Xingyuan Feng, Tongquan Sun, Chong Dong, and Xiang Yan. The Development of Digital Inclusive Finance in Chinese Counties: Index Construction, Measurement and Analysis, *China Rural Economy*, 2021(10), pp. 84–105.
2 Network red packets are Internet tools for friends, relatives, colleagues or classmates to play and bless, and Internet tools for Internet operators and businesses to organize Internet online activities, distribute red packets and send money.

References

CGAP, 2015, Digital Financial Inclusion: Implications for Customers, Regulators, Supervisors, and Standard-Setting Bodies, www.cgap.org/research/publication/digital-financial-inclusion.
Cheng, Aihua and Jiang Hang, 2018, Research on Inclusive Financial Development Index Based on G1-Variation Coefficient Method – Taking Hubei as an Example, Wuhan Finance, No. 4.

Fan, Gang, Wang Xiaolu, and Zhu Hengpeng, 2011, *China's Marketization Index – 2011 Report on the Relative Process of Marketization in Various Regions*, Beijing: Economic Science Press.

Feng, Xingyuan, Sun Tongquan, Zhang Yuhuan, and Dong Chong, 2019, *Research on Rural Inclusive Finance*, Beijing: China Social Sciences Press.

Financial Consumption Rights Protection Bureau of the People's Bank of China, 2018, China Inclusive Financial Indicators Analysis Report, 2017 August, www.pbc.gov.cn/goutongjiaoliu/113456/113469/3602384/index.html.

GPFI, 2016, G20 Financial Inclusion Indicators, www.cgap.org.

Gwartney, J., R. Lawson, J. Hall, and R. Murphy, 2020, *2020 Annual Report: Economic Freedom of the World*. Vancouver, B.C: Fraser Institute.

IMF, 2021, Financial Access Survey (FAS), https://data.imf.org/?sk=E5DCAB7E-A5CA-4892-A6EA-598B5463A34C

Li, Mingxian and Sichao Tan, 2018, Analysis on the Development Level of Rural Inclusive Finance and its Influencing Factors in the Five Provinces of Central China, Wuhan Finance, No. 4.

Li, Qiaosha, Weikun Yang, and Jinghao Yang, 2017, International Experience and Enlightenment of Building China's Rural Inclusive Finance Index System, Economic Research Reference, No. 21.

Research Group of Digital Finance Research Center of Peking University, 2017, *Chinese Practice of Digital Inclusive Finance*, Beijing: China Renmin University Press.

Sarma, M., 2008, Index of Financial Inclusion, Indian Council for Research on International Economic Relations Working Paper No. 205, http://hdl.handle.net/10419/176233.

The World Bank, and The People's Bank of China, 2019, *Toward Universal Financial Inclusion in China Models, Challenges, and Global Lessons*, Beijing: China Finance Press.

The World Bank, Bill and Melinda Gates Foundation, 2011, Global Findex Methodology, https://globalfindex.worldbank.org/sites/globalfindex/files/databank/Methodology2011.pdf.

Zhang, Heng, Jianchao Luo, and Yifan Hao, 2017, Analysis on the Development Level and Influencing Factors of Rural Inclusive Finance – An Empirical Investigation Based on the Data of 107 Rural Credit Cooperatives in Shaanxi Province, China Rural Economy, No. 1.

7
CHINA'S FINANCING SUPPORT FOR POVERTY ALLEVIATION

Tongquan Sun

1. Introduction

1.1 Lack of Funds for Development in the Rural Poor Areas of China

China's urban-rural dual economic structure has existed for a long time. Due to the bad climate, other related risks to agriculture, poor infrastructure (especially in poor areas), low labor productivity and a lack of investment opportunities, rural financial resources continue to flow out. From 1979 to 2000, the total amount of funds flowing from agriculture to industry and from rural areas to cities through the financial system was 1,478.5 billion yuan and 1,033.7 billion yuan, respectively. By the end of 2005, the deposit loan gap of banking institutions at and below the county level was as high as 3,012.8 billion yuan, and the deposit loan ratio was only 56.3%. Among the rural capital outflows areas, central and western regions were the most serious, with deposit loan ratios of 51.8% and 56.05%, respectively. Although in recent years, after a series of reforms in the rural financial market, rural financial institutions have increased, financial products have been innovated, and the supply of financial services has increased, the situation of continuous outflow of rural funds has not been fundamentally reversed.

In this case, it is difficult to form capital in China's rural areas. The difficulties for small enterprises and farmers in getting loans have been widespread and unsolvable for a long time, which hinders the economic development in poor areas and the increase of farmers' income. Especially for poor households, it is difficult for them to obtain financial services from formal financial institutions t because of their small loan amount and high management and transaction costs.

1.2 The Importance of Finance for Poverty Alleviation and Development

Poverty alleviation with finance is not only an integral part of the Chinese government's poverty alleviation policy but also a specific measure of poverty alleviation and development. Under the leadership of the central government, governments at all levels, financial institutions, enterprises or non-enterprise social organizations participated in poverty alleviation, provided comprehensive financial services for poor areas and poor people, supported the production and operation of low-income and poor farmers, helped them increase their income, got rid of poverty, achieved self-reliance and improved their economic and social status. In line with the development-oriented poverty alleviation strategy, poverty alleviation with finance is mainly carried out at three levels: first,

DOI: 10.4324/9781003369776-7

financial services to poor households, that is, to support the production and operation, as well as the living needs of education and medical treatment. Second, financial services to regional industrial development, to support enterprises in poor areas to develop production, promote employment and economic development so as to drive more people out of poverty and become rich. Third, financial support in infrastructure, including roads, hydropower, communication, education, medical treatment and other aspects related to production and life, to improve the basic material conditions and promote the equalization of public services required for long-term sustainable development.

2. Specialized Financial Policies for Poverty Alleviation

Until the beginning of reform and opening up, China's financial policy of offering funds for poverty alleviation was still deeply affected by the planned economic system. From 1978 to 1983, the funds for poverty alleviation basically came from national finance. In 1980, the central government established the "Fund for Supporting the Economy in Underdeveloped Areas" to specifically support the development of agriculture, township and village enterprises and cultural and medical undertakings in old revolutionary base areas, ethnic minority areas, remote areas and poor areas (i.e., old, young, border and poor areas). In 1982, the central government began to carry out the agricultural construction plan in Dingxi of Gansu province, Hexi and Xihaigu of Ningxia Hui Autonomous Region, focusing on supporting the three regions to improve agricultural infrastructure, develop planting and breeding industry, popularize and apply agricultural science and technology, and stably solve the problem of food and clothing of poor farmers' economic sources and the poorest farmers.

With the transformation from a plan to a market economy, regarding funds for poverty alleviation, China no longer only relies on official funds but increasingly relies on the continuous investment of financial resources. China's financial measures for poverty alleviation have gradually changed from Specialized Loans to complete and comprehensive financial services and from credit intervention to the development and cultivation of financial markets in poor areas.

2.1 Credits for Poverty Alleviation

2.1.1 Specialized Loan Policies for Poverty Alleviation in the Early Stage of Reform and Opening up

Specialized Loans refer to those being set up by the People's Bank of China (PBC) to meet the needs of economic development in different regions and periods and those of financial system reform. They are specified for special purposes and adopt preferential interest rates. The Specialized Loans for poverty alleviation were used to support poor counties in regional leading backbone projects with less investment and quick results, such as planting and breeding, processing of agricultural and sideline products and small mining so as to increase the economic strength of poor counties to become self-reliant, get rid of poverty and achieve the goal of solving the problems regarding food and clothing for the people in poor counties.

At the beginning of reform and opening up, Specialized Loans for poverty alleviation were mainly for old, young, border and poor areas, poor counties, industrial loans in counties, and specialized interest subsidized loans for poor areas. In 1983, PBC established the "Economic Development Loan for Ethnic Minority Areas" with preferential interest rates and began to use financial means to help the poor, mainly supporting the development of the local economy in the four ethnic autonomous regions of Inner Mongolia, Guangxi, Ningxia and Xinjiang and four remote and poor areas of Guizhou, Yunnan and Qinghai. In 1985, the loan was extended to poor counties nationwide, assured by the State Council and renamed "Economic Development Loan for Old, Young, Border and Poor Areas". In 1986, PBC formulated the "Interim Measures on the Administration of Specialized Loans". The fund for this loan was arranged by PBC. After the loan application was approved by PBC, it entrusted ABC to grant the credit.

In 1988, in order to help poor counties develop industries, get rid of poverty and become rich, the PBC set up industrial loans for 331 poor counties in industries of less investment and quick results. These loans were mainly put in regional leading backbone enterprises which had good economic and social benefits, promised development prospects, could take full use of local resources and were competitive locally. These enterprises can drive thousands of households to develop commodity production. These loans also supported the joint projects between the East and the West and horizontal cooperation between developed areas and poor counties in product diffusion and transfer of advanced technology, transformation and expansion projects to produce famous and special products in export to earn foreign exchange.

2.1.2 Subsidized Loans Policies for Poverty Alleviation

In 1986, PBC and the Agricultural Bank of China (hereafter referred to as ABC) jointly promulgated the "Interim Measures for the Administration of Specialized Interest Subsidized Loans to Support Poor Areas", proposing that from that year on, during the Seventh Five-Year Plan period, the central bank should allocate 1 billion yuan a year to mainly support key poor counties assured by the State Council in the projects of less investment, quick effects, marketable products, more households capable of joining-in and making use of local resources. The interest subsidized loans for poverty alleviation have been used so far and became the most important, largest and longest-lasting financial tool in poverty alleviation in China.

At the beginning of its establishment, the Subsidized Loans for poverty alleviation were operated and managed by the ABC – a specialized bank. After the establishment of the Agricultural Development Bank of China (ADBC) in 1994, these loans were transferred to be managed by the ADBC. However, since the ADBC has no business outlets at the grassroots level, it still needs to rely on the ABC to participate in the management. In 1998, the management of these loans was transferred back to the ABC again. In order to establish and improve the management system and operation mechanism, and to improve the operational efficiency to meet the market economy, the State Council Leading Group Office on Poverty Alleviation and Development (LGOP) and four other related governmental departments issued the Notice on Comprehensively Reforming the Management System of Subsidized Loans for Poverty Alleviation in 2008, which decided to delegate management authority, the usage and the benefits to local government. The document called to introduce a market competition mechanism, encouraging commercial banks to voluntarily participate according to commercial principles of open and fair competition. According to this policy, the issuing subject of the loans is no longer only the ABC, but all kinds of commercial banks with open and fair competition.

The funds initially came from the PBC and later came from the ABC and the refinancing of the PBC. After the release of the right in 2008, the funds were raised by the lending institutions themselves, and the PBC provided re-loans. In 2016, the PBC established the refinancing to poverty alleviation, which is specially used to guide local legal person institutions in poor areas to offer credits to poor areas.

At first, the Subsidized Loans were mainly used in national poverty-stricken counties, and after 2008, they were expanded to poverty-stricken villages in all counties of provinces. The loans were used in three areas: poor households, enterprises or farmers' cooperative organizations, and infrastructures.

The key objects and purposes of the loans have been adjusted several times. At first, the Subsidized Loans were mainly issued to poor households, focusing on supporting production projects such as planting, breeding and agricultural product processing to support their life. However, after more than two years of practice, there was a view that a lack of the necessary technical and management capabilities stopped the poorest households from making full use of their loans, and this policy made it difficult to use and allocate capital in scale. However, some economic entities in poor areas could run large-scale economic activities so as to promote the employment of poor households, increase their income and, at the same time, make a high recovery rate of loans, being more efficient. Therefore, since 1989, Subsidized Loans have been focused on economic entities in poor areas, in which at least half of the new employees must be from poor households.

The fact is that, with the Subsidized Loans mainly being invested in entities, poor households apparently got fewer Subsidized Loans. From 1989 to 1995, most of the Subsidized Loans were granted to township, village and county-run enterprises. As it is costly to employ a person, the predetermined policy in this respect had not been seriously implemented. In addition, the repayment rate did not rise as estimated. Later, in order to achieve the goal of the Seven-Year Priority Poverty Alleviation Program, households were focused back again. Therefore, after 1996, Subsidized Loans were gradually offered more to poor farmers, focusing on directly supporting the planting and breeding industry of poor households. Since 1997, most Subsidized Loans directly to poor households have adopted microfinance.

In 2001, the CPC Central Committee and the State Council issued *Outline of China's Rural Poverty Alleviation and Development (2001–2010)*, which re-emphasized the importance of supporting enterprise and industrial development for poverty reduction, continued to increase loans for poverty alleviation, and focused on supporting the planting and breeding industry, labor-intensive enterprises, agricultural product processing enterprises, market circulation enterprises and infrastructure projects, promoting microfinance to help households develop production. After entering the stage of targeted poverty alleviation in 2014, the Subsidized Loans were focused on the registered poor households in characteristic advantageous industries to increase their income.

The preferential interest rate has been adopted in Subsidized Loans and was subsidized by the Ministry of Finance. At the initial period, the ABC would determine the term of a loan according to the production and operation cycle of different loan purposes and the comprehensive income of the borrower, generally 1 to 3 years, and the longest is no more than 5 years. The loan interest rate is 6.1% per month, 2.1% is charged to borrowers, and 4% is subsidized by the central government. After 2001, the loan term was changed to one year, no more than three years, and the annual interest rate was unified to 3%. The gap in interest rate between the loan and the rate of the same grade in the same period published by the PBC was subsidized by central finance. After 2008, the loan term was flexibly determined by the lending institution according to the seasonal characteristics of local agricultural production, the production cycle of the loan project and the comprehensive repayment capacity. The interest rate of loans was no longer uniform, which was independently determined by the lending financial institutions in accordance with the related regulations of the PBC. The subsidy of the Subsidized Loans in key counties came from the central and provincial governments, and the subsidy of the Subsidized Loans to households in non-key counties came from the provincial government. Every year, the central government made a plan for the whole year, and provinces made their plans by themselves. In the period of Subsidized Loans, regarding loans for households, the central government would give subsidies to the interest rate by five percentage points annually, and regarding loans for projects, the central government would offer subsidies to the interest rate by three percentage points annually.

2.1.3 Microcredit Policy for Poverty Alleviation

In the early stage of reform and opening up, the implementation of the household contract responsibility system and the increase in the price of agricultural products resulted in the rapid and substantial decline in the number of rural poor. It showed the system's reform effects on poverty alleviation.

After the implementation of the poverty alleviation policy by strengthening the infrastructure construction in poor areas, improving basic production conditions, helping farmers develop planting and breeding industry and promoting regional economic development, the rural poor population has been greatly reduced again, which was the effect of regional economic development. Till the Seven-Year Priority Poverty Alleviation Program period, the remaining 80 million poor people were "hard bones" in poverty alleviation, which means that it was difficult to finish the task of poverty alleviation by the end of the 21st century just through the development of the rural economy or the regional economic development in poor areas. The government needed to release special policies and give special assistance to these poor people. Therefore, the Seven-Year Priority Poverty Alleviation Program placed special emphasis on households. At that time, although the large credit amount was put in use, the credits were hardly used by poor households with low social effects and low recovery ratio. Therefore, offering credit money directly to poor households became an important goal and task.

International experience and pilot projects in some domestic regions have proved that microfinance is an effective way to eliminate poverty, and it is also a way to get a high due repayment rate. Therefore, in 1998, the *Decision of the CPC Central Committee on Several Major Issues in Agriculture and Rural Work* required "to summarize and promote the effective practices like microcredits to households". In 1999, the *Decision of the CPC Central Committee and the State Council on Further Strengthening Poverty Alleviation and Development* once again clearly required "microcredit would be taken as an important measure to ensure the credit funds were used by households".

The history of China's microfinance policy and practice can be divided into two periods: first, some international and non-governmental organizations carried out some microfinance projects; second, the Chinese government-led microfinance projects with subsidized loans were expended.

Microfinance is a financial activity, so only financial institutions can engage in it according to law. However, in order to complete the arduous task of the Seven-Year Priority Poverty Alleviation Program, the Chinese government encouraged non-governmental organizations and international institutions to participate and mobilized social forces and resources to participate. On the one hand, it increased investment and promoted the innovation of poverty alleviation methods, and on the other, it also allowed more institutions and people to understand and support poor areas and poverty alleviation. Therefore, during this period, relevant central departments, local governments or non-governmental organizations, in cooperation with international multilateral and bilateral organizations and international non-governmental organizations, introduced the microfinance model.

Initially, most of these micro finances were carried out in the form of international cooperative projects. After the completion of these projects, many special microfinance operation institutions were established on the basis of the projects, mostly in the form of corporate or private nonenterprise legal persons, that is, later known as non-governmental organization microfinance institutions or public-interest microfinance institutions.

Public-interest microfinance institutions were not qualified to run businesses in finance, but they had good effects on poverty alleviation. As these funds are basically from domestic and foreign donations, which means they could hardly bring about possible financial risks for public deposit institutions. Therefore, the government gave these institutions some "concession" to carry out in the form of poverty alleviation projects. For example, in the poverty alleviation economic cooperative, a microfinance institution established under the guidance of the Chinese Academy of Social Sciences has obtained the permission of the PBC and the LGOP and continues to operate as a pilot. The microfinance projects carried out by the China International Center for Economic and Technological Exchange (CICETE) of the Ministry of Commerce and the United Nations Development Program (UNDP) in 48 counties of 17 provinces in China were operated in the form of international cooperation projects. The microfinance projects of the China Foundation for Poverty

Alleviation (CFPA) and the China Women's Federation were carried out as poverty alleviation or public-interest projects, and so on.

During the Seven-Year Priority Poverty Alleviation Program, in compliance with the central government, local grassroots Poverty Alleviation Offices established cooperatives and other institutions specializing in microfinance, which took the job of absorbing and returning loans to the ABC and directly issued small loans to poor farmers.

However, there were some problems raised from this operation: the poverty alleviation cooperatives couldn't solve the problems of non-performing loans and inverted interest rates (which means interest income is lower than lending cost). Moreover, the poverty alleviation cooperatives undertook many tasks to serve poor farmers, which made the operation cost too high to be met; that means it is hard for the cooperatives to be sustainable. In 1999, the poverty alleviation cooperatives no longer undertook loans; instead, the ABC directly lent money to households by itself. In this case, the cooperatives were only assistants of the ABC to provide services to households.

In 2014, China entered a new stage of "Targeted Poverty Reduction and Alleviation". In December, the LGOP and five other ministries and commissions jointly issued the *Guiding Opinions on the Innovative Development of Poverty Alleviation Microfinance*, which stressed taking the innovative development of microfinance as a key measure to achieve the goal. According to this document, the improvement of the availability of loans for registered poor households would be the basis of the work of target poverty reduction and alleviation. Financial institutions would coordinate to customize microfinance loan products for poor households, improve services to be accurate and effective, and promote the poverty-stricken population to get rid of poverty. The loans should focus on the groups who have the willingness to get loans, the potential ability to set up business, have skills and repayment ability. The loans would support the development of local characteristics and advantageous industries by the poor to increase their income. The support method was to provide a credit of less than 50,000 yuan and a term of less than 3 years to the qualified poor households and encourage financial institutions to reasonably determine the loan interest rate level with reference to the official basic rate. Local governments could make overall arrangements for financial funds and provide interest subsidies to qualified loan households, with the interest rate not exceeding the official basic interest rate. For the places which have better conditions, funds could be arranged to compensate for the bad debt of the loans. Microcredit insurance was supported, and the borrowers were encouraged to disperse loan risks through it.

2.1.4 Policy of Mutual Funds in Poor Villages

After entering the 21st century, with the changes in the economic environment and poverty alleviation situation, China's rural poverty alleviation was facing new challenges. Firstly, for a long time, China's financial poverty alleviation funds have adopted a top-down supply mechanism. The choice of projects and rural public services were made by the government, and there was no effective expression mechanism for farmers' demand. At the same time, there was no effective supervision mechanism for the supply of financial funds and rural public services. Secondly, the poverty at that time was not only the lack of income but also the poor people's low potential ability and weak impulse to improve their life. The only choice, in this case, was to promote joint and mutual assistance among farmers, improve the self-development and mutual assistance and cooperation ability of farmers and then realize the ability of poor farmers to get rid of poverty, truly making the development-oriented policy, and help poor farmers step into the development track. Third, China's rural poverty alleviation practice had always relied on the government administrative system to transfer resources to poor areas and poor households. This anti-poverty governance structure was easy to cause the problems of high cost and low efficiency due to insufficient information. Therefore, it was the key to optimize the anti-poverty governance structure to establish a mechanism that could give full play to the respective advantages of the government, community organizations and farmers and establish the cooperation between officials and people, poor groups and community subjects.

In 1995, Caohai Nature Reserve in Weining County, Guizhou province launched a "village credit fund" managed by the farmers themselves. In 2004, several places in China began to use financial funds to carry out pilot projects of community funds and mutual funds. In 2006, on the basis of summing up the experience, the LGOP and the Ministry of Finance issued the *Notice on Carrying out the Pilot Work of Establishing "Mutual Funds for Development of Poor Villages"*, launched the pilot of "mutual funds for development of poor villages" in 14 provinces (autonomous regions), arranged a certain amount of financial funds in some poor villages taking the whole villages into the "mutual funds". In these villages, farmers could expand the scale of mutual funds by taking shares with their own funds, and villagers could use "mutual funds" to develop production by borrowing.

2.2 The Policy of Insurance for Poverty Alleviation

Getting ill or paying tuition fees are the main causes of poverty or return to poverty. At the same time, agriculture is vulnerable to natural disasters, which directly reduces farmers' income. Therefore, insurance should be very important in reducing poverty. In May 2016, the China Insurance Regulatory Commission and LGOP jointly issued the *Opinions on Promote Insurance to Support Poverty Alleviation*, which stressed to accurately respond to the insurance needs of the registered poor population, meet the growing diversified insurance demands and take the key groups and tasks of poverty alleviation as the core. According to the document, the insurance should give inclusive cover basic risks for poor households, deliver insurance financing, increase the investment in poor areas, enhance the hematopoietic function, and promote the transformation and upgrading of agriculture in poor areas.

According to the above "Opinions", the central government encourage insurance companies to explore insurance for local characteristic and advantageous agricultural products according to local conditions, to actively develop and practice targeted price insurance, weather index insurance and insurance for facility-intensive agriculture, develop multi-level and high-protection agricultural insurance products and combine insurance products for new agricultural business entities which could drive the development and production of the poor, and explore and carry out insurance covering the agricultural, industrial chains, assisting new agricultural business entities in obtaining credit support. The government was to continuously improve the service level of serious illness insurance, improve the degree of protection by such insurance and alleviate the phenomenon of "poverty caused by illness and returning to poverty due to illness", actively develop and promote small life insurance products such as insurance for accidental injury, disease and medical treatment of the main labor force of poor households, actively develop poverty alleviation microcredit guarantee insurance, provide credit enhancement support for poor households' financing, and enhance the ability of poor people to obtain credit funds, actively carry out student loan guarantee insurance for college and middle school students from poor families. All level of government should try their best to give premium subsidies to the registered poor households, improve the efficiency of the use of poverty alleviation funds, establish and improve the risk sharing and compensation mechanism in poor areas, and specifically use it for loan guarantee insurance for the poor households and various poverty-stricken economic organizations that drive the employment of the poor people. By 2020, it had basically established an insurance service system and mechanism suitable for the national fight against poverty.

In 2016, the CIRC promoted the establishment of China's Insurance Industrial Investment Fund for Poverty Alleviation and China's Insurance Industrial Public-interest Fund for Poverty Alleviation to encourage and support the insurance fund in order to provide long-term support for the development of poor areas.

2.3 Participation of Capital Market for Poverty Alleviation

In order to support enterprises in poor areas in using multi-level capital financing, improve financing efficiency, reduce financing costs and continuously enhance the self-development ability of poor areas, in 2016, China Securities Regulatory Commission (CSRC) issued the *Opinions on Giving Full Play to the Role of Capital Market and Serving the National Poverty Alleviation Strategy*, which focused on the IPO, listing on the new third board, mergers and acquisitions and opening up a green channel. According to the above "Opinion", guided by the needs of economic development of poor areas and focusing on poverty alleviation, priority should be given to supporting enterprises in poor areas to make use of capital market resources and broaden direct financing channels. The enterprises that are registered and have main production and operation in poor areas, have run and paid income tax for three years or who are registered in poor areas have paid income tax of no less than 20 million yuan in poverty-stricken areas in the last year and promised not to change their registration places in the future three years, are eligible to enjoy the rapid listing policy of "reviewing the IPO application immediately after its submission and getting listed immediately after review and approval". The enterprises that are registered in poverty-stricken areas and apply for listing in the National SME share transfer system (i.e., the new third board), as well as those that issue corporate bonds and asset-backed securitization, are eligible to undergo a procedure of "specifically appointing a person in charge to care about the case and enjoying a special review". For those applying for listing on the new third board, the rapid listing policy of "once applied, will be reviewed immediately, get listed immediately after approval" shall be applied, and the initial listing fee shall be reduced or exempted. For the issuance of corporate bonds and asset-backed securitization, the policy of "once applied, will be reviewed immediately" shall apply.

3. The Evolution of Comprehensive and Targeted Financial Policies for Poverty Alleviation

China's poverty alleviation and development practice has proved that the solution to poverty problems fundamentally depends on economic development, and it can only be solved in development. In development, poor people can get fair development opportunities and share the fruits of development. Therefore, after the implementation of China's first poverty alleviation and development program, in view of the comprehensiveness and complexity of the remaining poverty problems, China's financial policies for poverty alleviation had gradually become more comprehensive. In addition to continually supplying financial services for poor groups, great efforts were to be made to build an inclusive financial system which could improve the availability and convenience of financial services at all levels of society.

3.1 Financial Poverty Alleviation Policy as a Basic Public Financial Service

The *Outline for Poverty Alleviation and Development in Rural China* (2011–2020), released by the Chinese government in 2011, emphasized the equalization of basic public services and required that the basic public services indicators in poor areas should be close to the national average by 2020. To this end, the *Outline* not only stressed to continue to improve the national subsidized loan policy but also stressed to promote the development of comprehensive financial services in poor areas, including actively promoting the innovation of financial products and financial service modes in poor areas, and encouraging the development of microcredit loans. The *Outline* requires:

to make the full coverage of financial services in villages and towns with the presence of no single outlet of any financial institutions in poor areas as soon as possible to guide the standardization of informal lending, and broaden financing channels in poor areas, encourage and support legal-person financial institutions within counties of poor areas to keep more than 70% of the newly increased loanable funds stay locally, encourage insurance institutions to establish grassroots service outlets in poor areas, improve the agricultural insurance premium subsidy policy from the central government, encourage local governments to develop insurance for local characteristic agricultural products according to the characteristic leading agricultural industries in poor areas, strengthen the construction of rural credit system in poor areas, and so on.

3.2 Policies for Developing Inclusive Finance

In November 2013, the Third Plenary Session of the 18th CPC Central Committee put forward the goal of "developing inclusive finance". In December of the same year, the CPC Central Committee and the State Council issued the *Opinions on Innovating Mechanisms to Solidly Promote Rural Poverty Alleviation and Development*, requested to establish a targeted poverty alleviation mechanism, to improve the financial service mechanism, to give full play to the guiding role of policy-oriented finance, and to support the construction of infrastructure and the development of leading industries in poor areas, guide and encourage commercial financial institutions to innovate financial products and services and increase credit supply in poor areas, accelerate the development of rural cooperative finance, enhance the agricultural support service function of RCC institutions, and standardize the development of village banks, microloan companies and mutual funds in poor villages, improve the policy of poverty alleviation subsidized loans and enlarge the scale, further promote microcredit loans, promote the extension of branches of financial institutions to poor townships and communities, and improve the rural payment environment, accelerate the selection through credit rating of creditworthy households, villages and townships (towns), develop agricultural guarantee institutions, expand the coverage of agricultural insurance, improve financial services for leading enterprises in agribusiness, family farms, farmers' cooperatives, and rural poverty alleviation bases for the disabled and other business organizations.

In 2014, the PBC and seven other ministries and commissions jointly issued the *Guiding Opinions on Comprehensively Supplying Good financial services for poverty alleviation and development* and stressed improving financial services in poor areas. By 2020, poor areas with sustainable commercial development should basically finish the full coverage of financial services in townships and administrative villages, build a multi-level with a sustainable rural payment service system and a sound rural credit system. The financial, ecological environment in poor areas would be further optimized so that the financial service level in poor areas would get closer to the national average. An inclusive financial system covering all classes and vulnerable groups in poor areas was to be preliminarily established by 2020. At the same time, the guidance focuses on infrastructure construction, economic development and industrial structure upgrading in poor areas, employment and entrepreneurship, poverty alleviation and prosperity of poor households, ecological construction and environmental protection.

In December 2015, China's State Council issued the *Plan for Promoting the Development of Inclusive Finance (2016–2020)*, which pointed out that China should develop inclusive finance based on the requirements of equal opportunities and the principle of commercial sustainability and provide appropriate and effective financial services at an affordable cost for all social strata and groups. Small and micro enterprises, farmers, urban low-income people, the poor, the disabled, the elderly and other special groups were the key target groups to be serviced by inclusive finance so that all market players could share financial services. By promoting mass entrepreneurship and innovation, enhancing social equity and social harmony, the country will become a well-off society in an all-round way.

3.3 Complete, Comprehensive and Targeted Financial Poverty Alleviation Policies

With the development of poverty alleviation practice, poverty alleviation with finance has entered all aspects of China's comprehensive economic and social development policy, especially in the overall strategy of the development of "agriculture, rural areas and farmers". In April 2014, the general office of the State Council issued *Several Opinions on the Development of Financial Services for "Agriculture, Rural Areas and Farmers"*, which stressed optimizing the network of county financial institutions, focusing on the central and western regions and economically backward areas, promoting the full coverage of rural basic financial services, deepening various forms of agricultural withdrawal, remittance, transfer services and mobile payment, and providing simple and convenient financial services, promoting the further development of the complementary advantages of policy finance, commercial finance and cooperative finance, and effectively improving financial services for vulnerable groups such as migrant workers, rural women and ethnic minorities.

In October 2015, the CPC Central Committee issued the *Proposal on Formulating the 13th Five-year-plan for National Economic and Social Development*, which clearly pointed out the need to accelerate the reform of the financial system and improve the financial institution system with reasonable division of labor and mutual supplement among commercial finance, development finance, policy-oriented finance and cooperative finance, focus on strengthening financial services for small, medium-sized and micro enterprises, rural areas, especially poor areas, increase central and provincial financial investment for poverty alleviation, give play to the complementary role of policy-oriented finance and commercial finance, integrate all kinds of poverty alleviation resources, and open up new funding channels for poverty alleviation and development.

In November 2015, the CPC Central Committee and the State Council issued the *Decision on Winning the Battle against Poverty*, making finance an important pillar of the poverty alleviation support system. The decision points out that it is necessary to encourage and guide commercial, policy, development and cooperative financial institutions to increase financial support for poverty alleviation and development, use a variety of monetary policy tools to provide long-term and low-cost funds to financial institutions to support poverty alleviation and development, establish poverty alleviation refinancing, implement more preferential interest rates than agricultural refinancing, and focus on supporting the development of characteristic industries in poor areas and the employment and entrepreneurship of the poor, use the financial subsidized funds and the surplus funds of some financial institutions to meet the capital needs of policy and development financial institutions, and broaden the sources of poverty alleviation funds, provide financing support for relocating to other places for anti-poverty. The China Development Bank (CDB) and the ADBC shall set up the "Financial Department for Poverty Alleviation", respectively. The ABC, PSBC, RCC institutions and other financial institutions should extend their service networks, innovate financial products and increase credit in poor areas. Provincial investment and financing entities for poverty alleviation and development should be established and improved. Guaranteed and free microcredit for poverty alleviation to poor households by RCC institutions, village banks and other financial institutions will be supported, for which the interest will be subsidized by the government at the official basic rate. The implementation of guaranteed loans for business startups, students' loans, women's small loans and rehabilitation and poverty alleviation loans will be strengthened. The priority of establishing village banks, microloan companies and other institutions in poor areas will be given. Support will also be given to the cultivation and development of farmers' mutual funds in poor areas and carrying out pilot credit cooperation of farmers' cooperatives, the establishment of loan risk compensation funds in poor areas, the establishment of government-funded financing guarantee institutions in poor areas, focusing on guarantee business. Small loan guarantee insurance and subsidy to guarantee insurance premiums for poor households should be introduced. The coverage of agricultural insurance should be expanded, and the characteristic agricultural product insurance in poor areas through the central government should be developed. The financial service infrastructure in poor areas should be strengthened, and the financial, ecological environment should be optimized. Price insurance for characteristic agricultural products in poverty-stricken areas and certain premium subsidies should be offered. The scope of properties used as collateral in poor areas should be effectively expanded.

In compliance with this decision, in order to enhance the accuracy and effectiveness of financial services, in 2016, seven ministries and commissions, including the PBC, issued the *Implementation Opinions on Financial Assistance for Poverty Alleviation* (*Opinions*), emphasizing to focus on the basic strategy of "targeted poverty reduction and alleviation", and to adhere to the combination of targeting and overall development, to the coordination between financial policies and poverty alleviation policies, and to the balancing between the overall planning of innovative development and risk prevention. The *Opinions* stressed that rural financial institutions should take inclusive finance as the foundation, try every effort to provide financial services to villages, households and people in poor areas, and strive to make every poor population in need of financial services easily enjoy modern financial services.

The *Opinions* requires that the branches of the PBC should strengthen coordination, cooperation and information sharing with relevant local government departments, timely collect local information such as the development of characteristic industries, infrastructure and basic public services in poor areas, guide financial institutions to carefully sort out the list of financial service demands of targeted projects, and identify the entry point of financial support. All financial institutions should actively connect with the registered poor households, establish specialized service files, accurately connect with the demands in the fields of the development of local characteristic industry, job-hunting and education of the poor, relocating and key projects in poor areas, enhance the development ability of the poor households and support the poor to get rid of poverty. The *Opinions* requires the vigorous promotion of the development of inclusive finance in poor areas, the strengthening of the construction of payment infrastructure in poor areas and the continuous promotion of the application of settlement accounts, payment instruments and payment and clearing networks to explore the sharing of and connection between the basic credit information of farmers and the information of registered poor households, improve the basic database of financial credit information, and explore the establishment of a credit evaluation index system for poor households.

The *Opinions* emphasizes the need to give full play to the main role of various financial institutions in helping to overcome poverty. The CDB and ADBC should speed up the establishment of "financial departments for poverty alleviation". Large and medium-sized commercial banks should stabilize and optimize the setting of grassroots outlets in counties, encourage and support the PSBC to establish a department for poor rural areas, and RCCs, rural commercial banks and rural cooperative banks should continue to play the main role in delivering rural financial services, support the steady and standardized development of farmers' mutual funds in poor areas and carry out pilot credit cooperation of farmers' cooperatives.

The *Opinions* points out that it is necessary to broaden the financing channels of enterprises in poor areas, support securities, futures, insurance and other financial institutions to set up branches in poor areas, encourage and support qualified enterprises in poor areas to raise funds through the main board, growth enterprise market (GEM), national SME share transfer system and regional equity trading market, and issue debt financing instruments such as enterprise bonds, corporate bonds, short-term financing bonds, medium-term notes, project income notes and regional collective SME bonds with credit enhancing by regional government, support poor areas to carry out price insurance for special agricultural products, improve and promote small loan guarantee insurance, and expand the density and depth of agricultural insurance.

The *Opinions* declares to improve the financial support and guarantee measures for targeted poverty alleviation, establish refinancing for poverty alleviation, reduce the interest rate by 1 percentage from the normal agricultural refinancing interest rate, and guide local legal-person financial institutions to increase their support to poor areas, effectively integrate all kinds of fiscal funds related to agriculture, rural areas and farmers and give full play to the role of fiscal policies in supporting and guiding financial resources. Financial institutions should increase support for the issuance of local government bonds in poor areas to replace the stock of debt and steadily resolve the risk of government debt in poor areas. Financial authorities should promote and enforce the credit due diligence exemption system, implement differentiated assessment of non-performing loan ratios according to the specific conditions of loan risk and cost and write-off of financial institutions in poor areas, and appropriately enlarge the tolerance of non-performing loans in poor areas.

The *Opinions* requires that the working mechanism of financial services for poverty alleviation should be continuously improved, to establish and improve the linkage mechanism of financial services for poverty alleviation with the participation of the PBC, China Banking Regulatory Commission (CBRC), the CSRC, China Insurance Regulatory Commission, the Commission of Development and Reform, the Office of Poverty Alleviation, Ministry of Finance, departments and bureaus of finance, and financial institutions, and strengthen policy interaction, work linkage and information sharing, establish and improve the special statistical monitoring system for financial services for poverty alleviation, timely and dynamically track and monitor the work of financial services for poverty alleviation in all localities and financial institutions, actively carry out special evaluation, enrich the application methods of evaluation results, and enhance the implementation effect of financial policies for poverty alleviation.

4. Monetary, Regulatory and Fiscal and Tax Support Policies in Compliance with Financial Poverty Alleviation

In order to accelerate the pace of development in rural areas (especially in the Central and Western Regions), the Chinese government has formulated a series of policies from the aspects of monetary, regulatory, fiscal and taxation policies to encourage financial institutions to increase the supply of rural financial services.

4.1 Monetary Policy

In order to encourage and guide rural financial institutions to allocate more new or revitalized credit resources to the field of "agriculture, rural areas and farmers", the PBC adopted policies such as differentiated deposit reserve ratios, re-lendings and rediscounting for supporting the development of agriculture, rural areas and farmers.

The first policy was differentiated deposit reserve ratios. In 2012, for the commercial banks, rural commercial banks, rural cooperative banks, RCCs and village banks which were legal persons in counties, if they could meet the requirements of prudent operation and give loans to "agriculture, rural areas and farmers" and small and micro enterprises at a certain percentage, the PBC decided to adopt a lower legal deposit reserve ratio. It was reduced again in 2014. For example, for the qualified financial institutions, the permitted deposit reserve ratio was set as 13%, but for other large financial institutions and small and medium-sized financial institutions, the ratio was 20% and 16.5%, respectively.

The second policy was central bank relending for supporting the development of agriculture, rural areas and farmers. This policy was adopted in 1999 to support rural financial institutions to increase the funds to rural areas by the PBC. Initially, the loans were used in RCCs, and then they were expanded to rural commercial banks, rural cooperative banks, RCCs, village banks and other deposit-taking banking financial institutions located in urban districts, counties or towns and townships and villages. The policy requires that during the period of relending, the increment of agricultural loans shall not be less than the total amount of relending, and the weighted average interest rate shall be lower than that of other loans related to supporting the development of the agriculture, rural areas and farmers of the same grade in the same period. In 2014, the PBC required that the proportion of the balance of relending in poor areas should be higher than that in the same period of last year, and the interest rate would be another 1 percentage point lower than the current preferential rate.

The third policy was central bank relending for poverty alleviation. In 2016, PBC offered relending business in 832 contiguous poverty-stricken areas, national key poverty counties and 411 provincial key poverty counties, implementing a more preferential interest rate than relending for supporting the development of agriculture, rural areas and farmers, and required financial institutions to give priority to the use the loans in the registered poor households and business entities that drive up the employment and development of poor households, which include family farms, large professional households, farmers' cooperatives and other economic entities. The loan interest rate issued by local legal-person financial institutions shall not exceed the benchmark rate of one year (including one year) published by PBC. At the end of 2020, the accumulative amount of the central bank relending for poverty alleviation was 668.8 billion yuan, with a balance outstanding of 215.3 billion yuan.

The fourth policy was the rediscounting management policy to guide financial institutions to optimize the credit structure and support credit for supporting the development of agriculture, rural areas and farmers. The PBC requires that all branches give priority to rediscount bills. The proportion of bills relating to the development of agriculture, rural areas and farmers in the balance of rediscounted bills at the end of each quarter in all provinces was higher than 30%. The discounting rate of rediscounted bills should be lower than the weighted average rate of the financial institutions at the same level in the same period so as to reduce rural financing costs.

4.2 Financial Regulatory Policies

In order to increase the supply of rural financial services, the Chinese government made a series of reforms in financial regulatory policies. The first is to moderately liberalize access to rural financial markets. In 2007, CBRC issued *Several Opinions on Adjusting and Relaxing Access Policies for Banking Financial Institutions in Rural Areas to Better Support the Construction of a New Socialist Countryside* and proposed to create three new types of rural financial institutions, namely village banks, loan companies and rural mutual funds. In order to encourage financial institutions to set up village banks in poor areas, in 2009, CBRC issued the *Notice on Overall Work Arrangement of New Rural Financial Institutions from 2009 to 2011*, requiring the main founding banking financial institutions to first consider the establishment of village banks in national poor counties and in the Central and Western Regions and decided to implement the access linkage measures, that is, to give priority to supporting the establishment of village banks in the Western Region. The number of village banks newly established in the Western Region should not be less than that in the Eastern Region. These measures increased rural financial supply and enhanced market competition. The second was to guide the increase of credit for serving the development of agriculture, rural areas and farmers, encourage the innovation of financial products for serving the development of agriculture, rural areas and farmers and set up institutional outlets in weak areas, and actively open up green channels for access. The third was to modify the calculation method of the loan-to-deposit ratio. With the new calculation method, the relending for supporting the development of agriculture, rural areas and farmers and the special financial bonds for supporting the development of agriculture, rural areas and farmers were deducted from the numerator in the calculation, and implement the assessment of flexible loan-to-deposit ratios and differential deposit deviation for rural grassroots financial institutions such as RCC institutions and village banks. Other regulatory policies also included reducing the risk weight of farmers' loans, enlarging the tolerance of non-performing loans among loans for serving the development of agriculture, rural areas and farmers, and so on.

4.3 Fiscal and Tax Policies

The main purpose of fiscal and tax policies is to encourage and support financial institutions to increase the supply of services in poor areas and for poor households.

The first policy was the targeted subsidy, which encourages financial institutions to solve the problem of weak and "blank" rural basic financial services in remote villages (towns or townships) in Western China. Since 2008, the central government has given subsidies of 2% of the average loan balance of the current year to three types of new rural financial institutions qualified: village banks, loan companies and rural mutual funds. In 2010, the central government also gave subsidies to the banking institution outlets of 2,255 villages and towns in 12 western provinces (regions) which had weak basic financial services.

The second policy was the incremental incentive to encourage financial institutions in counties or county-level cities to increase loans serving the development of agriculture, rural areas and farmers. Since 2008, the central government has given a 2% reward to the county financial institutions qualified in the pilot areas for the increase of the average balance of loans serving the development of agriculture, rural areas and farmers in the current year exceeding 15%, and the reward funds were given jointly by the central and local governments according to the specified proportion. In 2016, the Ministry of Finance formulated the *Measures of Special Funds for Inclusive Financial Development*, which included the targeted subsidies and incremental incentives for inclusive financial development as specialized loans, and further clarified and improved the rules of these two policies.

The third policy was the agricultural insurance premium subsidy. In order to enhance the ability to resist disasters, solve the "worries" of rural financial development, and transform the agricultural disaster prevention and relief methods from "government relief" and "post-disaster relief" to "insurance claim settlement" and "disaster prevention in advance", since 2007, the Chinese central government has implemented a policy for subsidizing agricultural insurance premium to promote agricultural insurance (for farmers and large-scale agricultural production and business entities) on the basis of voluntary participation of farmers and local governments, and provide certain premium subsidies, and the subsidized insurance types were gradually increased to 15 varieties in three categories: planting, breeding and forestry, basically covering major agricultural products relevant to the national economy, the people's livelihood and food security, and encourage local governments to carry out insurance types for local special agricultural products.

The fourth policy was preferential tax. In view of the high cost and high risk of agricultural loans and the difficulty of access of low-income farmers to loans, in 2010, the Ministry of Finance and the State Administration of Taxation decided to exempt the interest income of small loans from business tax for farmers with less than 50,000 yuan from financial institutions from January 1, 2009 to December 31, 2013 and included 90% of the total income in the calculation of taxable income. For the premium income obtained from planting and aquaculture, the income shall be reduced by 90% when calculating the taxable income. When calculating the taxable income, 90% of the interest income obtained from the Farmers' Self-service Cooperatives (centers) organized by Zhonghe Rural Credit Project Management Co., Ltd. and the CFPA was included in the total income. In 2014, the State Council also decided to extend this policy until the end of 2016, impose a reduced tax rate of 3% on the financial and insurance income, and increase the limit of small loans for farmers enjoying tax preference from 50,000 yuan to 100,000 yuan. Business tax was to be levied at a reduced rate of 3% on rural cooperative financial institutions and new types of rural financial institutions in the counties. In 2017, the *Notice on the Continuation of Tax Policies Related to Supporting Rural Financial Development* jointly issued by the Ministry of Finance and the State Administration of Taxation provided that from January 1, 2017 to December 31, 2019, the interest income from small loans of rural financial institutions for farmers in less than 100,000 yuan shall be exempted from value-added tax, and 90% shall be included in the total income when calculating the taxable income. For the premium income obtained from planting and aquaculture, 90% shall be included in the total income when calculating the taxable income.

5. Progress and Effectiveness of Finance for Poverty Alleviation

Financial institutions integrated poverty alleviation into supporting local economic and social development in poor areas, especially industrial development. Financial institutions that participated in poverty alleviation included not only the above-mentioned commercial banks and RCC institutions but also the PBC, development and policy-oriented banks and insurance companies.

5.1 Government-led Subsidized Loans

The central government-led subsidized loans played a great role in the process of poverty alleviation, but there were many problems.

5.1.1 Subsidized Loans were an Important Source of Funds for Poverty Alleviation

From 1986 to 2013, China issued a total of 471.767 billion yuan of specialized loans for poverty alleviation (see Table 7.1), with an average of 16.849 billion yuan per year. From the time series of poverty alleviation loans and specialized fiscal funds for poverty alleviation, there were several characteristics:

TABLE 7.1 Amounts of loans for poverty alleviation and specialized fiscal funds for poverty alleviation (Years 1986–2013) Unit: 100 million

Year	Loans for poverty alleviation (1)	Specialized fiscal funds for poverty alleviation (2)
1986	23.00	19.00
1987	23.00	19.00
1988	30.50	10.00
1989	30.50	11.00
1990	30.50	16.00
1991	35.50	28.00
1992	41.00	26.60
1993	35.00	41.20
1994	45.50	52.35
1995	45.50	53.00
1996	55.00	53.00
1997	85.00	68.15
1998	100.00	73.15
1999	150.00	78.15
2000	150.00	88.15
2001	185.00	100.02
2002	185.00	106.02
2003	185.00	114.02

(*Continued*)

TABLE 7.1 (Continued)

Year	Loans for poverty alleviation (1)	Specialized fiscal funds for poverty alleviation (2)
2004	185.00	122.01
2005	90.00	129.93
2006	141.61	137.01
2007	124.48	144.04
2008	214.32	167.34
2009	259.96	197.30
2010	436.30	222.68
2011	453.90	272.00
2012	538.00	332.05
2013	839.10	394.00

Source: Editorial Board of the State Council Office of the Leadership Group for Poverty Alleviation and Development. *Yearbook of Poverty Alleviation and Development in China 2014*. Beijing: Solidarity Press, 2016.

First, specialized loans were a very long-term and important tool for poverty alleviation, which could be seen from the proportion of the loans in the funds of poverty alleviation. In the 28 years from 1986 to 2013, there were only five years in which the annual release of loans was less than the specialized fiscal funds. It even reached 3.05 times that of the latter in 1988 and 2.13 times that of the latter in 2013 (see Table 7.1).

5.1.2 The Fiscal Subsidies Played a Good Leverage Role

From 2001 to 2013, the central government gave an accumulated subsidy of 7.105 billion yuan to specialized loans. As can be seen from Table 7.1, the corresponding amount of the loans during this period was 383.767 billion yuan, with a magnitude of mobilizing a total amount of loans which was 54.01 times that of the fiscal subsidy, which showed that the leverage ratio was very high. To some extent, the subsidized loans mitigated the trend of accelerated capital outflow from poor areas.

5.1.3 Hard to Aim at the Target

We should first be clear about the goal of the loan of poverty alleviation and then investigate whether the distribution and use of loans were consistent with the goal. Normally, specialized loans worked in two ways, i.e., the direct and indirect way, which raised a lot of disputes in the assessment of how far the loans aimed at the target. The direct way was reflected by that the loans were issued to the poor households directly, while the indirect way was reflected that the benefits of loans reached poor households. Sometimes, it is complicated to judge whether the distribution and use of loans deviated from the goal. Compared with loans issued to households directly, the evaluation of loan benefits to households is more difficult in terms of methods and data. The policy adjustment from loan issuance to households to that to economic entities in the late 1980s was mainly based on the assumption of the superiority of giving loans' benefits to poor households.

The research about the target has been focused on loans to households. There are two questions to be investigated: first, whether there was a problem of "lending to the rich instead of the poor"; and second, whether there was an overflow of loans. Some scholars found that comparing the proportion of loans received by different income groups with that of the population in 2004, the loaning in that year embodied an obvious inclination to more care to low-income farmers; that means there was no problem with "lending to the rich rather than to the poor". However, by making use of the flexibility of policies and the difficulty in defining poor and low-income households in its actual work, the ABC offered more loans to low-income and middle-income farmers, among which 1/3 were given to the low-income and 2/3 to the middle-income group who was beyond the targeted groups defined by the *Outline for Rural Poverty Alleviation and Development*. The overflow of loans is mainly concentrated in middle-income farmers in poor counties.

5.1.4 Fiscal Subsidy Had Some Negative Impacts

Subsidized loans distorted the allocation of rural financial resources, hindered the development of the rural financial market, and were not conducive to the continuous alleviation of poverty and the establishment of normal financial market order in poor areas. Moreover, because of the unsustainability of subsidies, any kind of subsidized loans can't become a sustainable way to solve the problem of the shortage of funds for the poor.

5.2 Microfinance of Non-governmental Organizations

5.2.1 It Eased the Rural Credit Constraints and Improved the Fairness of Credit Distribution

The central idea of microfinance of non-governmental organizations is to directly solve the problem of financial difficulties of the poor in production and life, help the poor generate income and get rid of poverty. In the absence of credit services from formal financial institutions, microfinance of non-governmental organizations has become the most important source of farmers' productive loans, alleviated the constraints of productive loans in the rural credit market, helped to improve the inefficient operation of the rural credit market, improved farmers' initial resource endowment or production opportunities, and has the potential to increase farmers' income. Microfinance of non-governmental organizations can reduce the Gini coefficient of credit by 5 ~ 8 percentage points and improve the unequal distribution of credit among farmers.

5.2.2 The Related Non-Financial Services Improved the Self-development Ability of the Poor

The non-governmental microfinance not only provides microfinance services for developing family production to low-income farmers but also provides other non-financial services to improve the development capacity of the poor, such as skill training, cultural education, financial training, capacity-building of community organizations, and some charity relief activities for poverty alleviation.

5.2.3 Some Public-interest Microfinance Institutions Achieved Sustainable and Long-term Development Ability

The development problems for public-interest microfinance are not only achieving the goal of poverty alleviation but also enabling its own sustainable development. Some microfinance projects in China have gradually achieved these goals through institutionalization and specialization. Since 1993, the Rural Development Institute of the Chinese Academy of Social Sciences successively introduced the microfinance model of Grameen Bank (GB Model) in Hebei, Henan and Shaanxi provinces, established poverty alleviation economic cooperatives with a status of juridical associations, carried out experiments and achieved a series of successes. At the same time, the microfinance projects cooperated by the CICETE and UNDP have also been transformed into special microfinance institutions with the status of juridical associations, which operate independently. Depending on its local microfinance projects, the CFPA established a private non-enterprise legal person entity, which is named Farmers' Independent Service (FIS). On the basis of the FIS, Chongho Bridge

Management Limited (named "Chongho Bridge") was established in 2008, which is a professional public-interest microfinance institution with the widest coverage, the largest number of customers and the largest scale in China. By the end of 2017, Chongho Bridge had covered 280 counties in 21 provinces (autonomous regions and cities) in China, most of which were national and provincial poor counties, with 381,929 effective customers, of which farmers accounted for 92.70% and female customers accounted for 82.90%. The cumulative loans were 27.843 billion yuan with more than 2 million accounts, the loan balance was more than 5.9 million yuan, and the average household loan balance was 15,555 yuan.

5.2.4 Difficulties for Public-interest Microfinance

First of all, public-interest microfinance lacks the legal status of financial institutions. Even Chongho Bridge, with such a wide range of services, did not get a license of finance. Without legal status, these institutions had few financing channels and could only mainly rely on donated funds. However, the limited donations make it difficult for institutions to expand the market, enlarge the service scale and improve their capacity. In this case, it is also difficult for these institutions to recruit high-level professionals. All these have limited their sustainability and their ability to boost poverty alleviation.

The reason for the development of public-interest microfinance in favor of becoming a financial institution is that one can expect institutional sustainability from it as a financial institution, and with such a financial institution, one can expect the sustainability of the outcome from poverty elimination which can be realized only through long-term intervention by some institutions as such. However, for the development of institutions themselves, there is need for continuous improvement and a rise in employee welfare. Therefore, the goal of institutionalized microfinance all over the world deviates to varying degrees; that is, they seldom or rarely service the poorest identified at the initial stage. China is no exception. Studies have shown that if microfinance still tries to target the poorest, special targeting tools should be needed and corresponding costs should be paid.

5.3 Rural Mutual Funds in Poor Villages

With the help of the platform of mutual funds in poor villages, the fiscal funds for poverty alleviation can be used according to the real demands of farmers in poor communities and can be used on a rolling basis, while its value should be maintained and increased. It is an innovation of the existing institutional arrangements and helped to establish a decision-making mechanism guided by the demand of poor farmers, which matches the government supply with the demand of poor farmers. This "hematopoietic" method not only makes the funds reach the targeted groups but also improves these groups' self-organizing and self-developing abilities. At the same time, the feature of internal information symmetry in mutual funds is helpful in reducing the transaction cost and risk of loan management, improve the repayment rate and further improve the efficiency and sustainability of the use of government funds.

According to the related statistics of the LGOP, by the end of 2013, the pilot of mutual funds had been carried out in 19,397 poor villages in 1,407 counties of 28 provinces (autonomous regions and municipalities directly under the central government) in China, with a total scale of 4.517 billion yuan, including 1.154 billion yuan from the central government, 2.279 billion yuan of provincial special funds, and 1.15 billion yuan of mutual funds and other funds invested by farmers. One-million nine-hundred-fourteen-thousand six-hundred farmers joined the mutual funds, accounting for 30.72% of the total number of households in the pilot villages, and 988,800 poor households entered the mutual funds, accounting for 41.2% of the poor households. A total of 8.873 billion yuan of loans were issued, including 4.819 billion yuan to poor households, accounting for 54.31%

of the total loans. The accumulated number of loans reached 2.4 million person-times, including 1.1624 million person-times relating to borrowings by poor households, accounting for 56.85%. The accumulated income of fund occupancy fees was 535 million yuan. Accumulated repayment was 6.905 billion yuan. The accumulated number of overdue loans was 37,651, with an accumulated overdue amount of 217 million yuan, and the overdue rate was 2.45%. The accumulated loss is 25.22 million yuan.

Since 2014, there have been three changes in the development of village mutual funds in poor villages. First, with economic development, the demand for capital scale has increased as a whole. The original loan ceiling of 3,000–5,000 yuan can no longer meet the needs of the development and production of poor villages. Second, the function of mutual funds changed. These funds were used as a guarantee for the loans from banks, where the leverage rate is 10. In this way, a village can have a credit line of 3–5 million yuan one year, which can meet the capital demand for industrial development in the village. Third, some funds can't go on. Their management ability was a problem, but some mutual funds were occupied by strong groups such as village cadres, in which case, these funds were generally stopped by the local government and then directly put to use for public welfare undertakings in the village, such as building roads or squares.

5.4 New Mechanism of Policy-Oriented Banks

China's policy-oriented financial institutions include the CDB and ADBC. There were three fields in which the CDB does poverty alleviation: First, it deepened cooperation with the related bureaus in strengthening the construction of joint poverty alleviation mechanisms. For example, it signed an agreement for development finance cooperation with the LGOP to jointly explore models for targeted poverty alleviation, such as supporting poor villages to develop characteristic industries. Second, it helped poor areas scientifically formulate development plans, for example, formulate plans and provide advisory services in the development of characteristic industries and the financing mechanism of infrastructure construction. Third, it increased support for key areas; for example, it increased credit support for the relocation of the poor, the urban-rural integration, shantytowns transformation, new countryside construction and development of characteristic industries, as well as infrastructure construction such as rural roads, safe drinking water, rural power grid and reconstruction of dilapidated houses. It also innovated the "four platforms and one association" model,[1] gave full play to the leverage of financial funds and the wholesale financing advantages of the CDB, provided financing services for poor farmers to develop production, and supported poor villages and farmers to develop characteristic industries. In addition, the CDB also launched education loans and provided loans to four designated counties in Guizhou. In 2016, the CDB set up a special division of poverty alleviation. In accordance with the idea of supporting the "relocation projects in cooperation with provincial governments, infrastructure projects in cooperation with county governments, industrial development projects in villages (and households), and education assistance projects targeting at households (and indivdiuals)", the CDB continued to strengthen its development financing and consultancy for poverty alleviation.

By the end of 2015, the CDB had granted 87.9 billion yuan of student loans to college students from poor areas, benefiting 15.24 million students from poor families in 2003 counties, and 27 billion yuan of loans to support the construction of campus safety projects in poor areas such as Qinghai, Shanxi and Inner Mongolia. The loans have covered 832 national poor counties and 727 counties in a concentrated cluster of extremely poor counties, with a total of 156 million yuan of loans.

In April 2016, ADBC was the first bank among all financial institutions to set up a special division for poverty alleviation with offices in 22 provincial-level branches. Its secondary branches, which had the task of poverty alleviation, added a plate of poverty alleviation in their customer department.

In 832 national poverty-stricken counties where there was a branch of the ADBC, it added a plate of "Poverty Alleviation Department of the ADBC in XX County (city)" for the counties with no branches, a specialist of the ADBC will be stationed. With the above steps, the service of the ADBC to poverty alleviation covered all the poor counties in the country. In addition, the ADBC gave credit support to 537 national poverty-stricken counties. At the end of 2015, 412 loan projects for relocation from other places were implemented, with an amount of 270 billion yuan, the average lending rate decreased by 15.7%, and the average loan term was 21 years, benefiting 5.18 million relocated people, of which 62.7% were registered poor households. The ADBC formulated corresponding financial products and service models according to the industrial characteristics, resource endowment and economic and social development trends in different counties. It also formulated a five-year policy-oriented financial plan, took the lead in successfully issuing special financial bonds and ordinary bonds in the inter-bank bond market, and created financial experimental demonstration areas in provinces with heavy poverty alleviation tasks. By the end of 2016, the loan balance of the ADBC in 839 poor counties reached 792.875 billion yuan.

5.5 Innovation in Financial Mechanism and Products of Other Commercial Banks

Including the ABC and RCC institutions (including rural commercial banks, rural cooperative banks and RCCs), as a whole, commercial banks are the largest investors in rural areas and even poor areas. Since 2011, the ABC has formulated policies and working systems for poverty alleviation, established a leading group for centralized financial services in contiguous poverty-stricken areas at the head office, signed a "financial poverty alleviation cooperation agreement" with the LGOP, and formulated comprehensive financial service plans and plans for leading industries in 14 areas. The ABC's lending traditionally focused on infrastructure construction and industries. By the beginning of 2016, the ABC had invested a total of 378.34 billion yuan in loans to support infrastructure construction, such as transportation and water conservancy in poor areas, and 133.19 billion yuan in loans to support thousands of leading enterprises in agricultural industrialization. In addition, the ABC also innovated financial products and services and granted credit loans of 37.6 billion yuan to farmers and herdsmen in Tibet, covering more than 90% of farmers and herdsmen in the region. A total of 640 million yuan of loans was granted for ecological resettlement projects in Guizhou, supporting the construction of 10,781 resettlement houses, benefiting 45,000 people. In Gansu province, a total of 15.29 billion yuan of loans were granted to farmers in the mode of "government policy-oriented guarantee companies + farmers", supporting 226,000 farmers. In Inner Mongolia, in the mode of "government risk compensation fund + farmers", a total of 6.31 billion yuan of loans were granted to support 112,000 farmers and 94 enterprises.

RCC institutions are the main force in China's rural financial market, and their credit services are an important force for poverty alleviation. In addition to cooperating with the government in issuing subsidized loans, the role of RCCs is mainly to issue loans serving the development of agriculture, rural areas and farmers. By the end of 2016, the balance of such loans and farmers' loans of RCC institutions were 8.19 trillion yuan and 3.96 trillion yuan, respectively, accounting for 55.93% and 29% of the balance of loans serving the development of agriculture, rural areas, farmers and farmers' loans of all financial institutions in China, respectively. The RCC institutions have also created many financial models according to local characteristics. For example, RCC institutions in Sichuan province launched the "financing new agricultural business entity + poor households" model, and RCC institutions in Jingyuan of Ningxia Hui Autonomous Region established the financial model of "funds follow the poor, the poor follow the capable people, the capable people follow the industries, and the industries follow the market", using bank loans to develop industrial projects that can increase the income of poor households, such as planting, breeding and processing.

In addition, other commercial banks in China participated in poverty alleviation in various forms. Through new countryside construction loans, urbanization loans and PPP model series loans, the China Construction Bank (CCB) has increased financial service support for the construction of infrastructure and public service facilities in poor areas. Baotou Commercial Bank explored a new model of "internet + poverty alleviation" and tried it out in Poyang County, the designated poverty alleviation County in Jiangxi province. Offline, the model relies on the volunteer post stations co-established with Youcheng Foundation, and the volunteers collect the information on loan demands of local farmers of Poyang, then online, relying on the original bank platform of the bank to raise funds from the society to meet the loan demands. From March 2014 to August 2015, this project raised a total of 12.896 million yuan through the internet platform, which offered 171 loans to farmers and agricultural cooperatives.

5.6 Innovation of Insurance Products for Poverty Alleviation

The specific products provided by the insurance industry for poverty alleviation are mainly medical insurance, agricultural insurance and credit guarantee insurance. Poverty or returning to poverty caused by illness is an important factor for trapping people in poverty. In China, triple medical securities have generally been carried out: basic medical insurance, serious illness insurance and medical assistance, with which premiums are reduced, coverage is increased, and the poverty incidence caused by illness is reduced. In 2016, the national serious illness insurance covered 920 million urban and rural residents. More than 7 million people have benefited directly, and the actual overall reimbursement proportion of medical expenses of seriously ill patients reached 70%. Agricultural insurance has played a certain role in reducing the losses of the planting and breeding industry caused by natural disasters. For example, in 2015, Liaoning province suffered a severe drought, agricultural insurance was paid 1.5 billion yuan, and there was no need for the local government to allocate any more disaster relief funds. Small loan guarantee insurance, borrower accident insurance and insurance policy pledge have played a certain role in credit enhancement for loans for the poor, driving the bank's loan issuance to poor households. At present, 25 provinces (cities) and 73 prefectures (cities) have carried out pilot microloan insurance in China. For example, the government of Jingning County, Zhejiang province used the special fund to uniformly purchase microloan guarantee insurance for low-income farmers and subsidized all loans, and banking institutions issued interest-free and guaranteed free loans against insurance policies.

5.7 Role of Capital Market for Poverty Alleviation

The *Opinions on Giving Full Play to the Role of the Capital Market and Serving the National Poverty Alleviation Strategy* issued by the CSRC in 2016 brought great convenience to the listing and financing of enterprises in poor areas. In 2016, it took an average of 799.956 days, or about 2.2 years, for Chinese enterprises to be listed successfully, from the acceptance of the IPO application to the completion of listing and issuance, and the time in 2017 was about 2.1 years. Two enterprises from Tibet took only 9.8 months and 11.2 months, respectively, from application to listing, which was lower than the average level. At the same time, this policy is also conducive to attracting foreign enterprises to invest in poor counties for listing and financing and is good for driving the rapid growth of tax revenue in poor counties.

Till March 2018, 12 enterprises in poor counties had been listed through the green channel, raising more than 3 billion yuan, another 63 enterprises had started listing, and 82 companies were listed on the new third board. On December 22, 2017, apple futures contract was officially listed and traded in Zhengzhou Commodity Exchange, which is the world's first fresh fruit futures variety.

After its launch, the apple futures can form an open and transparent market price, prevent farmers from reluctant selling or dumping, and form product standards. Quality deciding prices can improve the quality of agricultural products and promote industrial development.

5.8 Role of Rural Internet Finance

Internet finance, or FinTech, is a new form of China's rural financial policy tool for poverty alleviation. At present, it has made rapid progress and is on the ascendant. As early as 2009, Yixin Company established the "Yinongdai" p2p platform to raise low-cost funds from cities and provide them to public-interest microfinance organizations in poor areas to support the poor. By the end of 2016, it had subsidized 21,587 farmers and provided credit funds of nearly 230 million yuan, guiding the return of urban funds to poor rural areas. In 2015, the Ant Financial Group, a FinTech platform company which has close relationships with Alibaba, established a rural payment, insurance and loan platform. In 2016, Ant Financial established a rural finance division, which is responsible for rural payment, insurance, financing, wealth management, credit investigation and other businesses, injected capital into Chongho Bridge, provided digital technology services, and carried out business through it. In 2015, Jingdong Finance released a rural finance strategy to provide financial services for the whole rural industrial chains and the whole product chain and developed consumer credit, production credit, wealth management and crowdfunding products for the rural market. The Jingdong Finance has established comprehensive service stations in poor counties, townships and villages, integrating financial services, information services, e-commerce services, business supermarket services, logistics services and other functions. As of August 2016, the Jingdong Finance has built more than 1,500 county-level service centers and more than 1,500 service stores and recruited 270,000 rural market promoters, covering 270,000 administrative villages. On the one hand, the Jingdong Finance provides consumer credit services to farmers, with a cumulative transaction volume of more than 500 million yuan; on the other hand, it has provided loan services for the majority of planting and breeding farmers, with a cumulative loan amount of 345 million yuan. Other e-commerce enterprises also tried to explore the rural financial market.

5.9 Stimulation by the Monetary and Regulatory Policies

In terms of monetary policy, by the end of 2013, the PBC had issued relending and rediscount limits of 61.27 billion yuan and 3.03 billion yuan to 832 poor counties, with a year-on-year increase of 23.8% and 20%, of which the refinancing balance was 55.18 billion yuan, a year-on-year increase of 36.7%, 14.3 percentage points higher than the national average rate. On the basis of relending for agriculture, in 2016, the Chinese government launched relending for poverty alleviation, implemented more preferential interest rates than the former one, and focused on supporting characteristic industries in poor areas and the employment and business startups of the poor. At the end of 2016, the balance of relending reached 112.7 billion yuan.

In terms of regulatory policies, in order to guide the banking financial institutions which were the main founders of village banks to found village banks in underdeveloped areas, the CBRC has implemented policies such as "linking East and West, linking urban and rural areas, linking development with underdevelopment", "one village bank runs in more counties" and "prefecture-level village banks with head office and branches in underdeveloped areas such as old, minority people-concentrated, border and poor areas". These policies aimed at expanding the coverage of village banks in underdeveloped areas. As a new type of rural financial institution, the coverage of village banks has continually expanded, under which, by the end of 2016, 1,519 village banks were established, with an asset scale of 1.24 trillion yuan, with the balance of farmers' loans and loans serving the development of agriculture, rural areas and farmers 323.4 billion yuan and 555 billion yuan respectively, covering 1,259 counties of which 64.5% were located in the central and western regions, A total of 401 village and town banks were located in key counties and counties concentrated in contiguous areas with special difficulties, forming a supplement to the rural financial market in poor areas.

In addition, the CBRC has also implemented the policy of linking urban and rural financial service outlets, appropriate lending access standards for outlets in poor areas, established green access channels and shortened the approval time. By the end of 2015, 5,185 county-level banking financial institutions and 43,598 service outlets had been established in poor areas, with a total of 1,203,000 self-service devices, including 59,207 ATMs and 838,000 POS machines.

6. Summary

Financial policy is an important part of economic policy, and the change of the economic system determines the change of the financial system. Over the past 40 years of reform and development, the role of finance in helping the poor has been paid more and more attention and is playing a more and more important role. This trend is consistent with China's transformation from a planned to a market economic system. It is an important support for China's development-oriented poverty alleviation strategy and the result of China's financial system reform.

The policies and methods of finance for poverty alleviation continue to develop with China's economic development and poverty alleviation practice. The Chinese government not only did work on tackling the problems with the financing of poor families but also emphasized on giving the full play of the driving role of industrial and regional economic development. Not only the improvement of material conditions but also the improvement of institutional development policies conducive to the poor was focused. More emphasis was made not only on eliminating the causes that directly lead to poverty but also on counteracting the negative impact of environmental factors and basic conditions. There needs not only specific and direct intervention to poverty problems but also the construction of a complete, systematic and comprehensive inclusive financial system.

6.1 Experiences

In more than 40 years of poverty reduction and development, generally speaking, China has made great achievements in poverty alleviation through finance. The following are the basic experiences.

6.1.1 The Leading and Dominant Roles of the Government are Essential

Theoretically speaking, finance is a market-oriented behavior, but when it works for poverty alleviation, the government can provide an enabling environment and work with financial institutions in accordance with the principle of subsidiarity. First, the government should formulate clear and feasible strategic objectives and clearly describe the status, role and operation roadmap of finance in them. Secondly, a supporting and coordinated policy system should be formulated, in which all financial resources should be like a combined fist with a joint force, and there should be an effective incentive and restraint mechanism to create good conditions and atmosphere for financial institutions to participate in poverty alleviation. As a result, the various fiscal, taxation, monetary and regulatory policies and measures adopted by the Chinese government have effectively mobilized and guided financial institutions to carry out various poverty alleviation actions. Third, China's political and institutional advantages have played a protective role in the implementation of the poverty alleviation policy.

6.1.2 Good Understanding of the Relationship between Commercial Interests and Social Responsibilities by Financial Institutions is Important

Commercial financial institutions should not only serve the interests of shareholders but also serve the interests of society. They should not only operate their businesses well but also establish a correct concept of the relationship between justice and self-interest and do business in consideration of the national strategy and the overall situation of social development, balance the relationship between the pursuit of commercial interests and the performance of social responsibilities, give consideration to the principles of social benefits and commercial sustainability. In order to increase investment in poor areas, they should implement a preferential credit policy for poor areas in terms of internal authorization, performance appraisal and resource allocation.

6.1.3 Subjective Initiatives of the Poor is the Basis of Finance to Play its Role

Support by the finance institutions is different from fiscal capital, as the former emphasizes "borrow and repay". This principle is consistent with that of China's development-oriented poverty alleviation. Therefore, the basic requirement of finance is that borrowers have the possibility and ability of repayment and the willingness to develop, repay and enhance their income-generating capacity and repayment ability in the process of development; that means some poor people are suitable for it. Those who have no productive capacity, rely on relief to make a living or lack the willingness to repay are not suitable to be supported by financial measures.

6.1.4 Supporting the Poor by Finance is a Systematical and Cooperative Project

The policies of financial support for poverty alleviation were adjusted according to the deeper understanding of poverty: from giving direct financial assistance to the poor to financing industrial poverty alleviation in poor areas, then to financing infrastructure construction and relocation of the poor, from issuing loans to developing insurance and capital market support, from the innovation of credit products and service mechanism to the construction of an inclusive financial system. In this process, financial policies and measures have been gradually improved with the result of a comprehensive system of financial poverty alleviation policies, a system of poverty alleviation organizations, and a system of financial products and services for poverty alleviation. Financial institutions and local governments, enterprises and poor people have jointly created diverse financial poverty alleviation models, creating good conditions for finance to play a good role in poverty alleviation.

6.2 Outlook for the Future

After winning the battle against poverty in 2020 and eliminating absolute poverty, China's relative poverty will still exist for a long time. The task of solving unbalanced and insufficient development is still arduous, and it is still inseparable from the comprehensive and in-depth participation of finance so as to achieve rural revitalization and the common prosperity of all people. Therefore, China still needs to focus on the following four aspects.

First of all, we need to establish and improve the rural inclusive financial system; promote the combination of sound development of policy-oriented finance, commercial finance, cooperative finance and informal finance; give full play to the advantages of various financial institutions; innovate financial service institutions, products, tools and technologies conducive to poverty reduction based on the principles of capital security, controllable risk and social responsibility; and improve the availability of financial services in poor areas and poor people. We will increase the intensity and depth of financial poverty alleviation and form a financial service system that continues to support poverty reduction.

Second, we need to continue to strengthen the construction of payment infrastructure in poor areas and promote the application of settlement accounts, payment instruments and payment and clearing networks; consolidate and expand the coverage of agricultural withdrawal services in poor rural areas; and encourage the exploration of new electronic payment methods such as mobile payment and Internet payment to develop the payment service market in poor areas.

At the same time, we need to strengthen the construction of credit systems in poor areas, improve the basic database of financial credit information, and explore the establishment of a credit evaluation index system for poor households, so as to create a good social credit environment for financial poverty alleviation.

Third, we need to improve the financial risk dispersion mechanism in poor areas and better mobilize the enthusiasm of financial institutions to participate in supporting poverty alleviation and development. First, we should give full play to the positive role of the deposit insurance system, maintain financial stability in poor areas and protect the rights and interests of depositors in poor areas; Second, we should improve the rural credit guarantee system; Third, insurance companies should innovate targeted poverty alleviation insurance products and services, continuously expand the density and depth of agricultural insurance, support the development of characteristic agricultural product insurance in poor areas by means of fiscal awards instead of subsidies, improve and promote microfinance guarantee insurance, and provide credit enhancement support for the financing of poor households; Fourth, the government should optimize the financial ecological environment in poor areas, change the concept of financial development, reduce intervention in financial micro activities, respect the operational autonomy of financial institutions, strengthen the construction of local social credit system, safeguard judicial justice, severely crack down on debt evasion and abolition, and protect the legitimate rights and interests of creditors.

Fourth, in response to the rapid development and wide application of FinTech technology, we should actively explore solutions for financial poverty alleviation. Therefore, we need to pay attention to and support all kinds of FinTech enterprises to carry out rural financial business, strive to achieve "corner overtaking" and solve the problem of lack of financial services in poor areas.

Note

1 "Four platforms" means: taking the local government's state-owned asset operating companies as the financing platform, the guarantee companies as the guarantee platform, and the financial office as the management platform, and disclosing loan information through the social publicity platform. "One association" means creating a credit promotion association to enhance the credit of borrowers.

Reference

Editorial Board of the State Council Office of the Leadership Group for Poverty Alleviation and Development. 2016. *Yearbook of Poverty Alleviation and Development in China 2014*. Beijing: Solidarity Press.

INDEX

Note: Numbers in **bold** indicate a table. Numbers in *italics* indicate a figure on the corresponding page.

ABC *see* Agricultural Bank of China
Adams, D., and Fitchett, D. 5
ADB *see* Agricultural Development Bank
ADBC *see* Agricultural Development Bank of China
Agricultural Bank of China (ABC) 6;
   commercialization and restructuring of 28, 30;
   deficiencies of 27; establishment and cancellation
   of 23–24; Financial Division for Serving the
   Agriculture, Rural Areas and Farmers 39,
   40; "financial poverty alleviation cooperation
   agreement" with the LGOP signed by 128;
   Fourth National Branch Governors' Meeting
   of 61; *Interim Measures for the Administration of
   Specialized Interest-Subsidized Loans in Poor Areas*
   36, 111–112; loans by 114, 118, 124, 128; new
   financial institutions to complement/compete
   with 15; partial withdrawal from counties by
   28; poverty alleviation efforts by 114, 118, 128;
   *Requirements of the Overall Implementation Plan for
   the Joint-stock Reform of the ABC* 37; restoration/
   recovery of 25; restructuring of 31, 34; Rural
   Credit Cooperatives compared to 6, 14; Rural
   Credit Cooperatives managed by 26, 83n2; Rural
   Credit Cooperatives separated from xiii, 28–29,
   83n2; PBC, separation from followed by and
   merger into 23; shareholding system for 33; size
   and performance in rural financial sector of China
   12, **12**; Subsidized Loans 36, 111–112; withdrawal
   from county-level jurisdictions 14
Agricultural Development Bank (ADB) 37
Agricultural Development Bank of China (ADBC)
   29–31, 36, 111; "Financial Department for
   Poverty Alleviation" 118–119, 127; "Poverty
   Alleviation Department of the ADBC in XX
   County (city)" 128
AHP *see* Analytic Hierarchy Process (AHP)
   construction method

Alibaba 130
Alipay **89**, 91, **93**
Analytic Hierarchy Process (AHP) weight
   construction method 92, **93–94**
Ant Group xv, 48, 79, 88; rural finance division 130
Ants Credit Pay 48

Bank of China (BOC) 37; *see also* People's Bank of
   China (PBC)
Baotou Commercial Bank 129
BOC *see* Bank of China
Bodie, Z. 57

capital market for poverty alleviation 35, 129–130;
   green channels for 39
CBIRC *see* Banking and Insurance Regulatory
   Commission
CBRC *see* China Banking Regulatory Commission
CCB *see* China Construction Bank
CCCPC *see* Central Committee of the Communist
   Party of China
CDB *see* China Development Bank
Central Bank of China 57, 83
Central Committee of the Communist Party of
   China (CCCPC): *Decision of the CPC Central
   Committee on Several Major Issues in Agriculture
   and Rural Work* 113; *Decision of the CPC Central
   Committee and the State Council on Further
   Strengthening Poverty Alleviation and Development*
   113; *Decision on Winning the Battle against Poverty*
   118; No. 1 Document of the CCCCPC 26, 31,
   33, 37; *Outline of China's Rural Poverty Alleviation*
   112; *Proposal on Formulating the 13th Five- year-plan
   for National Economic and Social Development* 118;
   "Several Opinions by the CCCPC and State
   Council on Implementing New Development
   Concepts to Accelerate Modernization" 72;

"Strategic Plan for Rural Revitalization" 85;
Third Plenary Session of the CCCPC xiv, 35, 117
CFPA *see* China Foundation for Poverty Alleviation
China: "Big Four" banks 12; financial institutions in
rural China **5**; financial pluralization needed in 15;
four macroregions of 98–99; inclusive financial
system developed by 38; "Targeted Poverty
Reduction and Alleviation" stage in 114; *Report
of 19th National Congress of the Communist Party
of China* 35; Seven Year Priority 114; specialized
banking system, establishment of 25–27; state
banking institutions, formation of 23–25; top 100
counties, median scores of 101, **102–103**; *see also*
Communist Party of China; People's Republic
of China
China Bank and Insurance Regulatory Commission
(CBIRC) xviii, 5; "Guiding Opinions on
Financial Services for Rural Revitalization", 85,
120; "Interim Measures for Risk Classification
of Financial Assets of Commercial Banks"
80; "Notice on Further Strengthening the
Monitoring, Prevention and Control of Large
Risk of Small and Medium-sized Rural Financial
Institutions" 80; "Notice on Regulating Informal
Lending Activities and Maintaining Economic
and Financial Order" 16; "Opinions on Pushing
Rural Commercial Banks to Adhere to Their
Positioning, and Strengthen Their Governance
and Improve Their Financial Service Capacity"
78; penalty notices issued by 77; poverty
alleviation 120; reform initiative 74
China Banking Industry Association 84n3
China Banking Regulatory Commission (CBRC)
xiv, **68**; *Guiding Opinions on Accelerating the
Equity Transformation of Rural Cooperative Financial
Institutions* 34; *Guiding Opinions on Accelerating the
Restructuring of the Ownership System of the Rural
Cooperative Financial Institutions* 62; "Guiding
Opinions of the China Banking Regulatory
Commission on Accelerating Equity Reform
of Rural Cooperative Financial Institutions" 14;
*Interim Measures for the Postal Savings Institutions
in Business Management* 30; *Interim Provisions
on the Administration of Loan Companies* 32;
*Interim Provisions on the Administration of Rural
Mutual Fund Associations* 32; *Interim Provisions
on the Administration of Village Banks* 32; policies
aimed at expanding coverage of village banks
in underdeveloped areas 130–131; poverty
alleviation and 120; RCCs transitioned to rural
commercial banks by 70; rural mutual fund
societies not approved by 17; service goal for
financial institutions within the RCC system set
by 63; *Several Opinions on Adjusting and Relaxing
the Access Policies for Banking Financial Institutions in
Rural Areas to Better Support the Construction of New
Socialist Countryside* 32, 43, 121; supervision and
regulation of rural credit cooperatives by 61; three
new types of financial institutions introduced by
15, 121

China Construction Bank (CCB, Bank of
Communications) 37
China Counties Statistical Yearbook 88
China Development Bank (CDB) 37
China Foundation for Poverty Alleviation (CFPA)
114, 122, 125
China International Center for Economic and
Technological Exchange (CICETE) of the
Ministry of Commerce 113, 125
China Marketization Index 88
China Rural Inclusive Finance Survey 44
China Securities Regulatory Commission (CSRC)
120; "Guiding Opinions on Financial Services for
Rural Revitalization" 85; *Opinions on Giving Full
Play to the Role of Capital Market and Serving the
National Poverty Alleviation Strategy* 116, 129
China Women's Federation 114
Chinese Academy of Social Sciences 113
Chongho Bridge Management Limited
("Chongho Bridge") 125–126, 130
CICETE *see* China International Center for
Economic and Technological Exchange
(CICETE) of the Ministry of Commerce
Communist Party of China (CPC) xiv, 26, 31, 33,
35 37; Strategic Plan for Rural Revitalization 85;
see also Central Committee
credit services for farmers: countermeasures for
deepening 56–58
CRRC: "Guiding Opinions on the Experiments
with Microcredit Companies" 15

Decision of the State Council on Financial System Reform
(*1993 Decision*) 27
*Decision of the State Council on Rural Financial System
Reform* (*1996 Decision*) 27, 28
DIFDICC *see* Digital Inclusive Financial
Development Index for Chinese Counties
digital divide 106
Digital Finance Research Center of Peking
University 87
digital gap 43
digital inclusive finance 85–107; concept of 86;
development of 98–100; policy considerations
105–107; top 100 counties for 100–105
Digital Inclusive Financial Development Index
for Chinese Counties (DIFDICC) 87–95, 105;
construction of 88; data sources 88
Digital Inclusive Financial Development Index
System: movement, results, and analysis of
95–105; structure of **89–90**
Digital Inclusive Finance Index, Peking University 87
digital wealth management 91, 96, 105, 106
digitization 86
digitization degree 87

farmers and farm households, demand and access to
loans by 42–58: basic situation of 44; borrowing
sources **53**; constructing rural financial system
suitable for serving 39; credit demand and
accessibility 46; credit demand by, hierarchical

and structural characteristics of 50–55, **56**; credit
rationing and constraints **50**, **51**; deepening credit
services for, recommendations 55–58; difficulties
in obtaining loans by 109; formal credit secured
via guarantee and collateral 49, **49**; high degree
of self-exclusion from financial services by 49;
informal credit used by xvii, 47; low credit
satisfaction of 46; production and operating costs
and income characteristics of 44; unguaranteed
microcredit extended to 63
farmers' cooperatives xiv, 85, 111
Farmers' Independent Service (FIS) 125
financial repression 2, 80
financing demands of farm households 8–11
financing demands of SMEs in rural areas 11
financial market mechanisms, improving 17–19, 40
FinTech xiv, xv, 5, 44; digital inclusive finance
promoted by 85–86; entry into rural financial
markets by 79; poverty alleviation and 130, 133;
recommendation for county-level governments
to promote cooperation with 106, 107;
recommendation to develop 40; recommendation
to enhance sustainable operation using 81;
recommendation to strengthen knowledge of 58;
standardizing 33; *see also* Ant Group
fiscal allocation for agricultural loans 23
fiscal poverty alleviation funds 33; amounts of loans
123
FIS *see* Farmers' Independent Service

General Administration of Taxation 42–43
Goldberg, L. and White, L. 43
green access channel 39, 116, 121, 129, 131
Growth Enterprise Market (GEM) 37

Han, J. 11
Hausbank (house bank), Germany 82
Hayek, Friedrich August von xvi, 2, 4–5
hematopoietic method 115, 126
Huaxi Rural Commercial Bank 63

illegal fund-raising 16, 17
Imperfect Knowledge Paradigm 4
Incomplete Market Paradigm 4
informal bill discounting 38
Insurance Industrial Investment Fund for Poverty
Alleviation 115
Insurance Industrial Public-interest Fund for Poverty
Alleviation 115

Jingdong Finance 18, 130

Li, F. 11
Leading Group Office on Poverty Alleviation
and Development (LGOP) "financial poverty
alleviation cooperation agreement" with the ABC
128; *Guiding Opinions on the Innovative Development
of Poverty Alleviation Microfinance* 114; *Notice on
Carrying out the Pilot Work of Establishing "Mutual
Funds for Development of Poor Villages"* 115; poverty
alleviation work by 127; statistics on pilot of
mutual funds 126

LGOP *see* Leading Group Office on Poverty
Alleviation and Development
local banks 56
local culture and customs 10
local economic development 28, 106; PBC plans
for 110
local financial institutions 15
local government bonds 120
local governments 14, 27; debt carried by 78;
digital plans made by 99; financial offices of 61;
insurance for local agricultural products 117;
management authority of 36; management of
credit offices by 63; microfinancing introduced
by 113; non-performing loans and 30; regulatory
responsibility of 32
local knowledge 6, 7, 9, 18, 57; big data potentially
generated by 81; definition of 72
local legal-person financial institutions 120–121
Local Knowledge paradigm xvi, 2, 4–5, 17, 19

McKinnon, R. 2
macroeconomic policies 11
macro level financial adjustments *see* financial market
mechanisms, improving
macro regions of China xviii, 44, 86; comparing and
contrasting index systems/scores in different *98*,
99, **102–103**
micro and small credit 43
micro and small enterprise 6, 7, 35, 40, 43, 74;
digital loan interest rates for **90**, 91; loans to 120;
"Small and Micro Enterprise Index" (China PnR
Ltd.) 11; underserving of 85
micro-banks 72
microcredit xix, 17, 18, 19; to farmers 63; *Guiding
Opinions on the Innovative Development of Poverty
Alleviation Microcredit* (Poverty Alleviation
Office) 37; "Guiding Opinions on the Vigorous
Development of Rural Microfinance Business by
Banking Financial Institutions" (China Banking
Regulatory Commission 2007) 42; promoting
businesses to carry out innovations in 42;
Subsidized Loans 112
microcredit companies **5**, 15–17, 19; Guiding
Opinions on the Experiments with Microcredit
Companies" (CRRC and PBC) 15; as
lending-only financial institutions 16; licensing
of 19
microcredit guarantee insurance 115
microcredit loans, development of 116
microcredit policy for poverty alleviation 112–114
microcredit team, PSBC 37
micro-enterprise loans 43
microfinance: development of 36–37; farmers
granted 55; *Guiding Opinions on the Innovative
Development of Poverty Alleviation Microfinance*
(LGOP) 114; of non-governmental organizations
125–126; online 79; Poverty- alleviation
Subsidized Loans and Microfinance 35; "public
interest" 37, 38, 39, 41, 126, 130
microfinance companies 44, 48, 56, 57; "Guiding
Opinions on the Piloting of Microfinance
Companies" (CBRC) 43

microfinance loans 114
microfinance organizations/institutions 31–32, 57
microfinance policy in China: government-led 113
micro-insurance 19
microloan companies (MLCs) 22, 34, 35, 117; *Guidance on the Pilot of Microloan Companies* (CBRC and PBS) 32
microloan insurance 129, 133
microloans: applications for 72; PBC pilot program xix note 1; US study on 57
micro-management of financial institutions 76, 83
micro-withdrawals/payments 72
Ministry of Finance" Notice on Tax Policies Relating to Rural Finance 42
MFIs: diversification of 43; integrating regulatory mechanism of 57
MLCs *see* microloan companies
MYBank xv, xviii, 88, **90**

NERI *see* National Economy Research Institute (NERI)
National Branch Governors' Meeting (Fourth) of Agricultural Bank of China 61
National Bureau of Statistics 42, 46, 47, 98
national communication infrastructure, improving 106
National Congress of the Communist Party of China (19th) 35
National Economic and Social Development, Five-year Plan for 118
National Economy Research Institute (NERI) 88, 94
national fight against poverty 115
national finance: poverty alleviation and 110'National Financial Work Conference (Third) 37, 39
national inclusive financial development strategy, enforcement of 79
National Poverty Alleviation Strategy 116
national rural credit cooperative association, absence of 72
national serious illness insurance 129
National SME Share Transfer System 37, 119
national urban and rural individual and enterprise credit reporting system 107
non-governmental organizations 17; microfinance and 37, 38, 113; microfinance of 125–126

P2P lending platforms **6**, 33, 38, 130
pawnshops **5**, 38
PBC *see* People's Bank of China
Peng, Kenqiang 55
People's Bank of China (PBC) xiii, xiv; ABC administrated by 25; ABC separated from then merged with 23;; *Articles of a Rural Credit Cooperative Association at the County Level (Model)* 29; *Articles of a Rural Credit Cooperative (Model)* 29; Bureau of Rural Cooperative Financial Supervision and Administration 29; *Convention on Rural Credit Mutual-help Group (Draft,* 1972) 24; credit rating systems 18; direct loans to farmers not issued by 26; *Guiding Opinions*

on Comprehensively Supplying Good financial services for poverty alleviation and development 117; "Guiding Opinions on the Experiments with Microcredit Companies" 15; *Implementation Opinions on Financial Assistance for Poverty Alleviation (Opinions)* 119, 120; *Joint Notice on the Agreement on the Establishment of Postal Savings* 30; microloan pilot program of xix note 1; national banking conference of 1972 on RCCS 24; rediscount bills 121; rediscount limits 130; *Regulations on the Administration of RCCs* 29; *Regulations on the Administration of RCCs at the County Level* 29; relending in poor areas 121; relending limits 130; Rural Financial Administration of 23; Rural Financial Bureau 24; *Standard Rules for the Articles of the Rural Credit Cooperatives (Draft,* 1972) 24; survey of 2006 of farm households 8
People's Republic of China (PRC): *Decision of the State Council on Financial System Reform (1993 Decision)* 27; evolution of rural financial system of xvi–xvii, 22; founding of 30; Internet Finance (FinTech), development after 2013 of 33; *Law of the PRC on Commercial Banks* 27, 28; Ministry of Posts and Telecommunications 30; poverty alleviation and development practices of 35; restructuring of RCC system of 29; rural financial legislation of 41; rural inclusive financial system of 39, 40; two stages of xvi, 22, 24–25; Wen and Wang on 25
policy-oriented banks 14–15; new mechanism of 127–128
Postal Savings Bank of China (PSBC) xv, **5**, **6**, **12**, 28, 30, 31; policy-oriented banks and 14–15; savings from rural areas absorbed by 31; shareholding systems and 33
postal savings banks 44
poverty alleviation in rural China 109–133; comprehensive and targeted financial policies for 116–118; importance of finance for 109; innovation in financial mechanism and products of commercial banks 128–129; innovation of insurance products for 129; insurance for 115–116, 129; lack of funds for development 109; microfinance of non-governmental organizations 125–126; monetary, regulatory and fiscal and tax support policies in compliance with financial poverty alleviation 120–122; participation of capital market for 116; policy-oriented banks, new mechanism of 127–128; progress and effectiveness of finance for poverty alleviation 123–128; role of Capital Market for Poverty Alleviation 129; role of Rural Internet Finance 130; rural mutual funds in poor villages 126–127; specialized financial policies for 110–116; Seven-Year Priority Poverty Alleviation Program 36, 112, 113, 114; stimulation by the Monetary and Regulatory Policies 130; Subsidized Loans 123–125
Poverty-alleviation Subsidized Loans and Microfinance 35
Poverty Alleviation Offices, local 114

Poverty Alleviation Program *see* Seven-Year Priority Poverty Alleviation Program
PRC *see* People's Republic of China
PRCCA *see* Provincial Rural Credit Cooperative Association
Provincial Rural Credit Cooperative Association (PRCCA) *68*

RCCA *see* Rural Credit Cooperative Associations
RCC *see* Rural Credit Cooperative (RCC) institutions; Rural Credit Cooperative (RCC) System
RCCs *see* Rural Credit Cooperatives
RCFs *see* rural cooperative foundations
rice as savings and credit instruments 19n3
RoSCAs *see* rotating savings and credit associations
rotating savings and credit associations (RoSCAs) 16, 19n3, 38
rural commercial banks 14, 40
rural cooperative banks 34, 40, 64
rural cooperative foundations (RCFs), ban on 30
rural credit associations 70
Rural Credit Cooperative Associations (RCCA): ABCs, decoupling from 29; county level *69*; formation of 29; organizational structure of *69*; Provincial Rural Credit Cooperative Association (PRCCA) *68*; rural commercial banks transformed from 14; as "rural credit associations" 70; standard authentic 71; unified legal person entity status of *69*
Rural Credit Cooperative (RCC) institutions: accelerating reform of 83; agricultural support service function of 117; central bank relending for support of agriculture and 120; differential deposit deviations for 122; domination of credit market in counties and cities xiv, xv; downscaling to fit the best interests of 72; encouraging horizontal mergers among 82; factors affecting sustainable development of 75; financial repression impacting 80; Fair Play ground for 83; FinTech support, enhancing 81; German "Hausbank" as model for 81–82; implementing differentiated reform measures and regulatory policies for 82; improving management of 80; intense operating pressure on 79; intensified market competition for 79; internal control and compliance, strengthening 81; internal supervision of, improving 80–81; as main force in China's rural market 128; membership shares in 69; microcredit extended by 118; new management systems for 34; overall economic downturn impacting 79; overall non-performing loan ratio as being too high 80; ownership structure and governance of 75; poverty alleviation initiatives and 123; promoting sustainable development of 80; risks faced by 76–78
Rural Credit Cooperatives (RCCs): ABC compared to 7; ABC management of 26; ABCs, independence from 28; conditions for prospering of 70–71; as cooperative financial institutions 70; current ownership structures as detrimental to operations 64–68; establishment and development of 24; independent operation of 26; loan default rate 10–11; loans made in 1980 by 27; membership contributions to 73n3; "One RCC . . . one county" 18; online lending services by 33; ownership structure reform of 14; quasi-monopoly position of 17; reform of xiii, xviii, 60–63, 74, 82–83; *Report on Reforming the Management System of RCCs* (State Council) 25; restoration of cooperative nature of 28; restructuring and commercialization of 29; standard genuine, internal management system of 71
Rural Credit Cooperative (RCC) System: distribution of responsibilities and rights within 68–70; improving financial sustainability of financial institutions within 74–83; increased top-down management after alliances *68*; ownership, governance and interests of financial institutions within 60–73; poverty alleviation by 37
Rural Economic Research Department, Development Research Center of the State Council 42
rural inclusive financial system 35–39, 40–41
rural finance paradigms 2–5
rural financial institutions, structure of 5–6
rural financial legislation 43
rural financial market: change in and development of 1–19; initial formation of 25–26; further opening up of 31–35
rural financial services, demand for 7–8
rural financial system: establishment of 23; formation of 28–31; formation of modern system and further opening up of rural financial market 31–35; outlook of the reform and development of the rural financial system 39–41
rural financial system of the People's Republic of China, 70 years' evolution of 22–41; construction of a rural inclusive financial system 35–39; establishment of Rural Financial System and formation of State Banking Institutions 23–24; establishment of specialized banking system and initial formation of rural financial market 25–26; formation of rural financial system in which different-type institutions work together 27–30; further opening-up of the rural financial market and formation of a modern rural financial system 31–35; outlook of the reform and development of the rural financial system 39–41
Rural Financial System Paradigm 3–4
rural formal, semi-formal and informal finance 25; development of 12–17
Rural Internet Finance 130
Rural Mutual Fund Associations (RMFA) 16, 19n9
rural mutual funds 113–114, 126–127
rural mutual fund societies 17
Rural Revitalization Strategy (CCP) xiii

Seventh Five-Year Plan 111
Seven-Year Priority Poverty Alleviation Program 36, 112, 113, 114
Shaw, E. S. 2

SMCs *see* supply and marketing cooperatives
Small and Medium-Sized Enterprises (SMEs) 1;
  competitive rural financial order and 18; limited
  access to financial services of 7; loan demands of
  57; meeting financing demands in rural areas of
  xv, 11, **11**, 17; RCC institutions and 83; *see also*
  micro and small enterprise
SMEs *see* Small and Medium-Sized Enterprises
social responsibilities: commercial interests and 132
State Administration of Taxation 122–123; *see also*
  General Administration of Taxation
Statistical Bulletin of National Economic and Social
  Development 88
Stiglitz, J. 2, 4
subjective initiatives of the poor 132
Subsidized Credit Paradigm 2–3
supply and marketing cooperatives (SMCs) 24, 28
supporting the poor by finance 132

taxation 120, 131
tax benefits xiv
tax burdens 11
tax incentives 107
tax policies 120, 122–123

tax revenue 129
theory of financial deepening 2
theory of financial liberalization 2

UNDP *see* United Nations Development Program
United Nations Development Program (UNDP)
  113, 125
usury 16, 17

World Bank 86
World Index of Fraser Institute of Canada 88

Xi Jinping 35

Yinongdai p2p platform 130
Yinzhou Cooperative Bank (Yinzhou Bank) 14, 60,
  64, **65**, 72
Yinzhou District, Ningbo City 72
Yixin Company 130
Youcheng Foundation 129

Zhangjiagang Rural Credit Cooperative 14, 60,
  64, **65**
Zhengzhou Commodity Exchange 39

Printed in the United States
by Baker & Taylor Publisher Services